THE ULTIMATE
GOLF BOOK

ESSENTIAL GOLFING TECHNIQUES ● THE HISTORY OF GOLF ● THE MAJOR CHAMPIONSHIPS

THE ULTIMATE
GOLF BOOK

THE GREATEST PLAYERS ● AWE-INSPIRING COURSES ● RULES & ETIQUETTE EXPLAINED

NEIL TAPPIN AND FERGUS BISSET
COURSE DESCRIPTIONS BY GEOFFREY GILES

PaRragon

Bath · New York · Singapore · Hong Kong · Cologne · Delhi
Melbourne · Amsterdam · Johannesburg · Auckland · Shenzhen

First published by Parragon in 2011

Parragon
Queen Street House
4 Queen Street
Bath BA1 1HE, UK

www.parragon.com

Copyright © Parragon Books Ltd 2011

Created and produced by Jollands Editions

Creative director Tim Jollands
Editor Beverley Jollands
Book design JC Lanaway
Special photography Paul Severn
Course maps Compare Infobase Limited

ISBN 978-1-4454-4434-5

Cover design www.five-twentyfive.com
Printed in China

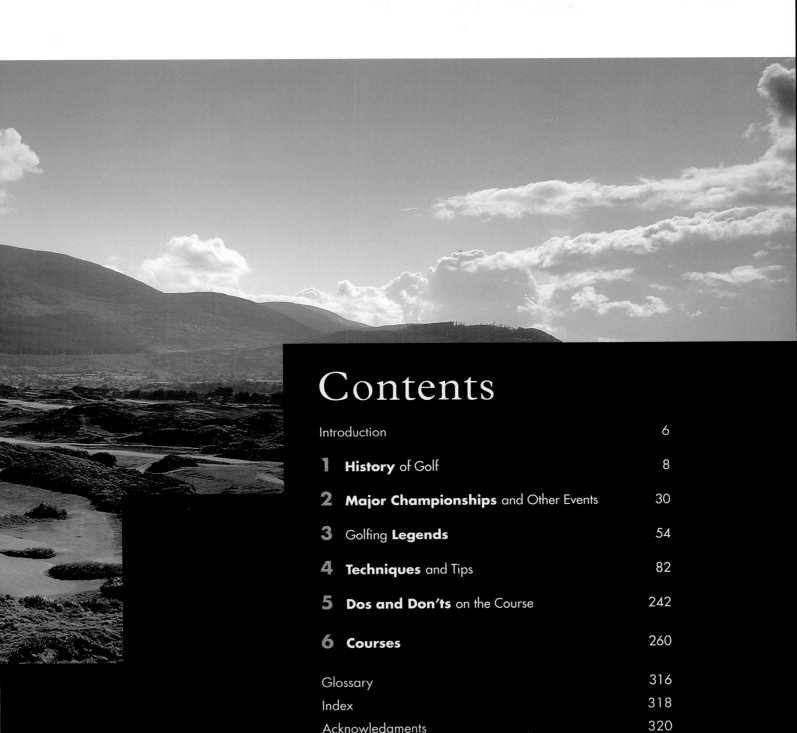

Contents

Introduction 6

1 **History** of Golf 8

2 **Major Championships** and Other Events 30

3 Golfing **Legends** 54

4 **Techniques** and Tips 82

5 **Dos and Don'ts** on the Course 242

6 **Courses** 260

Glossary 316

Index 318

Acknowledgements 320

Introduction

It was at St Andrews that I met my fellow author, Fergus Bisset. Playing golf for the University and in regular matches between friends, we were both lucky enough to spend four years immersed in the history and aura of the *auld grey toun*. Whether playing one of its many great courses or simply walking past the natural amphitheatre of the 18th on the Old Course on the way to lectures, golf was perpetually a part of the experience.

More than anything, it is the history of the place that gets you. Wherever you look, vivid images crystallize in your mind: Seve's iconic fist-pumping celebration that greeted his winning putt in 1984; Doug Sanders excruciatingly missing his short downhill putt on the 18th to lose to Jack Nicklaus in 1970; Tommy Nakajima being caught in the Road Hole bunker in 1978 – for any golf fan, there is nowhere like St Andrews.

The town has golf running through its veins. It is not unusual to see golf bags outside the supermarket or to hear the sound of spikes rattling on the pavement as golfers make their way down to this truly special stretch of links. There is a general sense that no matter what the weather and how many times you have plotted your way through the links before, a round on the Old Course is to be cherished. Walking in the exact footsteps of your heroes and taking on the same challenges they faced, you develop a new connection to the game. Indeed, it is this that makes our sport unique, and a pilgrimage to St Andrews, the epicentre of golfing life, is one that few true golf fans regret making.

Our aim in this book is to foster that kind of connection, and bring you closer to the varied dimensions of the game. We start by taking a look through the history books, chronicling the key events that have shaped the game since its origins in the fifteenth century, reliving the drama of golf's major championships, and celebrating the achievements and appeal of its greatest players. The core of the book is an extensive instruction section for those looking to make significant and lasting improvements to their own game; it sets out the keys to a sound long game as well as offering simple, practical advice to help you improve your score. We also guide you through golf's etiquette and rules, with tips on using the rules to your advantage and avoiding embarrassing mistakes. Finally, Geoffrey Giles takes you on a stunningly illustrated journey to some of the world's most aspirational golf courses, which will leave you with a strong desire to get out and play as many of these iconic layouts as possible.

In writing this book, we have aimed to spark in you a fresh interest for our uniquely rewarding game. So whether you are looking to improve your own playing ability or simply to enfold yourself in the rich tapestry of golfing history, we hope this book will bring you even closer to the game we all love.

Neil Tappin

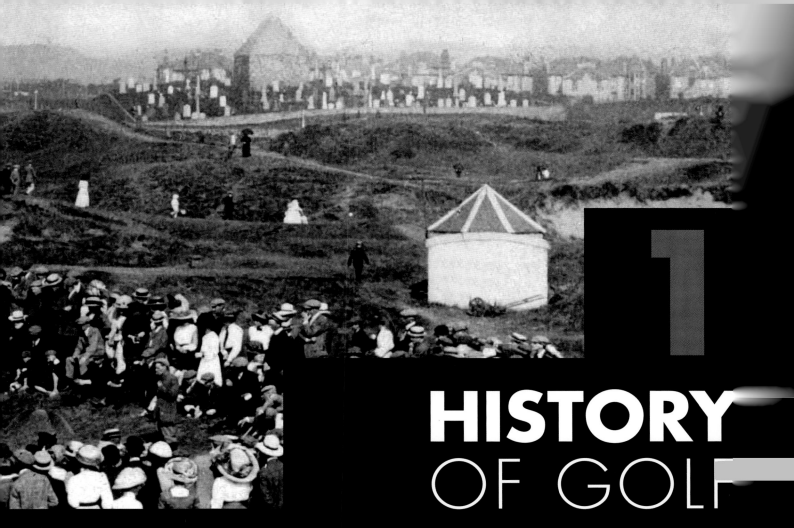

HISTORY
OF GOLF

In the Beginning **12**

Evolution **14**

The Great Triumvirate **16**

Between the Wars **18**

The Television Age **20**

US Domination **22**

Europe's Resurgence **24**

Tiger's Decade **26**

Recent Times **28**

Introduction

The origins of golf have been much debated. There is evidence that various stick and ball games were played across northwest Europe during the Middle Ages, and records from the Chinese Song Dynasty (960–1279) also describe a golf-like game, which might have found its way to medieval Europe. The key here, however, is that those stick and ball games were 'golf-like' rather than golf. The sport of golf as we know it today originated in Scotland: the first indisputable record of its existence comes from a Scottish Act of Parliament dated 1457, and the fact that this was an attempt to ban the game shows that it must already have been popular. The timeline on the following pages traces the development of golf from its medieval Scottish beginnings up to the present day.

The sport has evolved in an extraordinary way since the earliest games were played on the windswept, sandy coasts of Lothian and Fife. If the first golfers were able to glimpse modern players and playing conditions they'd find the sight quite unbelievable. Those golfing pioneers played over rough terrain, using crude wooden clubs and solid wooden balls, whereas today's players wield precision-engineered clubs to send multi-layered, urethane-covered balls across beautifully maintained fairways and greens. The objective of putting a ball in a hole in the ground remains the same, but the method is rather different.

Golf's popularity spread across Britain through the eighteenth and nineteenth centuries, and the process was expedited by the arrival of the railways. In the second half of the nineteenth century the number of golf clubs in Britain rose from fewer than 50 to more than 1,000. As the game expanded, so did the demand for club makers, ball makers and caddies, and from this group came the sport's first professionals. They began to compete in money matches, then in small tournaments. In 1860 the first Open Championship was contested at Prestwick in Scotland. By this time British émigrés had taken the sport to continental Europe and North America. In the United States, clubs were founded and national competitions inaugurated in the late nineteenth century.

Throughout the twentieth century golf's expansion gathered pace, and the sport developed a more universal appeal. Professionals became idolized superstars, equipment manufacturers made use of technology to mass-produce clubs and balls, and golf courses were adapted and manicured to offer optimum playing surfaces. Today, over 50 million people play golf across the globe. The game's top professionals are some of the most highly paid sportsmen in the world, and the golf industry is worth many billions of dollars. It's fair to say the sport has come a long way since the early days on Scotland's east coast.

1421–1786
In the Beginning

March 1421
Members of a Scottish regiment fighting alongside the French, against the English, at the Battle of Baugé in France are introduced to *chole*, a hockey-like game originating in Flanders, and possibly the origin of Scottish golf when the soldiers later take it back to Scotland.

The medieval game of chole

March 1457
The first written reference to golf appears in an Act of the Scottish Parliament. An edict issued by King James II prohibits the playing of 'gowf' and football, because these popular games are distracting the king's subjects from mandatory archery practice.

April 1603
James VI appoints William Mayne, an Edinburgh bow maker, as lifetime golf club maker to the Scottish royal court. Mayne is commissioned to make the king a set of matched clubs.

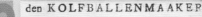

August 1618
A monopoly on the production of golf balls in Scotland is granted to James Melville and William Berwick, on condition that each ball shall cost no more than 4 shillings. Balls are no longer to be imported from Holland.

Dutch golf ball maker

October 1641
King Charles I is allegedly playing golf at Leith when he learns of the Irish rebellion that will lead to the English Civil War. Despite the distressing news, he finishes his game.

1743
Thomas Mathison's *The Goff: an Heroi-Comical Poem in Three Cantos* is the first published literary work devoted entirely to golf. It describes a match between two golfers on the links at Leith.

March 1744
The Honourable Company of Edinburgh Golfers is founded when Edinburgh Town Council presents a silver club to be played for annually by 'The Gentleman Golfers'. It's the world's first golf club. The Company draws up 13 'Articles & Laws in Playing at Golf': the game's earliest known rules.

Rules of the game

May 1754
A challenge match is played over the links of St Andrews for a silver club presented by 22 noblemen and gentlemen of Fife. The contest marks the founding of the Society of St Andrews Golfers, later the Royal and Ancient Golf Club of St Andrews (R&A).

Mary Queen of Scots

January 1502
The Treaty of Perpetual Peace between England and Scotland reduces the need for Scottish military training and enables enthusiastic player King James IV to relax the ban on golf (although the peace will last only until 1513).

February 1504
James IV's expenses include 42 shillings for the king 'to play at the golf' with his friend the Earl of Bothwell: the money was possibly for a bet. The accounts also show 9 shillings for 'golf clubbes and balles' for the king.

February 1567
Political enemies of Mary Queen of Scots accuse her of heartlessly playing golf at Seton House just days after the murder of her husband Lord Darnley, seeking to implicate her in the crime. Mary will be forced to abdicate later in the year.

December 1659
An ordinance is passed against the playing of golf in the streets of Fort Orange (later Albany, New York). This is the first reference to golf in America, although it's possible the game in question is the Dutch *kolven* rather than Scottish golf.

1681
At Leith, the Duke of York and John Paterson, representing Scotland, defeat two English noblemen in the first recorded international match. Andrew Dickson – the first caddy on record – carries the Duke of York's clubs.

April 1691
Alexander Monro, Regent of St Andrews University, describes St Andrews as 'the metropolis of Golfing' in a letter to his friend, the lawyer John Mackenzie of Delvine.

April 1724
A contest on the Leith Links in Edinburgh, between the Honourable Alexander Elphinstone and Captain John Porteous of the City Guard, is the first match to be reported in a newspaper. Elphinstone wins the match and the 20 guineas at stake.

1759
Stroke play is mentioned for the first time at St Andrews. It's the simplest method for counting an individual's score – each player just adds up the total number of strokes he or she has made during the round. Until now, all golf has been match play.

1764
The first four holes at St Andrews are combined to make two. As the same holes are played out and back, this means the course is reduced from 11 out and 11 back to 9 out and 9 back. It's the first 18-hole course and it sets the future standard.

St Andrews in the 1780s

September 1786
Scottish immigrants to the city of Charleston form South Carolina Golf Club, America's first golf club. The members play their games on Charleston Green.

1819–1890
Evolution

1819
The first reference is made to a professional golf tournament held in St Andrews. Sweepstakes contributed by St Andrews members are 'appointed to be played for by the ball-makers, club-makers and caddies'.

1833
King William IV becomes patron of the Perth Golfing Society, making it the first 'Royal' golf society. In 2011 there will be 62 clubs around the world that enjoy royal patronage.

January 1834
William IV becomes patron of the Society of St Andrews Golfers. From this point on the society is known as the Royal and Ancient Golf Club of St Andrews.

Pau Golf Club

April 1856
Robert Forgan takes over his uncle Hugh Philp's club-making firm in St Andrews, and begins using hickory imported from America to make the shafts of his clubs. Until this point ash or hazel has been favoured, but hickory is soon the wood of choice for club makers.

1856
Continental Europe's first golf club is founded at Pau in southern France. Scottish soldiers fighting in the Napoleonic Wars played golf in the countryside around Pau and have later returned as tourists to do the same, gradually establishing a British colony there.

1857
The Golfer's Manual by H.B. Farnie, writing under the pseudonym 'A Keen Hand', is the first book of prose devoted entirely to golf. The work contains details of instruction, history and equipment.

The spread of golf

1870
Britain is now criss-crossed by over 15,500 miles/ 25,000 km of railway track, a tenfold increase since 1837. Travel is now considerably easier and golf courses more accessible: it's a major factor contributing to the growth of the sport.

September 1872
Young Tom Morris wins a fourth straight Open Championship. Next year his name will go on a new trophy: a silver claret jug. In 1875 'Tommy' will die of a pulmonary haemorrhage, aged just 24, following the death of his wife and baby son in childbirth.

November 1883
Bob Ferguson, going for his fourth consecutive victory, loses the Open Championship to Willie Fernie in extra holes. Ferguson will play his final Open in 1889 because his playing career will be halted by a bout of typhoid.

Gutty ball

1836
University French teacher and amateur golfer Samuel Messieux hits the longest drive ever recorded using a 'featherie' ball. He fires a shot 361 yards/330 m down the Elysian Fields at St Andrews.

Featherie ball

1843
The first samples of gutta-percha arrive in Britain. This natural latex obtained from the sap of tropical trees is first employed as an insulator for telegraph wires, but within five years it will also be used to make golf balls, which will be known as 'gutties'.

1847
Scottish artist Charles Lees completes his masterpiece, *The Golfers*, a large group portrait depicting a match on the links of St Andrews on the day of the annual meeting of the Royal and Ancient Golf Club. In the twenty-first century the painting will hang in the Scottish National Portrait Gallery in Edinburgh.

September 1859
Allan Robertson, the first great golf professional, dies in St Andrews after an attack of jaundice. He was the first man to break 80 on the Old Course and was a mentor to Old Tom Morris.

October 1860
Lord Eglinton and Colonel James Ogilvie Fairlie decide to host a professional tournament to raise Prestwick's standing as a club. The Challenge Belt is on offer to the victor. It's the first Open Championship, and Willie Park Sr is the winner.

September 1867
Old Tom Morris wins his fourth and final Open Championship, defeating his great rival Willie Park Sr by two strokes. At 46, Morris is the oldest man ever to win the Open.

Allan Robertson

April 1885
The inaugural British Amateur Championship is held at Royal Liverpool Golf Club: 44 players enter, representing 12 clubs, and Allan Macfie runs out as the winner, beating Horace Hutchinson by 7 and 6 in the final.

Saint Andrews Golf Club, Yonkers

February 1888
The Saint Andrews Golf Club is founded in Yonkers, New York. In 2011 it will be the oldest surviving golf club in the United States, and will play over a Jack Nicklaus-designed course in Westchester County.

September 1890
An Englishman called John Ball is the first amateur and the first player from outside Scotland to win the Open Championship. He beats Archie Simpson by three shots. The same year Ball wins the second of his eight Amateur Championships.

1894–1914
The Great Triumvirate

OFFICIAL BULLETIN, U.S.G.A.

GOLF

One of the requirements of keeping posted on Golf is that you should read **The Evening Post.**

USGA bulletin

December 1894
Delegates from five American golf clubs – Saint Andrews, Shinnecock Hills, Newport, Chicago and Brookline – found the Amateur Golf Association of the United States, later to be known as the United States Golf Association (USGA).

October 1895
The first US Amateur and US Open championships are contested at Newport Golf Club in Rhode Island. Charles B. Macdonald wins the Amateur and Horace Rawlins the Open. In November, Lucy Barnes Brown will win the first US Women's Amateur Championship.

1897
Yale University wins the team event at the first collegiate golf tournament to be contested in the United States. Louis Bayard Jr, representing Princeton, is the individual champion.

June 1900
J.H. Taylor, Harry Vardon and James Braid finish 1–2–3 in the Open Championship at St Andrews. They become known as the 'Great Triumvirate' and, between them, win 16 of the 21 Opens contested from 1894 to 1914.

The Great Triumvirate, with Sandy Herd, 1905

October 1900
Golf features in the Paris Olympic Games. Charles Sands and Margaret Ives Abbott of the USA are the gold medal winners. Golf will again be on the schedule in 1904 but will disappear from the Olympic programme following a British boycott of the 1908 competition, not to return until 2016.

November 1901
Coburn Haskell and Bertram Work's new rubber-cored golf ball appears for sale. Patented in 1898, 'The Haskell' is twice the price of a 'gutty' but it flies considerably farther. Players using Haskell balls will win the British Open and Amateur championships of 1902.

April 1905
William Taylor applies for a patent to produce golf balls featuring a dimple pattern. He has realized that balls with depressions rather than bumps fly farther and higher.

June 1907
Arnaud Massy is the first non-British player to win the Open Championship when he lifts the Claret Jug at Royal Liverpool Golf Club. He will remain the only Frenchman to win the Open Championship.

January 1910
In an amendment to the rules of golf, the R&A judges centre-shafted putters such as the 'Schenectady' illegal. The USGA does not adopt the ruling and the Schenectady remains legal in America. It is the first time the R&A and USGA have disagreed on the rules.

Walter Travis, who won the 1904 British Amateur using a Schenectady putter

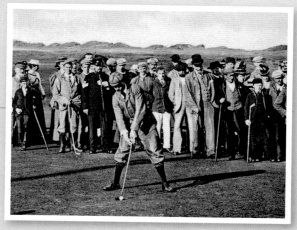

Freddie Tait

1898

January 1898

The Royal and Ancient Golf Club's newly founded rules committee meets for the first time and returns its first 'decision' – on a query from Enfield Golf Club about worm casts on inland courses.

1898

Freddie Tait backs himself to play from the St George's clubhouse in Sandwich, Kent, to the clubhouse at Deal in fewer than 40 shots. He manages it easily, firing his 32nd shot through a window of the Deal clubhouse.

1899

December 1899

Dr George Franklin Grant, a Boston dentist and Harvard's first African-American professor, receives a patent for an improved golf tee. Its top isn't concave, so the ball must be balanced on it. Although Grant never manufactures his product, he's generally considered to be the inventor of the wooden golf tee.

1903

December 1901

J.H. Taylor and a number of other leading players form the Professional Golfers' Association, or PGA, to protect the interests of golf professionals. Its initial membership consists of 59 professionals and 11 assistants. The association accounts list funds of just £47.

May 1903

The first golf course in Japan opens for play at Kobe Golf Club. Built by English expatriate Arthur Hesketh Groom, it's a nine-hole layout, but it will expand to a full 18 holes next year.

1904

June 1904

James Braid is the first player to break 70 in the Open Championship. He fires a 69 in the third round at Royal St George's. In the final round, J.H. Taylor and eventual winner Jack White also post sub-70 rounds.

Francis Ouimet

1911

September 1911

Harold Hilton fires his approach to the 37th hole of the US Amateur Championship towards rocks right of the first green. The ball ricochets back on to the putting surface, and Hilton takes the title. It's the first time the trophy has been won by an Englishman.

1913

September 1913

At the age of 20, American amateur Francis Ouimet causes a massive upset when he beats Harry Vardon and Ted Ray in an 18-hole play-off for the US Open Championship at Brookline in Massachusetts. Ouimet will remain a prominent figure in the world of golf until his death in 1967.

1914

June 1914

At Prestwick, Harry Vardon wins the Open Championship by three shots from J.H. Taylor. Vardon is the first and only man to win the Open six times. It's the last time one of the Great Triumvirate lifts the Claret Jug.

1920–1939
Between the Wars

Joyce Wethered

June 1920
The surprise winner of the English Ladies' Championship is 18-year-old Joyce Wethered. She will win it five times in a row from 1922 to 1926 and win the Ladies' British Amateur Championship on four occasions during the 1920s.

May 1921
The R&A amends the rules to stipulate that a ball should weigh no more than 1.62 ounces/45.93 g and have a diameter of no more than 1.62 inches/4.11 cm. In 1931 the USGA will introduce 'the big ball', with a minimum diameter of 1.68 inches/4.27 cm. The R&A won't adopt it immediately.

May 1921
A team of amateur golfers from the USA beats a team from Great Britain and Ireland in an unofficial match at Royal Liverpool Golf Club. In 1922 the sides will meet again to play for a trophy donated by George Herbert Walker, which will become known as the Walker Cup.

June 1927
Worcester Country Club in Massachusetts plays host to the inaugural Ryder Cup matches, in which a team of professionals from the USA defeats the visiting side from Great Britain by 9½–2½. The competition will go on to become one of the most anticipated and thrilling events in golf.

Bobby Jones (left) and O.B. Keeler

September 1930
Bobby Jones, the greatest amateur player in the history of the game, wins the US Amateur Championship, having claimed the British Amateur, British Open and US Open titles earlier in the year. The *Atlanta Journal*'s O.B. 'Pop' Keeler dubs his achievement the 'Grand Slam'.

May 1932
A competition held at Wallasey Golf Club in northwest England is played using a new scoring system devised by club member Dr Frank Barney Gorton Stableford. The Stableford system will become a staple of amateur golf from now on.

June 1934
England's Henry Cotton ends a run of ten straight American victories in the Open Championship when he takes the title at Royal St George's. He starts with incredible rounds of 67 and 65 to build a nine-shot lead. Even with a disappointing final round of 79, he wins by five shots.

Henry Cotton

April 1935
Gene Sarazen hits the 'shot heard round the world' en route to winning the second Masters Tournament. He holes a 4-wood from 235 yards/215 m for an albatross two on the 15th hole of the final round.

September 1936
Johnny Fischer wins the US Amateur using hickory-shafted clubs. It is the last time a national championship is won by a player using hickory shafts. Steel shafts were made legal by the USGA in 1924 and by the R&A in 1929.

Walter Hagen

1922

July 1922
Flamboyant showman Walter Hagen is the first US-born winner of the Open Championship. 'The Haig' will go on to lift the Claret Jug a further three times through the 1920s, winning 11 major titles between 1914 and 1929.

1923

July 1923
On the Monday before the US Open at Inwood Country Club, New York, Nassau Country Club professional Jim Maiden lends Bobby Jones his putter, nicknamed 'Calamity Jane'. Jones will go on to win the tournament and his 12 further major titles using the putter or replicas of it.

1925

June 1925
The first complete fairway irrigation system is installed at Brook Hollow Golf Club in Dallas, Texas. The development will change the playing characteristics of golf courses across the world.

May 1932
The first Curtis Cup match is played between amateur women from the USA and their counterparts from Great Britain and Ireland. The contest is held at the Wentworth Golf Club in Surrey, and the US team is victorious.

June 1932
Gene Sarazen wins the Open Championship at Prince's Golf Club in Sandwich, Kent. 'The Squire' is greatly aided by a new club of his own design – a precursor of the modern sand wedge. Sarazen's equipment sponsor, Wilson Sporting Goods, begins producing the R-90 sand wedge and will sell 50,000 within a year.

1934

March 1934
Horton Smith wins the first Augusta National Invitation Tournament, an event that will be officially known as the Masters from 1939. Smith will win again in 1936 and will play in every Masters until his death in 1963.

Inaugural Masters programme

1937

June 1937
The USA wins the Ryder Cup at Southport and Ainsdale Golf Club in Lancashire. It's the first time in the series the home side has lost. The USA will lose the Cup only once over the next 48 years.

1938

April 1938
Sam Snead wins the first Greater Greensboro Open. He will go on to win the North Carolina event eight times in his career – a PGA Tour record.

Sam Snead

1939

May 1939
The R&A follows the USGA's lead by limiting to 14 the number of clubs it is permissible to carry. The rule is designed to restore the requirement for shot making to the game.

1945–1959
The Television Age

1945

August 1945
Byron Nelson wins the Canadian Open by four strokes. It's his 11th consecutive victory on the PGA Tour, and it concludes the most famous winning streak in golf history. Nelson wins 18 of the 30 tournaments he enters in 1945.

September 1946
Patty Berg wins the inaugural US Women's Open, beating Betty Jameson by 5 and 4 in the 36-hole final. It's the only time the competition uses a match-play format.

June 1947
Jim Ferrier becomes the first Australian to win a major championship when he beats Chick Harbert in the final of the US PGA Championship at Plum Hollow Country Club, Michigan.

Ben Hogan

January 1950
A group of 13 women golfers, including Patty Berg and Babe Zaharias, found the Ladies Professional Golf Association. Two years from now the LPGA Tour will have a schedule of 21 events.

January 1952
The R&A and USGA issue a unified set of rules for the first time. In them the 'stymie' is abolished: lifting the ball on the green is now at the option of either the player or the opponent.

July 1953
After victories in the Masters and US Open earlier in the year, Ben Hogan crosses the Atlantic to play in the Open Championship for the only time in his career. He wins at Carnoustie by four strokes.

Babe Didrikson Zaharias

September 1956
Babe Didrikson Zaharias dies of cancer at the age of 45. After winning two Olympic gold medals in athletics, she turned her hand to golf in 1935. She won 48 tournaments between 1940 and 1955 and made three cuts on the men's PGA Tour.

October 1957
Under the captaincy of Dai Rees, Britain defeats the USA in the 12th Ryder Cup matches, held at Lindrick Golf Club in Yorkshire. It's Britain's first victory since 1933.

April 1958
Arnold Palmer wins the first of his four US Masters titles, beating Doug Ford and Fred Hawkins by one stroke. After the tournament, *Sports Illustrated* writer Herbert Warren Wind dubs the 11th, 12th and 13th holes at Augusta 'Amen Corner'.

June 1947
The US Open at St Louis Country Club, Missouri, is the first golf tournament to be televised, shown locally in St Louis by KSD-TV. The BBC will televise the British Open for the first time in 1955.

1949

February 1949
Ben Hogan and his wife are lucky to survive when their car crashes head-on into a Greyhound bus. Hogan suffers multiple fractures and doctors fear he will never play competitively again. Next year he will win the US Open.

Hollywood's take on the Hogan story

July 1949
Ireland's Harry Bradshaw finds his ball lodged in a broken beer bottle during the Open at Royal St George's. He blasts out, advancing the ball some 30 yards/27 m. After 72 holes Bradshaw is tied with Bobby Locke; the South African goes on to claim the first of his four Open titles through a 36-hole play-off.

1954

January 1954
Wilson Sporting Goods introduces the Wilson 'Staff' ball. It springs off the clubface 40 per cent faster than the speed of the clubhead, and heralds the arrival of modern power golf.

August 1954
The Tam O'Shanter World Championship in Niles, Illinois, is the first professional tournament to carry a purse of $100,000. Bob Toski picks up the winner's cheque for $50,000.

1956

July 1956
Australia's Peter Thomson wins a third consecutive Open Championship at Royal Liverpool. He is the first player to achieve the feat since Bob Ferguson in 1882.

Peter Thomson

1959

1959
Karsten Solheim invents a new 'heel and toe' weighted putter in his garage in Redwood City, California. He calls it the 'Ping 1A'. 'Ping' is the sound he hears when he first tries the putter on his kitchen floor.

Ping 1A

May 1959
Sam Snead shoots a 59 in the Greenbrier Open in West Virginia. It's the first sub-60 score posted in a competitive round. Snead's achievement does not go down in the record books, however, as the event is not sanctioned by the PGA Tour.

July 1959
A 23-year-old South African called Gary Player wins the Open Championship at Muirfield: it's the first of his nine major victories. Player makes a double bogey on the final hole and fears he's blown his chance, but none of those following him can match his total.

1960–1978
United States Domination

November 1960
Arnold Palmer wins the Mobile Sertoma Open in Alabama. It's his eighth PGA Tour title of the year. His victories include the US Masters and the US Open, where he beat a young amateur called Jack Nicklaus by two strokes.

June 1962
Aged 22, Jack Nicklaus wins the first of his 18 major titles at Oakmont Country Club in Pennsylvania, where he defeats crowd favourite Arnold Palmer in a play-off for the US Open. It signals a changing of the guard.

Arnold Palmer and Jack Nicklaus, 1962 US Open

August 1962
Playing in an amateur tournament in Texas, Homero Blancas fires a round of 55. He scores 13 birdies and an eagle and posts the lowest score ever recorded in competition.

July 1966
The 1964 Open Champion Tony Lema and his wife are killed in an air crash. Their chartered jet goes down en route from the PGA Championship in Akron, Ohio, to the Little Buick Open in Lincolnshire, Illinois. Lema is just 32 years old.

January 1968
Ram Golf produces the Ramlon, the first mass-produced ball with a Surlyn cover. Invented by DuPont, Surlyn is a durable plastic that makes golf balls far harder wearing.

April 1968
Argentina's Roberto de Vicenzo signs for a 66 in the final round of the US Masters when he's actually scored a 65. The rules state the higher total must stand and he loses the tournament by one shot.

Roberto de Vicenzo

April 1972
Home player Antonio Garrido wins the Spanish Open at Pals Golf Club near Girona. This is the first event to be contested on the newly established European Tour.

July 1974
The Open at Royal Lytham is the first in which the R&A stipulates the compulsory use of the 1.68-inch/4.27-cm diameter ball. The smaller 'British' ball will finally be made illegal by the R&A in 1990.

Lee Elder

April 1975
Lee Elder breaks down a significant barrier when he becomes the first African-American to play in the US Masters. The Texan misses the cut by four shots but will go on to play five more Masters, with his best finish tied 17th in 1979.

Bob Charles

July 1963
New Zealand's Bob Charles wins the Open Championship at Royal Lytham & St Annes, Lancashire. He defeats Phil Rodgers by eight shots in the event's last 36-hole play-off. Charles is the first left-handed player to win a major championship.

November 1965
A qualifying school for the PGA Tour is held for the first time. John Schlee is the inaugural medallist and will go on to be *Golf Digest*'s 'Rookie of the Year' in 1966.

January 1966
Bob Mader of Confidence Golf introduces the first investment-cast iron. Investment casting allows for the manufacture of perimeter-weighted clubs, which are more forgiving if the ball is not struck exactly in the centre of the clubface.

July 1969
England's Tony Jacklin wins the Open Championship at Royal Lytham & St Annes. He is the first British winner of the competition since Max Faulkner in 1951. Next year, Jacklin will become the first European US Open champion since 1925.

Tony Jacklin

September 1969
The Ryder Cup at Royal Birkdale, Lancashire, produces one of the most sporting gestures in the history of golf, when Jack Nicklaus concedes a 2-foot/60-cm putt to Tony Jacklin on the final green of their singles match. It means their game, and the whole competition, ends in a tie.

February 1971
Apollo 14 commander Alan Shepard uses a Wilson 6-iron to hit golf balls on the surface of the moon. He has two attempts, firing the second for, as he puts it, 'miles and miles and miles'.

June 1976
At the US Open in Atlanta the USGA introduces the use of a 'Stimpmeter' to measure the speed of greens. It is an aluminium bar 36 inches/ 91 cm long, tilted to the angle at which a golf ball will roll out of a notch and down the bar. The distance the ball travels over a flat section of green determines the speed of the surface.

June 1977
Al Geiberger is the first player to break 60 in a PGA Tour event. He shoots a 59 in the second round of the Danny Thomas Memphis Classic and goes on to win the event.

April 1978
South African Gary Player's victory at the US Masters ends a run of 13 straight major wins for players from the United States. During the 1970s non-American golfers win just seven of the 40 major championships contested.

Gary Player

1979–1996
Europe's Resurgence

1979

January 1979
At the PGA Merchandise Show, TaylorMade unveils a new steel-headed driver. It's christened the 'Pittsburgh Persimmon' and becomes a great success. By 1984 TaylorMade's metal woods will be the most played on the PGA Tour.

July 1979
On the 70th hole of the Open Championship at Royal Lytham, Seve Ballesteros fires his drive into a temporary car park. He receives a free drop, blasts onto the green and makes a birdie. His eventual three-shot victory opens the floodgates for European major success over the next decade and more.

Seve Ballesteros

September 1979
Following a suggestion by Jack Nicklaus, players from continental Europe become eligible for Ryder Cup selection for the first time. Spaniards Seve Ballesteros and Antonio Garrido are part of the new 'European' side, which loses to the USA at the Greenbrier.

1984

January 1984
Ping Golf incorporates 'square grooves', which produce more spin, into its 'Eye2' irons. The clubs will be banned by the USGA in 1988, although the ban will later be retracted after a legal battle.

1985

July 1985
Sandy Lyle wins the Open Championship at Royal St George's. He's the first British player to lift the Claret Jug since Tony Jacklin in 1969, and the first Scottish winner since Tommy Armour in 1931.

September 1985
On the 18th green at the Belfry, Warwickshire, Sam Torrance holes a 22-foot/6.7-m birdie putt to win the Ryder Cup for Europe. It's the first time since 1957 that the USA has lost the biennial transatlantic contest.

1989

December 1989
Richard Helmstetter, working for Callaway Golf, applies for a patent for a metal wood with a neckless head. The design, named 'Big Bertha', will be launched on the market in 1991, triggering the move towards oversized heads.

1990

January 1990
From 1 January, a new R&A ruling comes into force outlawing the smaller 1.62-inch/4.11-cm diameter ball from use in all competition. It ends 60 years of inconsistency between the R&A and USGA on the issue of ball size.

USA team, Solheim Cup winners

November 1990
The inaugural Solheim Cup, contested by teams of female professionals from the USA and Europe, is held at Lake Nona Golf & Country Club in Florida. The Americans win by 11½–4½.

1980

July 1980
Tom Watson is the winner at Muirfield, where the Open Championship finishes on a Sunday for the first time. Until now the competition has always concluded on a Saturday.

July 1980
A film comedy about golf, starring Bill Murray and Chevy Chase, is released. *Caddyshack* delivers a hilarious portrayal of American country club golf and will remain a firm favourite with golf fans across the globe.

1982

June 1982
Tom Watson runs a lap of the 17th green at Pebble Beach, California, after chipping in for a two in the last round of the US Open. He also birdies the closing hole to beat Jack Nicklaus by two shots.

Tom Watson

1986

April 1986
The Sony Ranking, later to become the Official World Golf Ranking, is introduced. Germany's Bernhard Langer is the inaugural No. 1, with Seve Ballesteros at No. 2 and Sandy Lyle at No. 3.

July 1986
Greg Norman is the first player to win a modern-era major using a non-wound ball. The Australian uses a Spalding 'Tour Edition' to secure victory in the Open Championship at Turnberry.

1987

Nick Faldo

July 1987
In testing conditions, Nick Faldo records 18 straight pars in the final round of the Open Championship at Muirfield to win by a single shot. It's the first of his six major titles.

1993

Bernhard Langer

April 1993
Bernhard Langer is the last player to win a major championship using a wooden-headed driver. He captures his second US Masters title playing with a persimmon-headed, Wood Brothers' 'Texan'.

1995

April 1995
Legendary golf professional, writer and coach Harvey Penick dies at the age of 90. He gives long-time student Ben Crenshaw lessons from his deathbed, and, just a week after Penick's passing, an emotional Crenshaw wins the US Masters.

1996

August 1996
Tiger Woods becomes the first golfer to win three consecutive US Amateur Championships when he takes the title at Pumpkin Ridge in Oregon. He is also the only person to win three straight US junior titles, a feat he accomplished between 1991 and 1993.

1997–2006
Tiger's Decade

1997

April 1997
Tiger Woods wins the US Masters by a record margin of 12 shots. It's his first major title and, at the age of 21, he is the tournament's youngest ever champion.

Tiger Woods

November 1997
John Daly finishes the PGA Tour season with a driving distance average of 302 yards/276 m. He is the first player to average over 300 yards/ 274 m from the tee for a full season on the circuit.

1998

July 1998
Mark O'Meara beats Brian Watts in a four-hole play-off to win the Open Championship at Royal Birkdale. Having already won the US Masters earlier in the season, 41-year-old O'Meara becomes the oldest man to win two majors in a single year.

1999

September 1999
In the Ryder Cup at Brookline, Massachusetts, Justin Leonard holes a crucial putt across the 17th green. The US team and fans invade the putting surface before Leonard's opponent, José María Olazábal, has a chance to putt for the half. It's regarded as one of the worst lapses of sportsmanship in golfing history.

October 1999
Just four months after winning the US Open at Pinehurst, Payne Stewart dies when the Learjet in which he is travelling from Orlando to Dallas suffers a loss of cockpit pressure and crashes.

Payne Stewart

2000

June 2000
At Pebble Beach, Tiger Woods wins the 100th US Open Championship by an astonishing 15 shots. It's the largest winning margin in the history of the majors. Woods will also win the next three major titles, to complete the so-called 'Tiger Slam'.

2001

July 2001
Ian Woosnam is tied for the lead in the Open Championship at Royal Lytham after birdieing the first hole of the final round, but on the second tee he discovers that his bag contains 15 rather than 14 clubs. He's penalized two strokes and finishes four behind eventual winner David Duval.

2002

August 2002
The USGA sets a limit on the coefficient of restitution (COR) for woods with a loft of 15° or less. Pertaining to the springiness of the clubface, the new COR restrictions are designed to curb the increasing distance players are able to hit the ball.

2004

November 2004
Vijay Singh is the first player to finish a season with over $10 million in prize money. He wins nine tournaments in 2004 and ends the year as world No. 1.

Vijay Singh

Jean Van de Velde

August 1998
Fiji's Vijay Singh wins the US PGA Championship by two shots from Steve Stricker at Sahalee Country Club near Seattle. Singh will go on to win two more major titles – the 2000 US Masters and the 2004 US PGA Championship.

November 1998
EA Sports releases a video game entitled *Tiger Woods 99*. It's the first in a series that will dominate the golf games market for the next 13 years. By 2011, 15 incarnations of the game will have been released.

July 1999
Jean Van de Velde of France has a three-shot lead on the final hole of the Open Championship at Carnoustie, but fires his second shot into a grandstand and his third into the Barry Burn. He makes a triple bogey and ends tied with Paul Lawrie and Justin Leonard. Lawrie wins the ensuing play-off.

1999

Tiger Woods

October 2000
In Las Vegas, Titleist introduces the 'ProV1' ball at the Invensys Classic on the PGA Tour. Billy Andrade uses the solid-core, non-wound ball to win the event. The ProV1 will become the most used golf ball in the professional game.

2001

Annika Sörenstam

March 2001
Annika Sörenstam becomes the first female golfer to shoot a 59 in competition. She posts the score in the second round of the Standard Register Ping tournament. She wins eight times this year and is the first woman to win $2 million in a single season.

2005

June 2005
The first US Open qualifier to be held in the UK takes place at Walton Heath, Surrey. New Zealand's Michael Campbell is one of nine players who make it through to play at Pinehurst, and he goes on to win the championship.

October 2005
Colin Montgomerie's victory in the Dunhill Links Championship helps him secure a record eighth European Tour Order of Merit. It's the first time the Scot has ended a season as Europe's leading player since topping the rankings seven times consecutively in the 1990s.

2006

August 2006
Tiger Woods wins the Buick Open at Warwick Hills in Michigan. It's his 50th PGA Tour victory and, at 30 years and 7 months, he's the youngest player to reach that milestone. Woods wins six straight events at the end of the season.

September 2006
Europe wins the Ryder Cup by a record-equalling 18$\frac{1}{2}$–9$\frac{1}{2}$. Following victories in 2002 and 2004, it's the first time Europe has won the Ryder Cup three times consecutively.

2007–2011
Recent Times

January 2007
The R&A publishes a World Amateur Golf Ranking for the first time. Scotland's Richie Ramsay is the inaugural No. 1. Ramsay's US Amateur Championship win in 2006 was the first British victory in that event since Harold Hilton's in 1911.

April 2007
Spain's Pablo Martín is the first amateur to win an event on the European Tour, claiming victory in the Estoril Open de Portugal. In 2009 two more amateurs will win titles on the circuit, Danny Lee winning the Johnnie Walker Classic and Shane Lowry, the Irish Open.

Pablo Martín

May 2007
Ryo Ishikawa wins the Munsingwear Open KSB Cup on the Japan Golf Tour. At 15 years and 8 months, he is the youngest ever winner of an event on one of the top-level men's professional tours.

June 2008
At the age of 10 years and 3 months, Allisen Corpuz of Hawaii plays in the US Women's Amateur Public Links Championship. She is the youngest person ever to play in a USGA championship, beating the record previously held by Michelle Wie.

June 2008
Tiger Woods wins the US Open, despite suffering from a torn ligament in his left knee and a double stress fracture in his left tibia. Wincing after almost every shot, he is tied with Rocco Mediate after 72 holes, and still after the 18-hole play-off. Woods wins on the first sudden-death hole.

Tiger Woods

Lorena Ochoa

April 2010
A beleaguered Tiger Woods returns to competitive golf at the US Masters. After receiving a very public dressing down before the first round from Masters Chairman Billy Payne, Woods finishes the tournament in a tie for fourth place.

April 2010
Women's world No. 1, Lorena Ochoa, announces her retirement from full-time competitive golf at the age of just 28. The Mexican is a two-time major champion and a winner of 27 events on the LPGA Tour.

June 2010
Graeme McDowell of Northern Ireland is the surprise winner of the US Open at Pebble Beach. He is the first European to lift the US Open trophy since Tony Jacklin in 1970.

October 2010
England's Lee Westwood takes over from Tiger Woods at No. 1 on the Official World Golf Ranking. Tiger's reign at the top has lasted an incredible 281 straight weeks. In total he's been the world's No. 1 player for 623 weeks – almost 12 years.

July 2007
Padraig Harrington reaches a play-off for the Open Championship at Carnoustie, despite finding the water twice on the 72nd hole. The Irishman defeats Sergio Garcia in extra holes to become the first European major winner since Scotland's Paul Lawrie in 1999.

Padraig Harrington

September 2007
Tiger Woods is the winner of the inaugural FedEx Cup on the PGA Tour. A season-long points race, culminating in four play-off events, the FedEx Cup carries a bonus pool of $35 million. As the champion, Tiger picks up $10 million.

November 2007
Sir Bob Charles makes the cut in the Michael Hill New Zealand Open. The 71-year-old is the oldest player to achieve this in a European Tour event.

November 2008
Jason Hak is the youngest player ever to make a cut on the European Tour. The 14-year-old amateur from Hong Kong fires two 70s to earn his place on the weekend at the UBS Hong Kong Open.

October 2009
After a vote taken by the International Olympic Committee, golf is approved for inclusion in the 2016 Olympic Games in Rio de Janeiro. There will be 72-hole stroke-play competitions for men and women.

November 2009
Tiger Woods crashes his car into a fire hydrant, then a tree, outside his house in Florida, after a story emerges claiming he has had an extramarital affair. Other women come forward with further allegations, and Tiger announces that he is taking a break from golf.

January 2010
New rulings on clubface grooves come into force for all clubs manufactured after 1 January. A limit is placed on the groove volume of clubs, excluding drivers and putters, and on groove-edge sharpness for clubs with a loft of 25° and above.

February 2011
Martin Kaymer moves ahead of Lee Westwood at the top of the Official World Golf Ranking. For the first time since 1992, the top four players on the list are European, the other two being Luke Donald and Graeme McDowell.

Martin Kaymer, Lee Westwood, Luke Donald

May 2011
The golfing world mourns the loss of a golfing genius, Seve Ballesteros, who at the age of 54 finally succumbs to cancer, first diagnosed in 2008. The Spanish maestro was European golf's on- and off-course inspiration for over 30 years.

Seve Ballesteros and José María Olazábal

2

MAJOR
CHAMPIONSHIPS
AND OTHER EVENTS

The Open
Championship **34**

The US Open **38**

The Masters
Tournament **42**

Introduction

Ever since the game of golf first emerged on Scotland's east coast, it has been played competitively. Indeed, the court records of King James IV suggest that he was laying wagers on his own golf matches at the start of the sixteenth century.

Organized golf tournaments began somewhat later. The first golf clubs held internal competitions, then, in 1857, Britain's principal clubs sent players to compete in a 'Grand National Tournament' hosted by the R&A at St Andrews. Three years after that, a tournament for the leading professional and amateur golfers was played at Prestwick, and the event became an annual fixture known as the Open Championship.

The idea of organized golfing championships spread, and open and amateur championships were inaugurated on both sides of the Atlantic, while professional players set up organizations and, latterly, 'tours'. Over the 150 years since the first Open Championship, golf has developed into one of the most popular sports in the world. Countless competitions are now held every week, from club medals up to elite international tournaments.

At the pinnacle of today's men's competitive game are the four major championships. They are the Open Championship, the US Open Championship, the Masters and the US PGA Championship.

These events, featuring the very best professional golfers and the leading amateurs, are watched by huge television audiences around the world, and the victors become superstars.

Each of the majors has witnessed phenomenal sporting achievements and has seen the game's most famous players emerge, dominate and depart. From Willie Park Sr's first Open victory onwards, winning a major has been the dream of every young golfer. In 1860, the Open Championship was the sole annual competition for professional players. Now the top pros compete in up to 50 events a year on organized tours across the world.

As golf is an individual sport, most of today's professional tournaments are individual, and the vast majority are played to a stroke-play format. But there are match-play team events in both the professional and amateur games, and these deliver a different level of excitement for both competitors and spectators.

The following pages offer a closer look at each of golf's four principal individual events – their beginnings, their administration, their history and the key players. In addition there is a guide to the game's premier team event, the Ryder Cup, and outlines of the professional and amateur games for both men and women.

The Open Championship

Decided over the third weekend of July on one of Britain's revered 'links' courses, the Open Championship, also known as the British Open, offers the most historic and coveted individual prize in men's golf. This great event was first contested in 1860, and celebrated its 150th anniversary at St Andrews in 2010.

Administered by the R&A, the Open Championship is the only one of the four men's major championships to be held outside the USA. As it is an open event, entries are accepted from any professional golfer or any amateur player whose handicap does not exceed scratch.

QUALIFICATION AND FORMAT

Players can qualify for the tournament proper in a variety of ways. The top players receive exemptions according to their world ranking or their performances in other significant events. Others make it through International Final Qualifying events, held on five continents. Lastly, players can progress through Regional Qualifying, then Local Final Qualifying

competitions held in Britain. From an initial entry of thousands each year, 156 get through to play in the main event.

Like the other major tournaments, the Open is 72 holes of stroke play with a cut after 36 holes. The top 70 and ties make it through to play the last two rounds. In the event of a tie after four rounds are completed, a four-hole play-off ensues. If a winner has still not emerged, the event goes to 'sudden death'.

BEGINNINGS

The Open was born when James Ogilvy Fairlie, a co-founder of Prestwick Golf Club and a close friend of Old Tom Morris, decided that a professional tournament would raise Prestwick's standing as a golf club. At Fairlie's instigation, Prestwick sent letters to

Most victories
6 – Harry Vardon, 1896, 1898, 1899, 1903, 1911, 1914

Youngest winner
Young Tom Morris, 1868, aged 17 years 5 months

Oldest winner
Old Tom Morris, 1867, aged 46 years 3 months

Lowest 72-hole total
267 (13 under par) – Greg Norman, 1993

Lowest round
63 – eight players

Biggest margin of victory
13 shots – Old Tom Morris, 1862

Most appearances
46 – Gary Player, 1956–2001

Below left Old Tom Morris and Young Tom Morris, both four-time winners of the Open. Young Tom was its youngest-ever champion.

Below J.H. Taylor, who won the Open five times, on the tee during the 1900 Open at St Andrews. Behind him is the bearded Old Tom Morris.

the leading British clubs, inviting them to send their professionals for a competition to be held over the links in October 1860. There were eight entrants, and Willie Park Sr of Musselburgh was the winner.

At that first Open Championship a red morocco leather and silver Challenge Belt was presented to the winner. No prize money was up for grabs, although the professionals were able to earn some pay by caddying for Prestwick members during the week of the competition. When Young Tom Morris won three consecutive titles, from 1868 to 1870, he was allowed to keep the belt, so a new prize was required. At the 1873 competition, a silver claret jug was awarded to the winner, Tom Kidd.

The first 12 championships were contested at Prestwick: Willie Park Sr, Old Tom Morris and Young Tom Morris shared 11 victories between them, and Andrew Strath (in 1865) was the only

other man to feature. Scottish players dominated the event until 1890, when John Ball recorded two firsts – not only was he the first English winner but he was also the first amateur to lift the Claret Jug. The 1890s saw the arrival of the 'Great Triumvirate': J.H. Taylor, Harry Vardon and James Braid won 16 Open titles between them between 1894 and 1914.

GLOBAL COMPETITION

After World War I the balance of power began to shift, as visitors from the USA came to the fore. Walter Hagen was a winner four times in the 1920s, while Bobby Jones picked up his third title in 1930. Henry Cotton struck back for the host nation in 1934; this started a run of eight British wins in nine championships, interrupted only by World War II and Sam Snead of the USA in 1946.

Above Walter Hagen is congratulated by his wife on winning the 1924 Open at Hoylake. The dashing American stormed Britain in the 1920s, winning the Open four times.

Below Bobby Jones driving from the 17th tee at St Andrews, where he went on to win the 1927 Open with a then record score of 285.

In the immediate postwar years, South African Bobby Locke and Australian Peter Thomson dominated the championship, with four wins each. Locke won three Opens between 1949 and 1952, then Thomson achieved a hat trick of victories between 1954 and 1956. In between, Ben Hogan confirmed his status as one of golf's all-time greats by winning the Open at his first and only attempt, in 1953, on the back of his wins in the US Masters and the US Open.

THE MODERN ERA

Arnold Palmer's victories of 1961 and 1962 were instrumental in reigniting a dwindling American interest in the Open Championship. His performances inspired the likes of Jack Nicklaus, Tony Lema, Lee Trevino and Tom Watson to travel across the Atlantic to compete, and players from the United States achieved 14 victories between 1964 and 1983.

Swashbuckling Spaniard Seve Ballesteros stemmed the red, white and blue tide with his win at Royal Lytham in 1979, and Nick Faldo further bolstered European fortunes with three wins between 1987 and 1992.

Tiger Woods got to grips with the links game at the start of the new millennium, collecting three titles in 2000, 2005 and 2006. In 2007 Ireland's Padraig Harrington was the first European to lift the Claret Jug since Scotland's Paul Lawrie in 1999. Harrington successfully defended the title the following year at Royal Birkdale. At Turnberry in 2009, Stewart Cink crushed Tom Watson's dream of becoming the oldest major champion when he beat the 59-year-old in a play-off for the title. In the 150th anniversary Open at St Andrews, South Africa's Louis Oosthuizen showed the field a clean pair of heels to become the 78th man to win the championship.

Top Arnold Palmer poised to drive at Troon in 1962. His wins here and at Royal Birkdale the previous year acted as a clarion call to his fellow Americans.

Above In 1977 Turnberry witnessed the greatest of Opens when (right) Tom Watson (65, 65) narrowly defeated Jack Nicklaus (65, 66) over an epic final 36 holes.

Far left Seve Ballesteros was renowned for his phenomenal recoveries. At Lytham in 1979, en route to his first major, he hit his tee shot at the 16th into a car park, yet made a birdie.

Left In 2000, Tiger Woods brought the Old Course to its knees with a 19-under-par aggregate of 269.

Below Padraig Harrington celebrating after eventually winning the 2007 Open at Carnoustie. In scenes reminiscent of Jean Van de Velde's collapse in 1999, the Irishman put two shots into the Barry Burn on the 72nd hole, forcing him into a play-off.

The US Open

Played in mid-June, the US Open is the second major championship to be held each year. Run by the United States Golf Association (USGA), the event has a reputation for being the most challenging of the majors, featuring brutally difficult courses that set exacting examinations of golfing prowess and mental fortitude.

As in the British Open, any professional or amateur whose handicap is better than the USGA's set maximum (currently 1.4) can attempt to qualify for a place in the 156-man US Open field, and there are exemption categories and international qualifiers as well as local and sectional qualifying competitions. In 2010 there were 9,052 entries for the tournament.

The two great national Opens differ greatly, however, with regard to venue choice. While the British Open has visited just 14 courses through its history, the US Open has been contested over 50 different courses across the USA since its inauguration in 1895.

ULTIMATE TEST

The courses used for the US Open are set up to be extremely difficult. Sloping greens are shaved to become super-fast, fairways are narrowed and the rough is grown thick. The winning four-round score is often around – or even over – par. In both 2006 and 2007 the winning total was five over par, a score almost unheard-of elsewhere in modern professional tournament golf.

The US Open tends to be an event where avoiding disasters is as important as making birdies. The courses generally reward steady and consistent play rather than outright aggression.

Most victories
4 – Willie Anderson, Bobby Jones, Ben Hogan, Jack Nicklaus

Youngest winner
John McDermott, 1911, aged 19 years 10 months

Oldest winner
Hale Irwin, 1990, aged 45 years

Lowest 72-hole total
272 – Jack Nicklaus, 1980 (8 under par); Lee Janzen, 1993 (8 under par); Tiger Woods, 2000 (12 under par); Jim Furyk, 2003 (8 under par)

Lowest round
63 – Johnny Miller, 1973; Jack Nicklaus, 1980; Tom Weiskopf, 1980; Vijay Singh, 2003

Biggest margin of victory
15 shots – Tiger Woods, 2000

Most appearances
44 – Jack Nicklaus, 1957–2000

Below The course at Oakland Hills was set up as a monster for the 1951 US Open. Ben Hogan, seen here on the 17th, tamed it with a closing 67, one of the greatest rounds of his life.

EARLY BRITISH DOMINATION

The first US Open was held at Newport Country Club on Rhode Island, on the day after the inaugural US Amateur Championship had been contested over the same course. There were 11 entrants, and the winner was an Englishman named Horace Rawlins. He had recently taken a post as professional at the host club.

Golf was a burgeoning sport in the United States at the end of the nineteenth century, and more experienced British players controlled the event in its early years – indeed, they won the first 16 championships. Willie Anderson was the most successful of the British emigrants, claiming four titles in total and three consecutively between 1903 and 1905.

Left John McDermott, the first American-born winner of the US Open, and also the youngest.

Above At Oakmont in 1962 the balance of power in golf shifted from Arnold Palmer (right) to Jack Nicklaus (left), who defeated Palmer in the two-round play-off to win the first of his four US Opens and 18 majors.

AMERICANS FIGHT BACK

John McDermott was the first native-born American to win the US Open, in 1911, and from that point the USA barely looked back. Home players captured all but four of the next 47 championships. In fact, when Gary Player of South Africa won the 1965 US Open at Bellerive, he ended a run of 33 straight American victories.

Bobby Jones was four times a champion in the space of eight years – from 1923 to 1930. Ben Hogan topped that by capturing four titles in just six years, from 1948 to 1953. Jack Nicklaus is the only other player to have won four US Opens. His victories were spread over 19 years, from 1962 to 1980, the first coming at Oakmont in his rookie season on the PGA Tour. In that event a fresh-faced Nicklaus defeated crowd favourite Arnold Palmer in a Sunday play-off. Palmer had won the fans' affection with his charismatic and cavalier approach to the game. In the 1960 US Open at Cherry Hills he began the final round seven shots off the lead, but he fired a closing 65 to roar through the field and take the title by two.

SURPRISE RESULTS

As in all great championships, there have been some notable US Open upsets over the years. In 1913 a 20-year-old local amateur named Francis Ouimet defeated the formidable British duo, Harry Vardon and Ted Ray, in an 18-hole play-off at Brookline Country Club. Ouimet's improbable victory planted golf firmly in the American conscience.

In 1955, Iowan municipal golf course professional Jack Fleck came from nowhere to tie with the great Ben Hogan after 72 holes at the Olympic Club. Fleck went on to beat the four-time champion by three shots in the next day's play-off. His win ranks as one of the most unexpected results in sporting history.

Above Bobby Jones (right), seen here with Gene Sarazen, had a stranglehold on the US Open in the 1920s. Between 1922 and 1930 he won four times and came second four times.

INTERNATIONAL WINS

Although American players continued to dominate through the latter part of the twentieth century, a more eclectic selection of nations has enjoyed US Open glory in recent years. Ernie Els of South Africa was twice a winner in the 1990s, and his countryman Retief Goosen also picked up two victories, in 2001 and 2004. Goosen's second win started a run of four consecutive championship wins by overseas players, since he was followed by New Zealand's Michael Campbell, Geoff Ogilvy of Australia and Angel Cabrera of Argentina.

Tiger Woods broke the international run in 2008, when he took his third US Open title at Torrey Pines, California, despite suffering from a torn knee ligament and a double stress fracture to his left tibia. In 2011, Rory McIlroy made it back-to-back US Open victories for players from Northern Ireland. The 22-year-old's outstanding eight-shot win at Congressional Country Club in Maryland followed Graeme McDowell's success at Pebble Beach in 2010.

Right Tiger Woods takes a swing on the 9th fairway at Pebble Beach against one of golf's most spectacular backdrops. He won the 100th US Open by the astonishing margin of 15 shots.

Tribute to Payne Stewart, Pebble Beach, 2000

21-BALL SALUTE

Pebble Beach has witnessed some of golf's great moments, not least Tom Watson's chip-in on the 17th to win in 1982. In 2000, the course hosted the 100th US Open. At sunrise on the Wednesday morning, Payne Stewart's fellow golfers lined the 18th fairway and hit balls into the Pacific Ocean in a poignant tribute to the late US Open champion, who had died in a plane crash just months after winning the coveted title for a second time in 1999.

The Masters Tournament

The Masters is unique among golf's four professional men's major championships in that it's always contested over the same course – the distinctively beautiful and immaculately presented Augusta National in the state of Georgia.

Most victories
6 – Jack Nicklaus, 1963, 1965, 1966, 1972, 1975, 1986

Youngest winner
Tiger Woods, 1997, aged 21 years 3 months

Oldest winner
Jack Nicklaus, 1986, aged 46 years 2 months

Lowest 72-hole total
270 (18 under par) – Tiger Woods, 1997

Lowest round
63 – Nick Price, 1986; Greg Norman, 1996

Biggest margin of victory
12 shots – Tiger Woods, 1997

Most appearances
52 – Gary Player, 1957–2009

Each April, the world's best players travel to this iconic layout to compete for the year's first major championship. Amid the azaleas, dogwoods and towering pines, competitors play across lush, green, undulating fairways, over perilous water hazards, to lightning-fast and supremely testing greens. After four days of enthralling stroke-play competition, the winning golfer is presented with a silver trophy, a gold medal and, famously, a Green Jacket.

The great amateur Bobby Jones was co-founder of Augusta National Golf Club. Together with a Wall Street banker named Clifford Roberts, he had the vision to turn 365 acres/148 ha of an old indigo plantation into America's most famous golf course. Jones worked with British course architect Dr Alister MacKenzie to design the layout.

AMEN CORNER

The course at Augusta National is one of the most recognizable to armchair golf fans. Holes 11–13, christened 'Amen Corner' by American writer Herbert Warren Wind in 1958, provide perhaps the most challenging stretch. But the par-5 15th and short 16th, where shots to the green must carry water, have also foiled many over the years. The greens at Augusta are extremely fast and sloping, and the course delivers a stringent examination of the short game.

Jones was the public face of the club, and his fame was central to the success of the early invitational tournaments hosted annually at Augusta. The first of these, in 1934, was called the Augusta National Invitation Tournament. It was not until 1939 that the event became known as 'the Masters'.

Above left Gene Sarazen (left) shakes hands with Bobby Jones after the naming of a bridge in his honour in 1955. Clifford Roberts, who ruled Augusta with an iron hand, looks on. Twenty years previously Sarazen had struck possibly the most famous shot in golf history when he holed a 4-wood approach to the par-5 15th for an albatross.

Opposite Tiger Woods negotiates the 12th, the apex of Amen Corner. The tee shot has to carry Rae's Creek, and the wind can be capricious, making club selection crucial. Jack Nicklaus has described it as the toughest par 3 in tournament golf; Tom Weiskopf once took 13 here.

MASTERS TRADITIONS

The Masters remains an invitational event and its field of around 90 players is considerably smaller than those of the other three major tournaments. Invitations are granted according to a number of published criteria: players who receive them include the top 50 on the Official World Golf Ranking the week prior to the tournament, recent major champions, and winners of various amateur tournaments, including the British, US and Asian Amateur Championships. Previous Masters

Right Jack Nicklaus's legendary back-nine charge on the final afternoon of the 1986 Masters, in which he took just 30 shots to come home, earned the 46-year-old his sixth Green Jacket and his 18th major.

Below Seve Ballesteros blasts his way out of trouble on his way to a second Masters victory, in 1983.

champions are given a lifetime entitlement to play in the tournament, but are discouraged from entering if they are no longer competitive.

There are a number of traditions at Augusta. On the Tuesday night prior to the tournament a 'champions' dinner' is held at the club, attended by past winners of the competition, and the defending champion is given the honour of selecting the menu. On the Wednesday, a par-3 contest is held over the club's par-3 course. This is a great family occasion, introduced in 1960, but there's a well-known 'jinx' that no winner of the par-3 event has gone on to win the tournament proper.

Since 1963 an honorary starter has usually struck a tee shot to get the tournament under way. Jock Hutchison, Fred McLeod, Byron Nelson, Gene Sarazen, Sam Snead, Arnold Palmer and Jack Nicklaus have all had this responsibility in the past.

NOTABLE WINNERS

Although he'd retired from competitive golf four years earlier, Bobby Jones played in the inaugural invitational tournament of 1934. He finished 13th, while Horton Smith took the victory.

The 1935 event witnessed one of the most famous shots in golf's history, when Gene Sarazen holed a 4-wood from 235 yards/215 m on the 15th hole for an albatross two. He went on to win in an 18-hole play-off against Craig Wood.

Americans dominated the tournament through its first 25 years. Sam Snead was three times a winner and Ben Hogan took the title twice. South Africa's Gary Player was the first overseas golfer to win the Masters when he triumphed in 1961. He was also victorious in 1974 and 1978. But US players continued to reign supreme, with Jack Nicklaus and Arnold Palmer leading the charge. Palmer took four titles and Nicklaus six. His last came in 1986, when he was 46 years old.

In 1980 Spanish sensation Seve Ballesteros was the first European to don a Green Jacket. This victory, and his second in 1983, heralded a new, international era for the tournament. Germany's Bernhard Langer won in 1985 and 1993. Sandy Lyle of Scotland was the first British champion in 1988,

and his success was quickly followed by that of Nick Faldo, who won twice consecutively in 1989 and 1990, and for a third time in 1996. Ian Woosnam of Wales made it four straight British winners in 1991, and José María Olazábal's victories in 1994 and 1999 meant that European players had won 11 of the 20 tournaments of the 1980s and 1990s.

Tiger Woods announced his arrival as a 'major' force by winning the 1997 tournament by a record 12 shots. He also won in 2001, 2002 and 2005. Tiger's great rival Phil Mickelson has been the most successful player at the Masters in recent years. He's won three times since 2004.

Top Drama is almost guaranteed at the short 16th: a possible birdie perhaps, or an undesired skirmish with the water.

Above The youngest-ever winner of the Masters raises his arms in victory after winning the 1997 tournament with a record 18-under-par 270. The decade of the Tiger had begun.

The US PGA Championship

Of the four men's major championships, the US PGA Championship is the last to be contested each year, and is usually held in the second week of August. Although, in many people's eyes, it's regarded as the least significant of the majors, it tends to feature the strongest field of the four.

The US PGA Championship is the only major that does not explicitly grant entry to the top 50 players on the Official World Golf Ranking. Invitations are, however, generally extended to all players in the top 100.

The tournament owes its inception to the Philadelphia department store owner Rodman Wanamaker. In January 1916 he convened a meeting of leading American golfers and other important golf industry figures to discuss the formation of a professional golfers' association. The result was the founding of the PGA of America. Seven months later the organization contested the inaugural PGA Championship at Siwanoy Country Club in Eastchester, New York.

Most victories
5 – Walter Hagen, Jack Nicklaus

Youngest winner
Gene Sarazen, 1922, aged 20 years 5 months

Oldest winner
Julius Boros, 1968, aged 48 years 4 months

Lowest 72-hole total
265 (15 under par) – David Toms, 2001

Lowest round
63 – ten players

Biggest margin of victory
Match play, 8 and 7 – Paul Runyan beat Sam Snead, 1938; stroke play, 7 shots – Jack Nicklaus, 1980

Most appearances
37 – Jack Nicklaus, 1962–2000; Arnold Palmer, 1958–94

MATCH-PLAY TOURNAMENT

Wanamaker put up the prize money and trophies for that first tournament and suggested that the event should be similar to the British News of the World Tournament – a match-play event. From 1916 right up until 1957, the US PGA Championship was played to a match-play format.

British-born professional Jim Barnes captured the first title, beating Jock Hutchison, originally from St Andrews, Scotland, in the final. After World War I, Walter Hagen emerged as a US PGA specialist, winning five championships, including four in a row from 1924–27.

Above Bob Tway chips in from a greenside bunker on the final hole to steal the 1986 PGA Championship from Greg Norman.

Left Match-play supremo Walter Hagen (right) dominated the US PGA Championship throughout the 1920s.

He won 22 consecutive matches before Leo Diegel took the title in 1928. Gene Sarazen was another stalwart of the championship: he won for the first time in 1922 and made his last appearance in 1972, at the age of 70.

THE STROKE-PLAY ERA

In 1958, Dow Finsterwald won the first US PGA Championship to be played to a stroke-play format. He had been a beaten finalist the previous year. American players continued to rule the roost, as they had in the match-play era. In 1962 South Africa's Gary Player became only the fifth foreign-born player to win the title. Through the 1960s, 70s and 80s, Player, who won again in 1972, and Australia's David Graham, the winner in 1979, were the only overseas golfers to triumph. During those decades, Jack Nicklaus was the man to beat. He took five championships between 1963 and 1980 and finished in the top ten a further ten times.

As with the other three majors, recent winners have reflected the globalization of golf – since 1990, players hailing from five different continents have taken the title. In 2008 Padraig Harrington of Ireland was the first European-born winner since Tommy Armour in 1930.

The following year Y.E. Yang of South Korea defeated four-time champion Tiger Woods to become the first Asian man to win a major. Then, in 2010, Germany's Martin Kaymer defeated Bubba Watson of the USA in a sudden-death play-off at Whistling Straits, Wisconsin, to become the first continental European winner of the US PGA Championship.

Below The look says it all: an astounded John Daly celebrates the most unexpected of victories in the 1991 US PGA Championship at Crooked Stick, Indiana. Going into the event, the American was ranked 168th in the world.

The Ryder Cup

A biennial team contest between the leading professional golfers from Europe and the USA, the Ryder Cup is one of the most eagerly anticipated events on the golfing, indeed sporting, calendar. Alternately held in the USA and Europe, it generates huge excitement among both players and fans.

Most appearances	11 – Nick Faldo (GB&I/Eur), 1977–97
Most points scored	25 – Nick Faldo (GB&I/Eur), 1977–97
Most times as captain	6 – Walter Hagen (USA), 1927–37
Youngest player	Sergio Garcia (Eur), 1999, aged 19 years 8 months
Oldest player	Raymond Floyd (USA), 1993, aged 51 years
Biggest margin of victory	23½–8½ – USA win at Champions Golf Club, Houston, Texas, 1967

In 1926, at an unofficial match between professionals from the USA and Britain played at Wentworth, a 68-year-old seed merchant called Samuel Ryder was an interested spectator. He took it upon himself to make the competition a permanent fixture and to that end commissioned Mappin & Webb of Mayfair to create a gold trophy, the cost of which was split: Ryder paid £100, *Golf Illustrated* paid £100 and the R&A put in £50. Since 1927, the Ryder Cup has been played for on 38 occasions, and the USA leads the series by 25 to 11, with two tied matches.

THE FORMAT

There have been numerous changes to the team structure and playing format of the Ryder Cup over the years, but this is the current situation. Each team consists of 12 men, who have either qualified via a performance-based points system or have been picked by the captain, who is generally a former player.

The Cup is decided by a series of matches played to a match-play format in pairs or singles. Each match is worth one point. Over the first two days there are four sessions of pairs matches, half played as foursomes (alternate shot), half played as four-ball (better-ball). In each session there are four matches, with eight men from each team competing. On the final day there are 12 singles matches, accounting for 12 of the 28 points on offer. A team needs to reach 14½ points to be the outright winner. In the event of a tie, the defending team retains the Cup.

Above left The British Ryder Cup team on Cunard liner *Aquitania*, on their way to America to compete in the inaugural Ryder Cup. Second from the left is businessman Samuel Ryder, who founded the competition.

Above Tony Jacklin (left) and Jack Nicklaus shake hands in 1969, after Nicklaus had sportingly conceded a short putt to ensure that both their match and the Ryder Cup would be halved.

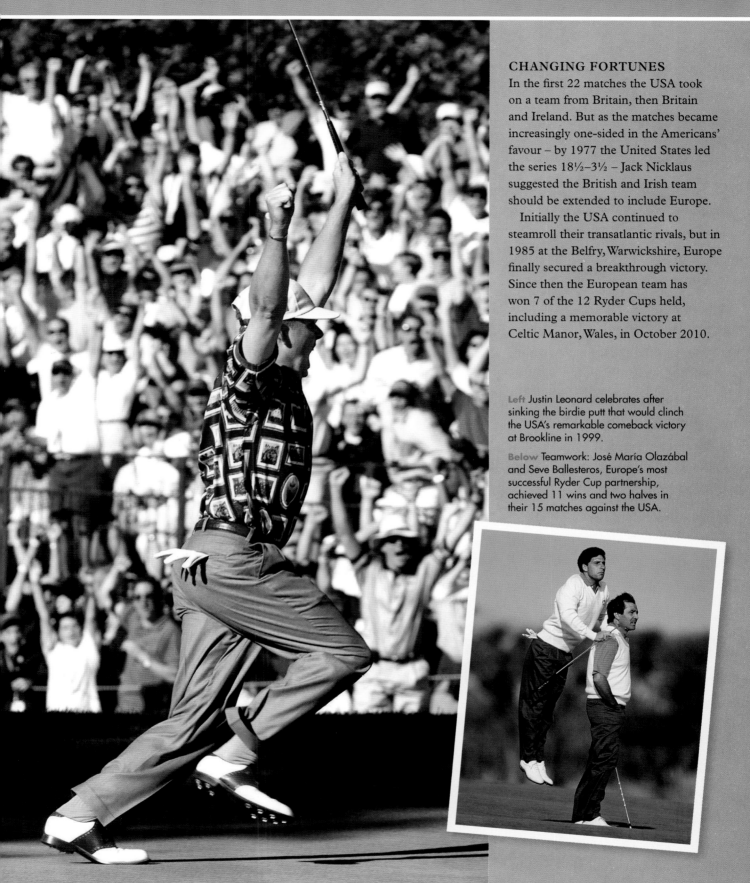

CHANGING FORTUNES

In the first 22 matches the USA took on a team from Britain, then Britain and Ireland. But as the matches became increasingly one-sided in the Americans' favour – by 1977 the United States led the series 18½–3½ – Jack Nicklaus suggested the British and Irish team should be extended to include Europe.

Initially the USA continued to steamroll their transatlantic rivals, but in 1985 at the Belfry, Warwickshire, Europe finally secured a breakthrough victory. Since then the European team has won 7 of the 12 Ryder Cups held, including a memorable victory at Celtic Manor, Wales, in October 2010.

Left Justin Leonard celebrates after sinking the birdie putt that would clinch the USA's remarkable comeback victory at Brookline in 1999.

Below Teamwork: José María Olazábal and Seve Ballesteros, Europe's most successful Ryder Cup partnership, achieved 11 wins and two halves in their 15 matches against the USA.

Professional Golf

Over the last century things have changed dramatically for tournament golf professionals. They have become some of the highest paid and most recognizable sports personalities on the planet, competing for huge prizes on organized 'tours', while their earnings are supplemented by lucrative sponsorship deals.

The two principal organizations in men's professional tournament golf today are the PGA Tour and the PGA European Tour. Although a tour existed in the USA from the 1930s, it was not until 1968 that the PGA Tour formally separated from the Professional Golfers' Association of America (the PGA). The name 'PGA Tour' was adopted in 1975.

THE USA

The circuit was, and predominantly still is, based in the USA. Currently there are 45 official events, contested over 41 weeks. The majors and World Golf Championship events are co-sanctioned by the PGA Tour, and the circuit features a number of other key competitions, such as the Players Championship.

Since 2007, the focus of the PGA Tour season has been the FedEx Cup. Throughout the regular season, from January to late August, players collect points from tournament performances with a view to qualifying for the FedEx Cup Play-offs. These four events, culminating in the Tour Championship, decide the winner of the FedEx Cup and the distribution of a huge bonus pool – amounting to $35 million in 2011. The winner of the FedEx Cup itself receives $10 million, the richest prize on the Tour.

The PGA Tour also operates the second-tier Nationwide Tour and the Champions Tour, for players over 50.

Above The 2010 season was a phenomenal one for European golf. Europe reclaimed the Ryder Cup, European Tour players Graeme McDowell, Louis Oosthuizen and Martin Kaymer won three of the year's four majors, and Lee Westwood displaced Tiger Woods as World No. 1.

Left Davis Love III drives on the 18th at Harbour Town Golf Links, South Carolina, during the PGA Tour's Verizon Heritage tournament of 2008. Love won the event five times between 1987 and 2003.

EUROPE AND THE REST OF THE WORLD

The PGA European Tour was introduced in 1972. At that time it consisted of 20 tournaments, 13 of which were held in Britain and Ireland. Since then the European Tour has grown considerably: it's now a truly global circuit, visiting Europe, North America, Africa, Asia and Australasia.

Like the PGA Tour's FedEx Cup, the European Tour features a season-long points race to decide the player of the year. The Race to Dubai carries a current bonus pool of $7.5 million, with a prize of $1.5 million going to the leading player after the season-ending Dubai World Championship. Also like the PGA Tour, the European Tour is responsible for the administration of two further circuits – the Challenge Tour, a feeder for the main circuit, and the European Seniors Tour.

In 1996 the International Federation of PGA Tours was founded. Beside the PGA Tour and European Tour, its first members were the Japan Golf Tour, the PGA Tour of Australasia and South Africa's Sunshine Tour. The Asian Tour joined in 1999, and since then numerous other circuits across the globe, both men's and women's, have joined the federation.

WOMEN'S PROFESSIONAL GOLF

The Ladies Professional Golf Association (LPGA) Tour, based largely in the USA, is the principal women's circuit, but there is also a Ladies European Tour and a Ladies Asian Golf Tour. As in the men's game, there are four events in women's golf that are classified as 'majors'. Over the years the list of women's majors has been altered on several occasions, but currently they are the Kraft Nabisco

Above left Annika Sörenstam challenged the status quo in 2003 by becoming the first woman to play a PGA Tour event in 58 years. After rounds of 71 and 74 in the Bank of America Colonial Tournament, she missed the cut by four shots.

Above Se Ri Pak took the LPGA tour by storm in 1998, winning two majors in her rookie year. Her performances paved the way for a new generation of South Korean golfers. Today, South Korea has more players in the top 100 of the Rolex Women's World Golf Ranking than any other country.

Championship, the LPGA Championship, the US Women's Open and the Women's British Open.

First played in 1990, the Solheim Cup is a biennial team event contested between the USA and Europe in the style of the men's Ryder Cup. It has swiftly become one of the most exciting and intense events in women's golf.

Amateur Golf

In days gone by, the top amateur players were generally part-time golfers. They would hold down a regular job and play golf on the side. As an example, the greatest amateur in the history of the game, Bobby Jones, was a successful lawyer. Things are a little different now.

Today's top-level amateur tends to be a full-time golfer, with a coach, psychologist, physiotherapist and other support. In fact there are few real differences between the professional and amateur games. There is one key distinction, however: amateurs are not paid to play. There are strict rules governing amateur status, but the most basic of these is that prize money is not on offer at amateur tournaments.

The most prestigious individual amateur events in men's golf are the (British) Amateur Championship and the US Amateur Championship. In women's golf they are the British Ladies' Amateur Championship and the US Women's Amateur Championship.

AMATEUR CHAMPIONSHIP

The Amateur Championship – informally known as the British Amateur – was founded in 1885 by Royal Liverpool Golf Club, at the instigation of the club secretary Thomas Owen Potter. There were 44 entrants from 12 British clubs for the inaugural event, and Lancashire's Allan Macfie was the winner.

In 1921 the R&A took over the running of the championship. Now, the event sees entries from all over the world, with 288 applicants offered starting places. Qualification for entry is largely

Below left Harold Hilton crouching over a putt en route to winning the 1911 Amateur Championship at Prestwick. Later that year he would also win the US Amateur.

Below As an amateur, Tiger Woods broke innumerable records and won three US Amateurs in a row.

Opposite Joyce Wethered leads Glenna Collett over the Swilcan Bridge at St Andrews during the final of the 1929 British Ladies' Championship. Wethered fought back from 5 down to win one of golf's finest-ever matches.

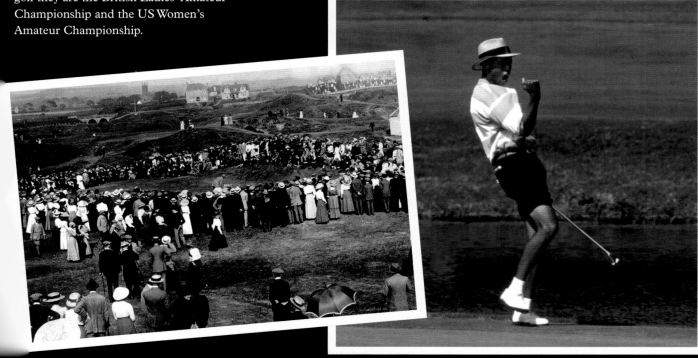

based on the World Amateur Golf Ranking; significant golf nations are allocated places on a quota basis.

The annual competition consists of two qualifying rounds of stroke play, with the leading 64 going on to contest the match-play stages. The winner of the event is invited to play in that year's Open Championship and in the US Masters the following April.

US AMATEUR CHAMPIONSHIP

The US Amateur, run by the USGA and dating back to 1895, has a very similar format to its British equivalent – 36 holes of stroke play with the top 64 progressing to decide the tournament by match play. As with the British Amateur, the winner is granted invitations to play in the Open and the Masters. He is also invited to participate in the US Open. Like the British Amateur, before World War II the US Amateur used to be considered one of the four major championships.

OTHER MEN'S EVENTS

Established in response to golf's rapid expansion in the region, the Asian Amateur Championship, first played in 2009, is earning a reputation as one of the predominant fixtures on the amateur calendar. The winner of that tournament receives an invitation to the following year's US Masters and entry into International Final Qualifying for the Open Championship.

The Walker Cup is the most famous team event in the men's amateur game. Inaugurated in 1922, it sees a side of ten players from Great Britain and Ireland take on a team from the USA. Between 1947 and 1985, the USA lost just once, but in recent years honours have been more equally divided.

Another key team event is the Eisenhower Trophy. Effectively the World Amateur Team Championship, it's played biennially, with teams of three representing each participating country.

WOMEN'S AMATEUR EVENTS

First contested in 1893, the British Ladies' Amateur Golf Championship has been won by some great players, including Joyce Wethered (four times), Babe Zaharias and Mickey Walker. As with the men's British Amateur Championship, the tournament is decided over two qualifying rounds of stroke play before the top 64 go on to contest the match-play stages.

The format is the same for the other principal prize in women's amateur golf, the US Women's Amateur Championship. Another historic tournament, it was first played in 1895.

The Curtis Cup is the women's equivalent of the Walker Cup. First played in 1932, the match is contested by a team from the USA and one representing Great Britain and Ireland. The USA has dominated the event in recent years, winning the last seven straight matches.

including

Byron Nelson **64**   Sam Snead **65**

Kathy Whitworth **70**   Tom Watson **71**   Severiano Ballesteros **72**   Bernhard Langer **73**   Greg Norman **73**

GOLFING **LEGENDS**

3

Old Tom Morris **59**

Harry Vardon **61**

Walter Hagen **62**

Bobby Jones **63**

Henry Cotton **64**

Ben Hogan **66**

Peter Thomson **67**

Arnold Palmer **68**

Gary Player **69**

Jack Nicklaus **69**

Introduction

Golf is one of the few individual sports where a participant's performance is totally within his or her own hands. It's a game where one competitor cannot physically impact on another's play. Psychological blows can, of course, be struck, so the paragons of the game have all been mentally strong as well as physically talented. Players are often revered as much for their focus and determination as for their shot-making prowess.

In every generation since golf was first played competitively, a selection of legends has emerged. Any player who masters the game commands the respect of fellow golfers, but there are those who transcend the sport to become well known even by people who have never picked up a golf club. Some have gained fame for their unparalleled skill, some for their flamboyant personalities, others simply for their ability to win. First by word of mouth, then in newspaper reports and latterly on television, golf's greatest players have forged their places in the public consciousness by mastering a sport that's widely recognized to be one of the most challenging in the world.

The following pages present a selection of the most famous names in golf over the last 150 years. From the early Scottish professionals of the nineteenth century to the bright young stars of the new millennium, each has left an indelible imprint on the game's history.

In the beginning, golf's biggest stars were British. Scottish pros such as Old Tom Morris and Willie Park Sr were the first men to capture the public's imagination with their on-course rivalry. Then came the 'Great Triumvirate' of Vardon, Taylor and Braid. Their successes in the Open Championship, and farther afield, greatly increased golf's popularity in Britain.

Walter Hagen led the American assault on the top of the game in the 1920s, and he was followed by the likes of Bobby Jones, Gene Sarazen and Sam Snead. These men were golf's first global superstars. America has been the dominant country in world golf since that time, although many players from outside the United States have also enjoyed considerable success over sustained periods.

Longevity is a key reason why golf produces so many figureheads. The sport offers players an opportunity to enjoy success over a long timespan, and the public can follow golfers' careers for decades rather than years, growing old with them. In 2009, at the age of 59, Tom Watson came within a whisker of securing his sixth Open title at Turnberry. His romantic yet brilliant effort earned him fans who were the children and grandchildren of those who'd cheered him to his first Open victory in 1975. It's little wonder golfers become legends in their own lifetimes.

Willie Park Sr

Born
30 June 1833,
Musselburgh, Scotland

Died
25 July 1903

Majors
4

Open Championship
1860, 1863, 1866, 1875

IN 1854, **WILLIE PARK**, a caddy from East Lothian, challenged Allan Robertson, Tom Morris or Willie Dunn – the leading players of the day – to a match with £100 at stake. Tom's brother George accepted the wager of the young upstart from Musselburgh, and was soundly beaten.

Park was a confident and competitive character who feared no opponent. He was a tall and powerful player, able to hit an impressively long ball, but it was for his skill at putting that he was most feared.

He won the inaugural Open Championship at Prestwick in 1860, defeating the course's creator and tournament favourite Tom Morris by two shots. A great rivalry developed between the two men, and they shared the spoils in seven of the first eight Open Championships – Park taking three titles and Morris four.

Willie Park Jr

Born
4 February 1864,
Musselburgh, Scotland

Died
22 May 1925

Majors
2

US Open
Cut 1919

Open Championship
1887, 1889

WILLIE PARK JR played in professional matches as a teenager and competed in his first Open Championship in 1880, aged just 16. He finished only 16th in that event, but he managed 12 championship top tens over the next 20 years, including two victories. As with his father, the strength of his game lay around the greens, and his putting often made up for his less than perfect long game. He once famously said: 'A man who can putt is a match for anyone.'

Park was also a fine club maker, with shops in London and New York, and a pioneering golf course architect. He contributed to the design of some 170 layouts in Britain, Europe and North America, including Sunningdale's Old Course and the North and South courses at Olympia Fields in Chicago.

Old Tom Morris

Born
16 June 1821,
St Andrews, Fife, Scotland

Died
24 May 1908

Majors
4

Open Championship
1861, 1862, 1864, 1867

AFTER LEAVING SCHOOL at the age of 14, Tom Morris was taken on as an apprentice by the St Andrews ball maker and caddy Allan Robertson. He worked under Robertson until 1851, when he was employed to lay out a new course at Prestwick and appointed 'Keeper of the Green'. The course hosted the inaugural Open Championship of 1860.

Morris was a smooth swinger who had a cool temperament but a famous fragility on short putts. He may have lost out to Willie Park in 1860, but he struck back to win the next two Opens. In 1862 he finished 13 shots clear of the field – a margin that has never been equalled.

Tom Morris returned to St Andrews in 1864 and continued to tread the links when he was well into his 80s. Golf's Grand Old Man remains one of the game's most iconic figures.

Young Tom Morris

Born
20 April 1851,
St Andrews, Fife, Scotland

Died
25 December 1875

Majors
4

Open Championship
1868, 1869, 1870, 1872

THE SON OF Old Tom Morris, young 'Tommy' was born and bred to golf. He hit the ball over prodigious distances, with a low, penetrating flight, and had a natural touch around the greens. In 1868, at the age of 17, he became the youngest-ever winner of the Open Championship. He defended the title in 1869 and became the first man to win three straight in 1870. There was no championship in 1871, but in 1872 Tommy won again. He's the only player ever to have won four consecutive Opens. His first-round 47 in 1870 over Prestwick's 12-hole layout is said to have been one of the greatest rounds of golf ever played.

In the history of the game no player's star has shone so brightly, so briefly. Tommy died in tragic circumstances aged just 24, suffering a pulmonary haemorrhage just three months after his wife and baby son had died in childbirth.

Harold Hilton

Born
12 January 1869, West Kirby,
Merseyside, England

Died
5 March 1942

Majors
7

Open Championship
1892, 1897

US Amateur
1911

British Amateur
1900, 1901, 1911, 1913

A MEMBER OF Royal Liverpool Golf Club, Harold Hilton became the second amateur to win the Open when he captured the championship over 72 holes at Muirfield in 1892. He won the Open again in 1897 and was British Amateur champion on four occasions between 1900 and 1913. In 1911 he shocked the American golfing establishment by becoming the first foreign-born winner of the US Amateur Championship.

Hilton was a powerful player with a wild swing and a great ability for shot making. He put so much effort into his shots that his cap would regularly fall off his head at the end of a full swing. He was also a writer, and published a number of popular books on golf. When *Golf Monthly* magazine was founded in 1911, Hilton was its first editor.

J.H. Taylor

Born
19 March 1871,
Northam, Devon, England

Died
10 February 1963

Majors
5

US Open
2nd 1900

Open Championship
1894, 1895, 1900, 1909, 1913

JOHN HENRY TAYLOR was a pioneering golf professional – a co-founder and the first chairman of the British Professional Golfers' Association in 1901. Five times Open champion, he played in all 30 Open Championships held between 1893 and 1927, and finished in the top ten an amazing 23 times. He was a single-minded and focused competitor with a burning desire to win. He forged a great rivalry with Harry Vardon and James Braid, and the three became known as the 'Great Triumvirate'.

At the age of 62, Taylor captained the 1933 British Ryder Cup team to victory at Southport and Ainsdale. He continued his involvement with golf in later life by writing books, making golf clubs and designing courses. He died a month before his 92nd birthday.

James Braid

Born
6 February 1870,
Earlsferry, Fife, Scotland

Died
27 November 1950

Majors
5

Open Championship
1901, 1905, 1906, 1908, 1910

A TALL, RANGY and robust golfer, James Braid at one time held the world record for the longest drive – 395 yards/361 m, measured at Walton Heath, the club where he was professional from its inception in 1904 until his death in 1950. He had a strong grip and hit the ball from right to left.

The first decade of the twentieth century saw Braid, a member of the Great Triumvirate, at the peak of his playing career. Between 1901 and 1910 he won five of the ten Open Championships held, and was runner-up on three occasions.

Not content with excelling on the links, Braid also turned his hand to course design. He was an architect of some skill and was involved in the construction and remodelling of over 200 courses, including Gleneagles and Nairn.

Harry Vardon

Born
9 May 1870, Grouville, Jersey

Died
20 March 1937

Majors
7

US Open
1900

Open Championship
1896, 1898, 1899, 1903,
1911, 1914

HAILING FROM THE Channel Island of Jersey, Harry Vardon is the only man to have won the Open Championship on six occasions. He was a member of the Great Triumvirate and an accurate and highly skilled golfer, famed for his control over the ball and his manipulation of hickory-shafted clubs. He also developed a unique style of gripping the club, in which the little finger of the right hand overlapped the index finger of the left hand – this is still known as the 'Vardon grip'.

Vardon was diagnosed with tuberculosis after picking up his fourth Open title in 1903 and spent much of the first decade of the twentieth century recuperating. It's generally felt that he would have collected more major titles had it not been for his illness.

Walter Hagen

Born
21 December 1892,
Rochester, New York, USA

Died
6 October 1969

Majors
11

Masters
Tied 11th 1936

US Open
1914, 1919

Open Championship
1922, 1924, 1928, 1929

US PGA
1921, 1924, 1925, 1926, 1927

WALTER HAGEN'S flamboyant style ushered in a new era for professional golf. Champagne and limousines, parties at the Savoy, golfing with the Prince of Wales – Hagen was quite a showman. But he backed up his bravado with a sparkling game. He was a fierce competitor and a great match player. He won 22 straight 36-hole matches at the US PGA Championship, and 32 out of 33 matches between the first round in 1921 and the quarterfinals of 1928.

When he began his career, professionals were considered second-class citizens in the socially exclusive world of golf, but Hagen was instrumental in changing that perception. Speaking at a dinner held in Hagen's honour in 1967, Arnold Palmer said: 'If it were not for you, Walter, this dinner tonight would be downstairs in the pro shop, not in the ballroom.'

Gene Sarazen

Born
27 February 1902,
Harrison, New York, USA

Died
13 May 1999

Majors
7

Masters
1935

US Open
1922, 1932

Open Championship
1932

US PGA
1922, 1923, 1933

GENE SARAZEN was born Eugenio Saraceni, but changed his name as he felt it sounded like that of a violinist. His poor health as a young man led him to try golf as a way to take fresh air, and he quickly realized he was a natural. He won the 1922 US Open as a 20-year-old, then proved it was no fluke by capturing the US PGA Championship later in the same year.

Sarazen is one of only five men who have won all four professional major titles (the others being Jack Nicklaus, Tiger Woods, Ben Hogan and Gary Player) and was an ever-present figure in golf through the twentieth century. He presented the American television series *Shell's Wonderful World of Golf* and remained an honorary starter at the Masters until 1999.

Bobby Jones

Born
17 March 1902,
Atlanta, Georgia, USA

Died
18 December 1971

Majors
13

US Open
1923, 1926, 1929, 1930

Open Championship
1926, 1927, 1930

US Amateur
1924, 1925, 1927, 1928, 1930

British Amateur
1930

THE FINEST AMATEUR golfer ever to swing a club, Robert Tyre 'Bobby' Jones was a great man as well as a great champion. He overcame a fiery temper in his early golfing years and went on to set the benchmarks for sportsmanship and integrity at the game's highest level.

Bobby Jones possessed a fluid and elegant swing and an excellent golfing brain that helped him dominate the amateur game through the 1920s. In 1930 he completed what became known as the 'Grand Slam' by winning the US and British Amateur Championships as well as the US and British Opens. It's an achievement that will surely never be replicated.

Jones retired from competitive golf at the age of 28 and went on to co-found Augusta National Golf Club and the Masters Tournament.

Joyce Wethered

Born
17 November 1901,
Brook, Surrey, England

Died
18 November 1997

Majors
N/A

English Ladies' Championship
1920, 1921, 1922, 1923, 1924

Ladies' British Amateur Championship
1922, 1924, 1925, 1929

PRIOR TO THE 1930 British Amateur Championship, Joyce Wethered played 18 holes at St Andrews with Bobby Jones. 'I have not played golf with anyone, man or woman, amateur or professional, who made me feel so utterly outclassed,' he said afterwards.

Joyce Wethered (later Lady Heathcoat-Amory) was one of the most talented golfers of the early twentieth century. She was an unheard-of 18-year-old when she entered the 1920 English Ladies' Championship, but she won the event, beating the favourite, Cecil Leitch, in the final. She won the English Championship five times consecutively and picked up the Ladies' British Amateur title on four occasions, perhaps most memorably at St Andrews in 1929, when she defeated top US lady amateur Glenna Collett in the final.

Henry Cotton

Born
28 January 1907, Holmes
Chapel, Cheshire, England

Died
22 December 1987

Majors
3

Masters
Tied 13th 1957

US Open
Tied 17th 1956

Open Championship
1934, 1937, 1948

HENRY COTTON'S Open Championship victory at Sandwich in 1934 was the first by a home player for 11 years, and it did much to rejuvenate British golfing fortunes. He picked up a second Open title at Carnoustie in 1937, but World War II interrupted his career and he won just one more major, the 1948 Open at Muirfield.

During the war Cotton served with the RAF, but he also raised money for the Red Cross by playing in exhibition matches. He was a champion of junior golf, an instructor, author and course designer. In 1947 and 1953 he captained the British Ryder Cup team. A trailblazing professional and a true English gentleman, Cotton's tireless efforts earned him an MBE and later a knighthood, which was officially conferred upon him one week after his death.

Byron Nelson

Born
4 February 1912,
Waxahachie, Texas, USA

Died
26 September 2006

Majors
5

Masters
1937, 1942

US Open
1939

Open Championship
5th 1937

US PGA
1940, 1945

WHEN BYRON NELSON retired from competitive golf in 1946, aged just 34, he did so having set golfing records that are likely never to be beaten. Between 1944 and 1946 he won an incredible 34 tournaments, from 75 starts. In the 1945 season he won 18 times, including 11 events in a row. His scoring average for the year was 68.33 (67.45 in the last round).

Tall and powerful, Nelson is widely considered to have been the first man to successfully employ a modern golf swing. He had an upright action with full shoulder turn. Hickory shafts had called for a wristy technique, but the introduction of steel in the late 1920s allowed Nelson to use the larger muscles in his legs and torso to generate power.

Babe Didrikson Zaharias

Born
26 June 1911,
Port Arthur, Texas, USA

Died
27 September 1956

Majors
10

Western Open
1940, 1944, 1945, 1950

Titleholders Championship
1947, 1950, 1952

US Women's Open
1948, 1950, 1954

GOLF WAS NOT the first sport in which Mildred 'Babe' Didrikson Zaharias enjoyed success. At high school she excelled in swimming, tennis, basketball and athletics. At the 1932 Olympic Games in Los Angeles she won gold medals in the javelin and the 80-m hurdles. She first played golf at the age of 21 and within three years was Texas women's amateur champion.

America's first female golfing celebrity, Babe won four major titles as an amateur before turning professional in 1947. She famously competed against the men, and she remains the only woman to make the cut in a PGA Tour event – a feat she achieved three times. She was a founder of the LPGA Tour and won 41 events on the circuit. She died of cancer at the age of just 45.

Sam Snead

Born
27 May 1912,
Ashwood, Virginia, USA

Died
23 May 2002

Majors
7

Masters
1949, 1952, 1954

US Open
2nd/tied 2nd 1937, 1947,
1949, 1953

Open Championship
1946

US PGA
1942, 1949, 1951

IN THE 1979 Quad Cities Open, a 67-year-old Sam Snead matched and then beat his age as he fired rounds of 67 and 66. The performance was indicative of his enduring talent and huge will to succeed. More than 40 years after emerging on the PGA Tour, he was still able to compete at the highest level. In a career spanning six decades, Snead collected 82 PGA Tour victories (more than any other player), seven majors and over 160 professional titles.

Renowned for his powerful and accurate ball striking, Snead had a rhythmical, free-flowing swing, earning him the moniker 'Swingin' Sam' when he first appeared on tour. Golf writers later changed it to 'Slammin' Sam' – the nickname that lived with him to the end of his life.

Ben Hogan

Born
13 August 1912,
Stephenville, Texas, USA

Died
25 July 1997

Majors
9

Masters
1951, 1953

US Open
1948, 1950, 1951, 1953

Open Championship
1953

US PGA
1946, 1948

FOR STUDENTS OF the golf swing, no action epitomizes 'classic' more accurately than Ben Hogan's. Although the Texan won nine major championships between 1946 and 1953, it's for his graceful and rhythmic swing that he is best remembered. During his early career he was afflicted with an erratic hook, but he practised tirelessly to turn his right-to-left shot shape into a.slight fade. In doing this he lost a little distance but increased his accuracy. From then on he was a clinical player, with total control over his game.

Hogan was a prolific Tour winner until injuries sustained in a car crash forced him to restrict his appearances. Despite this, in 1953 he came closest of any golfer to completing the modern Grand Slam: he won the Masters, US Open and Open Championship but was unable to get back from Britain in time to compete in the US PGA.

Bobby Locke

Born
20 November 1917,
Germiston, South Africa

Died
9 March 1987

Majors
4

Masters
Tied 10th 1948

US Open
3rd/tied 3rd 1947, 1951

Open Championship
1949, 1950, 1952, 1957

US PGA
Tied 33rd 1947

ARTHUR D'ARCY LOCKE was nicknamed 'Bobby' at an early age because of his admiration for Bobby Jones. Like Jones, he was a prodigy. He won both the South African Amateur and Open titles of 1935 at the age of just 18. In all, he won 72 professional tournaments during his career, including six events on the US Tour in 1947, but his greatest successes came in the Open Championship, an event he won four times between 1949 and 1957.

Locke played with a wristy, inside-to-out swing, producing a consistent draw that repeated unerringly. It was on the greens, however, that he truly excelled. He used an old rusty putter with a hickory shaft and employed an unorthodox technique to formidable effect. Gary Player believes that Locke was the greatest putter in the history of the game.

Max Faulkner

Born
27 July 1916, Bexhill-on-Sea,
East Sussex, England

Died
26 February 2005

Majors
1

Open Championship
1951

A FLAMBOYANT and talented player, Max Faulkner brought flair and fun to the golf course in a career spanning four decades. He was a fantastic striker of the ball and was renowned for his ability to manufacture shots. He also manufactured his own clubs and had a huge collection of putters, including many made by his own hand.

He had a colourful dress sense and an infectious personality. During one round of golf he claimed he needed to get more blood to his brain, so he walked from the green to the next tee on his hands. Although he won 18 professional tournaments between 1946 and 1970, his greatest triumph was winning the Open Championship of 1951, a victory he described as, 'All I ever wanted.'

Peter Thomson

Born
23 August 1929,
Melbourne, Australia

Majors
5

Masters
5th 1957

US Open
Tied 4th 1956

Open Championship
1954, 1955, 1956, 1958, 1965

ALTHOUGH HE WON 81 professional tournaments between 1947 and 1988, it is Peter Thomson's stunning record in the Open Championship that has secured his place in golfing history. Between 1951 and 1973 he made 23 consecutive cuts in the tournament. During that time he recorded 18 top-ten finishes and five victories, and he was the only player in the twentieth century to lift the Claret Jug three times consecutively.

Thomson was self-taught and employed an uncomplicated and natural technique. His simple playing style meant that his game was extremely consistent and reliable. This, coupled with his ability to thrive under pressure, made Thomson a steely competitor and a regular winner.

Arnold Palmer

Born
10 September 1929,
Latrobe, Pennsylvania, USA

Majors
7

Masters
1958, 1960, 1962, 1964

US Open
1960

Open Championship
1961, 1962

US PGA
Tied 2nd 1964, 1968, 1970

'THE KING' was 28 when he blazed into the public eye at the 1958 Masters. Employing an aggressive style of golf, he birdied the last two holes to win by a single shot. He developed a reputation for swashbuckling and exciting play, and gained an army of fans who cheered him on to six further major championships and 62 PGA Tour victories.

Palmer's back-to-back Open wins in 1961 and 1962 did a great deal to encourage other pros from the USA to travel to Britain to compete in golf's greatest championship, and his charisma and good humour won him many British supporters. His flair and style captivated television audiences, and he became golf's first global superstar, boosting the sport's popularity enormously.

Mickey Wright

Born
14 February 1935,
San Diego, California, USA

Majors
13

Western Open
1962, 1963, 1966

Titleholders Championship
1961, 1962

LPGA Championship
1958, 1960, 1961, 1963

US Women's Open
1958, 1959, 1961, 1964

FOR A SPELL in the early 1960s Mickey Wright was untouchable on the LPGA Tour. She topped the money list for four seasons in a row, from 1961 to 1964, and won an astounding 44 tournaments on the circuit in that time. In total she won 82 LPGA Tour events, and is second only to Kathy Whitworth on the all-time list.

Ben Hogan described Wright's swing as the best he ever saw, and many, including Kathy Whitworth, felt Wright could have won over 100 tour events had she not chosen to step back from competitive golf in 1969 at the age of 34. She served as president of the LPGA in 1963 and 1964 and throughout her career she worked tirelessly to promote women's professional golf.

Gary Player

Born
1 November 1935,
Johannesburg, South Africa

Majors
9

Masters
1961, 1974, 1978

US Open
1965

Open Championship
1959, 1968, 1974

US PGA
1962, 1972

A TENACIOUS COMPETITOR, Gary Player's will to win has been second to none. Standing just 5 feet 7 inches/1.7 m tall, he is known for his exceptional work ethic, not only in golfing technique but also with regard to his physical fitness and strength.

He was the first golfer from outside the United States to win the Masters and is the only international player to have won all four major titles. A truly global sportsman, he has won 165 tournaments as a professional and has racked up over 15 million miles/24 million km of travel: Player estimates he's spent more than three years of his life in an aeroplane. He's also a successful businessman and renowned golf course designer. Through a career spanning seven decades he has been a great ambassador for golf and for South Africa.

Jack Nicklaus

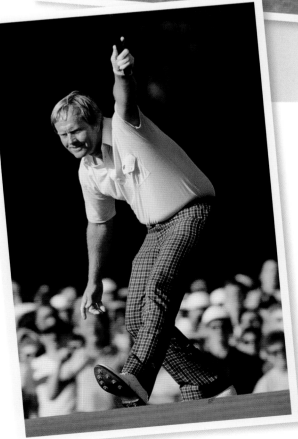

Born
21 January 1940,
Columbus, Ohio, USA

Majors
18

Masters
1963, 1965, 1966, 1972,
1975, 1986

US Open
1962, 1967, 1972, 1980

Open Championship
1966, 1970, 1978

US PGA
1963, 1971, 1973, 1975, 1980

WHEN IT COMES to golf's major championships, Jack Nicklaus is the greatest golfer of all time. He was just 22 when he won his first – the US Open of 1962 – and he was 46 when he won his 18th and last, the 1986 US Masters.

In his prime Nicklaus was one of the game's fiercest competitors. Although no aspect of his game was particularly outstanding, he had an uncanny ability to produce the necessary shot or hole the required putt at the crucial moment. As a result he won 115 titles in the course of an illustrious career. As a course designer, a businessman and a spokesman for the sport, the 'Golden Bear' has represented golf proudly and flawlessly for the last half century.

Kathy Whitworth

Born
27 September 1939,
Monahans, Texas, USA

Majors
6

Western Open
1967

Titleholders Championship
1965, 1966

Kraft Nabisco Championship
Tied 2nd 1983

LPGA Championship
1967, 1971, 1975

US Women's Open
2nd 1971

OVER A 23-YEAR SPAN between 1962 and 1985, Kathy Whitworth secured an incredible 88 tournament victories on the LPGA Tour. No professional golfer has won more events on a single circuit. Between 1966 and 1973 she was LPGA Tour Player of the Year seven times and the tour's money list leader eight times. In 1981 she became the first female golfer to surpass $1 million in career earnings.

A great driver of the ball, an excellent putter and a steely competitor, Whitworth won at least one LPGA Tour event every year from 1962 to 1978. She has served as president of the LPGA and captained the victorious US team in the inaugural Solheim Cup of 1990.

Lee Trevino

Born
1 December 1939,
Dallas, Texas, USA

Majors
6

Masters
Tied 10th 1975, 1985

US Open
1968, 1971

Open Championship
1971, 1972

US PGA
1974, 1984

LEE TREVINO is famous for his gritty determination and positive approach to golf. Both qualities were a product of his tough upbringing: he was raised in Texas by his mother and grandfather, and sent to work in the cotton fields at the age of five. Trevino's unique, self-taught technique and formidable gamesmanship were honed in his early career by gambling in head-to-head matches – he'd often wager more than he could afford to lose.

The glory years for 'Super Mex' came in the early 1970s. He won the US Open in 1971, the Open Championships of 1971 and 1972 and a further 12 PGA Tour events between 1970 and 1974. Trevino was a favourite with the fans. He laughed and joked with the galleries and played every game with a smile on his face.

Tom Watson

Born
4 September 1949,
Kansas City, Missouri, USA

Majors
8

Masters
1977, 1981

US Open
1982

Open Championship
1975, 1977, 1980, 1982, 1983

US PGA
2nd 1978

LONG AND ACCURATE, with a deadly short game, Tom Watson is one of the most complete golfers in the history of the game, and has won 68 tournaments as a professional. Watson's great rivalry with Jack Nicklaus did much to increase golf's popularity in the late 1970s. Their most epic battle – a tussle that became known as the 'Duel in the Sun' – came in the 1977 Open Championship at Turnberry. They were tied going into the final 36 holes, and Nicklaus closed with 65, 66, only to be defeated by a single stroke as Watson posted 65, 65. Watson captured the public's imagination at Turnberry again in 2009, when he came agonizingly close to securing a sixth Open title at the age of 59.

Nancy Lopez

Born
6 January 1957,
Torrance, California, USA

Majors
3

Kraft Nabisco Championship
Tied 3rd 1995

LPGA Championship
1978, 1985, 1989

US Women's Open
2nd/tied 2nd 1975, 1977,
1989, 1997

du Maurier Classic
2nd/tied 2nd 1979, 1981, 1996

NANCY LOPEZ played her first full LPGA Tour season in 1978 at the age of 21, and was a sensation. She won nine tournaments, including five consecutively, and was named Player of the Year and Associated Press Female Athlete of the Year. Lopez won eight times on the circuit in 1979, and won a further 31 LPGA Tour events between 1980 and 1997. Four times LPGA Tour Player of the Year, she reignited the public's interest in professional women's golf.

On the course, Lopez had an unusual action, with an early wrist break and slow backswing. But it repeated extremely effectively and held up under pressure. She retired from regular tournament play in 2002 but was captain of the US Solheim Cup team in 2005.

Severiano Ballesteros

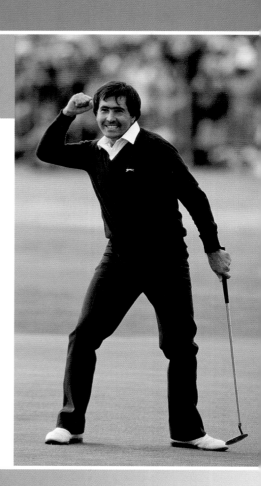

Born
9 April 1957,
Pedreña, Cantabria, Spain

Died
7 May 2011

Majors
5

Masters
1980, 1983

US Open
3rd 1987

Open Championship
1979, 1984, 1988

US PGA
5th 1984

THE DASHING SPANIARD was one of the most charismatic and naturally gifted golfers in the sport's history. In the 1970s and 80s he revitalized European golf and spearheaded the continent's return to the pinnacle of the game.

Seve first grabbed the headlines as a 19-year-old, when he finished runner-up in the 1976 Open at Royal Birkdale and captivated spectators with his swashbuckling and impulsive style. His audacious recoveries, improbable birdies and unrivalled creativity saw him win a record 50 tournaments on the European Tour, including five majors. He played in eight Ryder Cups and captained Europe to victory in 1997.

In 2008 he was diagnosed with a brain tumour. To the end, he fought the illness with the same courage and determination he displayed throughout his playing career.

Bernhard Langer

Born
27 August 1957,
Anhausen, Germany

Majors
2

Masters
1985, 1993

US Open
Tied 4th 1987

Open Championship
2nd/tied 2nd 1981, 1984

US PGA
Tied 21st 1987

BERNHARD LANGER is the model golf professional. Dedicated and precise, he has maintained an impressive level of consistency at the very top of the golfing tree for over 30 years. During his career he has battled the dreaded putting 'yips', but has overcome the affliction to win 83 times around the world.

In 1985 Langer won seven tournaments on five continents, including the US Masters. When the Official World Golf Ranking was introduced in 1986, he was the inaugural No. 1. He's also a Ryder Cup stalwart, playing in ten matches and captaining Europe to an emphatic win in the United States in 2004. Langer's golfing successes have been instrumental in raising the sport's profile in his home country and inspiring a new generation of German professionals.

Greg Norman

Born
10 February 1955,
Mount Isa, Australia

Majors
2

Masters
2nd/tied 2nd 1986, 1987, 1996

US Open
2nd 1984, 1995

Open Championship
1986, 1993

US PGA
2nd 1986, 1993

THE 'GREAT WHITE SHARK' was a dominant force in golf through the 1980s and 90s. He spent an incredible 331 weeks as World No. 1 (only Tiger Woods has resided in the top spot for longer), recorded 87 tournament victories between 1976 and 2001, and finished in the top ten at 30 majors. Although he won the Open Championship twice, he is often remembered for his historic defeats: he's the only player to lose play-offs in all four majors.

In his prime, Norman was known as an unerringly straight driver of the ball and a powerful iron player with the ability to destroy high-quality fields. He has also forged a successful off-course career, with business interests ranging from golf course design to wine making.

Nick Faldo

Born
18 July 1957,
Welwyn Garden City, England

Majors
6

Masters
1989, 1990, 1996

US Open
2nd 1988

Open Championship
1987, 1990, 1992

US PGA
Tied 2nd 1992

NICK FALDO is the most successful British golfer of the modern era. His early career showed promise, but his competitive drive and quest for golfing perfection led him to completely rebuild his swing in the mid-1980s, under the guidance of David Leadbetter. The process took three years, but Faldo emerged with a technically excellent action that could stand up to the highest pressures of the professional game.

His efforts were vindicated when he won the Open Championship at Muirfield in 1987 and claimed five further major titles in the following ten years. He played in 11 consecutive Ryder Cups between 1977 and 1997 and is the competition's all-time leading points scorer. In recognition of his contribution to British golf, Faldo received a knighthood in 2009.

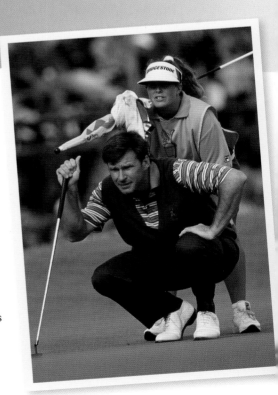

Payne Stewart

Born
30 January 1957,
Springfield, Missouri, USA

Died
25 October 1999

Majors
3

Masters
Tied 8th 1986

US Open
1991, 1999

Open Championship
2nd/tied 2nd 1985, 1990

US PGA
1989

IN HIS TRADEMARK plus fours and flat cap, Payne Stewart was one of the most recognizable figures in golf in the late twentieth century. He turned pro in 1979 but, despite his elegant game, failed to make an immediate impact in the United States and spent a couple of years playing in Asia. After he finally earned his PGA Tour card in 1982, his game developed steadily and he took his first major title at the 1989 US PGA Championship. He went on to win two US Opens and was also a member of five Ryder Cup teams, making his last appearance at Brookline in September 1999. One month later he was tragically killed in an air crash, and the game lost one of its most flamboyant characters.

John Daly

Born
28 April 1966,
Carmichael, California, USA

Majors
2

Masters
Tied 3rd 1993

US Open
Tied 27th 1997

Open Championship
1995

US PGA
1991

SINCE HE APPEARED from nowhere (in his first year on the US Tour) to win the 1991 US PGA Championship, John Daly's career has been a rollercoaster ride. He has struggled with alcohol, lost millions of dollars gambling and been married four times. But, on occasion, his golf has been pure genius, and his all-or-nothing mentality has captivated golf fans around the world. His swing is unconventional: taking the club back way past parallel at the top, he generates huge power, and he was famous in his early career for his prodigious length from the tee.

Daly's 'grip it and rip it' style has produced 19 tournament victories but has also caused countless meltdowns. He is the only eligible two-time major winner never selected to play in a Ryder Cup.

Nick Price

Born
28 January 1957,
Durban, South Africa

Majors
3

Masters
5th 1986

US Open
4th/tied 4th 1992, 1998

Open Championship
1994

US PGA
1992, 1994

IN 1994 NICK PRICE of Zimbabwe secured back-to-back major titles – the Open Championship and the US PGA Championship. Between 1991 and 1994 he won 18 tournaments and climbed to No. 1 in the Official World Golf Ranking. His quick-tempo swing is one of the most efficient in the game, and he has earned a reputation as a pure ball striker with a particular aptitude for long-iron play. His greatest triumph came in the 1994 Open Championship at Turnberry. Three behind Jesper Parnevik with three to play, Price finished birdie-eagle-par, to take the Claret Jug by a single stroke.

Price has been a great ambassador for golf and has received the USGA's Bobby Jones Award and the PGA Tour's Payne Stewart Award in recognition of his contribution to the game.

Colin Montgomerie

Born
23 June 1963, Glasgow, Scotland

Majors
0

Masters
Tied 8th 1998

US Open
2nd/tied 2nd 1994, 1997, 2006

Open Championship
2nd 2005

US PGA
2nd 1995

'MONTY' IS ONE of the most successful golfers in the history of the European Tour. He has been European No. 1 on eight occasions – seven times consecutively between 1993 and 1999 – and has won 31 tournaments on the circuit. Although he has never won a major title, he has finished as runner-up five times, losing twice in play-offs.

The Scot is best known for his heroics in the Ryder Cup. Playing in the event on eight occasions, he has amassed a total of 23.5 points and has never lost a Ryder Cup singles match. He captained Europe to victory at Celtic Manor in 2010. He is one of golf's great personalities and has worn his heart on his sleeve throughout his career.

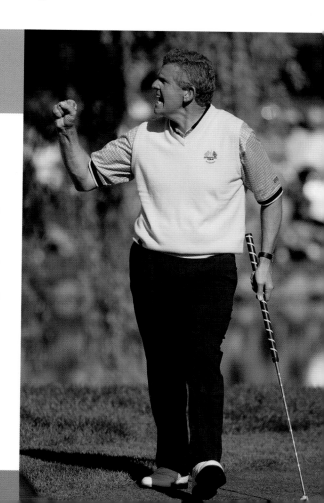

Laura Davies

Born
5 October 1963,
Coventry, England

Majors
4

Kraft Nabisco Championship
2nd 1994

LPGA Championship
1994, 1996

US Women's Open
1987

du Maurier Classic
1996

Women's British Open
Tied 8th 2004

RENOWNED AS ONE of the longest hitters in the women's game, Laura Davies is the most successful female British golfer of modern times. She has won the Ladies European Tour Order of Merit a record seven times and was the first non-American golfer to top the LPGA Tour money list – a feat she accomplished in 1994.

Davies turned professional in 1985 and was Rookie of the Year as well as leading money winner in her debut season on the Ladies European Tour. She has won a total of 81 tournaments as a professional, including four major titles, and has competed in all 11 Solheim Cups held from 1990 to 2009, winning a total of 23.5 points in 43 matches.

José María Olazábal

Born
5 February 1966,
Hondarribia, Spain

Majors
2

Masters
1994, 1999

US Open
Tied 8th 1990, 1991

Open Championship
3rd/tied 3rd 1992, 2005

US PGA
Tied 4th 2000

IN 1984, 18-year-old José María Olazábal defeated Colin Montgomerie in the final of the British Amateur Championship at Formby Golf Club. The Spaniard is the only player since World War II to win the Amateur Championship and go on to claim a professional major title.

Known for his deft touch around the greens, 'Ollie' won his two majors on a course famed for providing the ultimate examination of the short game – Augusta National. In addition to his Masters victories, he has won 29 professional tournaments around the world.

Olazábal forged a formidable Ryder Cup partnership with fellow Spaniard Severiano Ballesteros: in the 15 matches they played together they notched up 11 wins and two halves, suffering just two defeats. He is captain of the 2012 European Ryder Cup team.

Ernie Els

Born
17 October 1969,
Johannesburg, South Africa

Majors
3

Masters
2nd 2000, 2004

US Open
1994, 1997

Open Championship
2002

US PGA
3rd/T3rd 1995, 2007

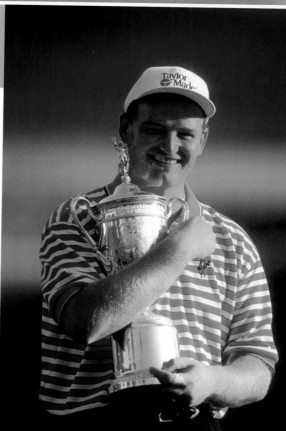

THE SOUTH AFRICAN Ernie Els has been one of the most consistently successful golfers of the last 20 years. He has scored 64 victories around the world since turning professional in 1989, and has spent a total of more than 15 years in the top ten of the Official World Golf Ranking – longer than any other player. Throughout his career he has been a truly global golfer, playing tournaments on all five continents almost every season.

Tall with a long, languid swing, Els – who has picked up the nickname 'The Big Easy' – generates seemingly effortless power and is one of the cleanest strikers of the ball in the modern game. He has inspired a new generation of South African golfers.

Annika Sörenstam

Born
9 October 1970, Bro, Sweden

Majors
10

Kraft Nabisco Championship
2001, 2002, 2005

LPGA Championship
2003, 2004, 2005

US Women's Open
1995, 1996, 2006

du Maurier Classic
2nd 1998

Women's British Open
2003

ANNIKA SÖRENSTAM'S retirement from tournament golf at the end of 2008 marked the conclusion of one of the most successful playing careers in the history of professional golf. Winning 93 tournaments across the globe, including ten major titles, she greatly raised the profile of the women's game and set new standards for female professionals.

In 2001 Sörenstam shot the first 59 on the LPGA Tour, claimed eight LPGA Tour titles and was the first woman to earn more than $2 million in a single season; the following year, she won an incredible 11 LPGA Tour titles. She was LPGA Tour Player of the Year eight times and was inaugural No. 1 in the Women's World Golf Ranking when it was introduced in 2006. She retired as the all-time leading money winner in women's golf.

Tiger Woods

Born
30 December 1975,
Cypress, California, USA

Majors
14

Masters
1997, 2001, 2002, 2005

US Open
2000, 2002, 2008

Open Championship
2000, 2005, 2006

US PGA
1999, 2000, 2006, 2007

ELDRICK 'TIGER' WOODS has changed the face of golf since he turned professional in 1996. He's the world's most highly paid athlete, and his fame transcends the sport. He has inspired a generation of players and set new standards of excellence in the professional game.

Woods is known for his powerful ball-striking, clinical short game and stunning clutch putting. He also possesses unrivalled focus and an uncanny ability to win, even when the chips are down. As an example, he took the 2008 US Open title despite suffering from a fractured tibia. Woods holds a myriad of records in the professional game and, if he's able to surpass Jack Nicklaus's total of 18 major titles, his status as greatest player of all time will be confirmed.

Phil Mickelson

Born
16 June 1970, San Diego, California, USA

Majors
4

Masters
2004, 2006, 2010

US Open
2nd/T2nd 1999, 2002, 2004, 2006, 2009

Open Championship
3rd 2004

US PGA
2005

ONE OF THE MOST popular players of the modern era, Phil Mickelson burst onto the scene in 1991 when he won the PGA Tour's Northern Telecom Open as an amateur. The Californian turned professional the following year and has enjoyed a hugely successful career, winning almost 50 tournaments including four majors (though not the US Open, in which he has been runner-up a record five times).

Although right-handed, Mickelson plays left-handed because he learned to swing by mirroring his father's right-handed action. He's one of the longest hitters in world golf but not one of the straightest. 'Lefty' is able to counter his inaccuracy, however, with supremely creative shot making and skills in escapism to rival Houdini. His ability around the greens is legendary – the towering flop-shot is a Mickelson trademark.

Padraig Harrington

Born
31 August 1971, Dublin, Ireland

Majors
3

Masters
T5th 2002, 2008

US Open
5th/T5th 2000, 2006

Open Championship
2007, 2008

US PGA
2008

A PROFESSIONAL since 1995, Harrington has worked extremely hard and displayed dogged determination in order to ascend to golf's very highest echelon. The Irishman's arrival at the pinnacle of the game came in the Open Championship of 2007 at Carnoustie in Scotland. Defeating Sergio Garcia in a four-hole play-off, he became the first European major winner since 1999 and the first player from the Republic of Ireland to lift the Claret Jug. He successfully defended the title the following year at Royal Birkdale, then went on to claim the US PGA Championship the next month.

Harrington is a superb scrambler and his ability to save shots is second to none. He's an excellent putter with a steely nerve and a never-say-die approach to the game.

Lee Westwood

Born
24 April 1973,
Worksop, England

Majors
0

Masters
2nd 2010

US Open
3rd 2008, tied 3rd 2011

Open Championship
2nd 2010

US PGA
T3rd 2009

IN OCTOBER 2010 Lee Westwood ended Tiger Woods' 281-week reign as the world's No. 1 ranked golfer. The Englishman is current holder of that most unwanted tag, 'best player not to have won a major' – a tag once held by Phil Mickelson, who has since gone on to bag four of them.

Westwood enjoyed considerable success in his early professional career and was European No. 1 in 2000. But he suffered a dramatic loss of form over the next two seasons and dropped as low as 266 on the Official World Golf Ranking. He bounced back, however, and is now renowned for his consistent performances in golf's big events. He's a brilliant driver of the golf ball and a highly accurate iron player. His expertise from tee to green is the secret to his success.

Westwood is a Ryder Cup stalwart and has finished in the top three in six majors since 2008. That elusive first win must surely come soon.

Martin Kaymer

Born 28 December 1984, Düsseldorf, Germany	**US Open** Tied 8th 2010
Majors 1	**Open Championship** Tied 7th 2010
Masters Cut 2008–2011	**US PGA** 2010

MAKING HIS DEBUT on the European Tour in 2007, Martin Kaymer finished the season as the Sir Henry Cotton Rookie of the Year. His first victory on the circuit came at the 2008 Abu Dhabi Golf Championship, an event he has since won twice more. In 2010 he became only the second European to win the US PGA Championship, en route to securing the European Tour Golfer of the Year award. In February 2011 the ice-cool German climbed to No. 1 in the Official World Golf Ranking.

Rory McIlroy

Born 4 May 1989, Hollywood, Northern Ireland	**US Open** 2011
Majors 1	**Open Championship** Tied 3rd 2010
Masters Tied 15th 2011	**US PGA** Tied 3rd 2009, 2010

THE YOUNG Northern Irishman has enjoyed a swift rise to the highest echelons of the game since joining the paid ranks in 2007. A long hitter with a technically excellent swing, McIlroy has all the makings of a World No. 1. After a final-round collapse at the 2011 Masters, McIlroy bounced back admirably in the US Open. His winning total of 16 under par was the lowest in US Open history and it left the field floundering in his wake.

Rickie Fowler

Born 13 December 1988, Anaheim, California, USA	**US Open** Tied 60th 2008
Majors 0	**Open Championship** Tied 14th 2010
Masters Tied 38th 2011	**US PGA** Tied 58th 2010

AS THE USA claimed victory in the 2009 Walker Cup, Rickie Fowler turned professional after winning all four of his matches. He secured his playing rights for the 2010 PGA Tour through the gruelling Qualifying School and was named Rookie of the Year at the end of his debut season. The charismatic Californian has an unorthodox technique and plays quickly and naturally. Corey Pavin recognized Fowler's ability and named him as a captain's pick for the 2010 US Ryder Cup team.

Matteo Manassero

Born 19 April 1993, Negrar, Italy	**US Open** Tied 54th 2011
Majors 0	**Open Championship** Tied 13th 2009
Masters Tied 36th 2010	**US PGA** Has not played

IN 2009, Matteo Manassero, aged 16, was the youngest-ever winner of the British Amateur Championship. Since then the records have tumbled. That summer he finished 13th in the Open Championship, becoming the youngest winner of the Silver Medal presented to the leading amateur. In 2010 he became the youngest player to make the cut at the US Masters and, after he turned professional, his capture of the Castelló Masters made him the youngest-ever winner on the European Tour.

Michelle Wie

Born 11 October 1989, Honolulu, Hawaii, USA	**LPGA Championship** 2nd 2005
Majors 0	**US Women's Open** Tied 3rd 2006
Kraft Nabisco Championship Tied 3rd 2006	**Women's British Open** Tied 3rd 2005

IN THE FIRST years of this millennium, Michelle Wie set numerous records for reaching milestones at an extremely young age. But she was pushed too far too soon and spent a few years in the wilderness as a result. Since joining the LPGA Tour full time in 2009, she's made steady progress back towards the top of the game. She's won twice on the circuit and has climbed into the top ten in the Women's World Golf Ranking.

Ryo Ishikawa

Born 17 September 1991, Matsubushi, Japan	**US Open** Tied 30th 2011
Majors 0	**Open Championship** Tied 27th 2010
Masters Tied 20th 2011	**US PGA** Tied 56th 2009

ISHIKAWA HAS BEEN a sensation in his home country since 2007, when he won a tournament on the Japan Golf Tour as a 15-year-old amateur. Since then he has won eight more times on the circuit and was the leading money winner in 2009. In September 2009, he became the youngest player ever to break into the top 50 in the Official World Golf Ranking. In May 2010, Ishikawa fired a final round of 58 to win The Crowns tournament on the Japan Golf Tour.

4

TECHNIQUES
AND TIPS

Swing Essentials **86**　　Driving **108**　　Fairway Woods **126**

Introduction

If you have read the previous chapter you'll know about the main achievements of the greatest players in the game. Take time to study these legends closely, however, and you will notice that there is no such thing as an identikit golf swing. Each player moves in a slightly different way, possessing his or her own unique set of strengths and weaknesses.

There are, however, some core principles that it pays all players, no matter what their standard, to follow. This chapter focuses on the essential techniques that will allow you to make the best swing possible. From standing to the ball in the correct way to making a full turn, we aim to describe these key moves as clearly as possible, so that you are armed with all the knowledge you need. Of course, the long game is only one part of the puzzle. Bunker play, chipping and putting are also covered, to help you back up a great swing with the ability to score well.

To avoid complicated repetition, the advice that follows has been written in terms of right-handed players. All the same principles naturally apply for left-handers, who will be able to adopt a mirror image of the positions shown in the photographs.

No matter what your standard or natural physical capabilities, understanding the important elements discussed on the following pages will help you get more enjoyment from this great game.

Swing Essentials

ONE OF THE CHARACTERISTICS that sets golf apart from many other popular sports is the varied nature of the challenge. While in some games you are required to make the same move time and again, in golf, the demands on your body and mind depend on the scenario in front of you. Being able to adapt your game and understanding how to manipulate the flight of your ball lie at the heart of becoming a truly rounded, successful player. The plethora of different shots available to the most accomplished golfers in the world means they are rarely stuck without a solution to any difficult scenario.

This section is devoted to nailing down those key fundamentals, to ensure that you consistently give yourself the best possible chance of making a successful swing. The vast majority of destructive shots arise through failing to set the perfect building blocks of a solid address position and a technically sound swing. So, to help, we will start by taking a close look at how to establish the correct grip, alignment, stance and posture. These are the static positions that will become the foundations of your success on the course. Once these are nailed down we will examine the individual moves that, when knitted together, will combine to create a swing that is repeatable, rhythmic and athletic.

If you can master the points on these pages, the intricacies of how to adapt to different areas of the game should fall into place with ease. Take some time to understand what the correct positions look and – more importantly – feel like, and then hit plenty of practice balls, so it all becomes second nature. Once you start competing on the course for real, you will not regret the time spent mastering these basic principles.

Holding the Club Correctly

The first fundamental that requires careful attention is your grip. Placing your hands on the club in the correct way gives you the best possible chance of keeping the clubface square to the target and on line through the hitting area, preventing the wayward shots caused by excess sidespin.

CHOOSING YOUR GRIPS

Being the only part of the club that is in contact with the body, the grip is a crucial but often neglected piece of equipment. Throughout this section, we will talk about the importance of *feel*: that is, relying on your natural instincts to play the game without over-analysing the mechanics of each shot. For this reason it is essential that your grips do two things: (a) provide you with a firm hold and (b) help you feel the club through your hands.

There is a wide range of different grips available, so it's worth taking the time to look for a design that feels good but also offers plenty of traction. Indeed, those who often play in difficult weather conditions should think about using grips with cord running through them, as this will offer greater control. Above all, remember that over time all grips will become less tacky. How often you change them clearly depends on how much you play and practise, but most regular golfers should think about swapping their grips every 18 months.

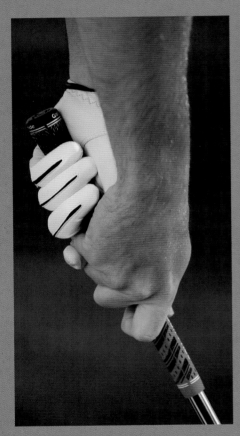

Below There are many different grips to choose from that offer different levels of feel.

⌃ THE PERFECT HOLD

The two photographs above show what the correct grip looks like. The simple point to make here is that the palm of the right hand is facing towards the target, and the left palm is aiming directly away from it. Neither hand is sitting on top of or underneath the shaft. Keeping your hands facing each other, on line with the target as they sit on the grip at the address, will allow your wrists to move correctly during the swing. Any mistakes here will not only cause the clubface to open or close but will also affect the plane of the swing. Keep your hands in the position shown and you should have a great chance of hitting a straight ball that does not carry too much sidespin.

❯ TEAM WORK

A great way to work out the way your hands should come together on the grip is to place them flat together with the club between them. These photographs show how the two hands can overlap each other. You can either lock the two fingers together (left) or let the right little finger overlap the left index finger (right). In each case your hands will join each other on the grip to work together throughout the swing. If you have no immediate preference, hit some shots using both grips in turn and opt for the one that feels most comfortable and natural. A final point to notice is how the hands almost mirror each other, with the fleshy part of the right hand sitting on top of the left thumb.

❮ RIGHT AND LEFT HAND CHECKPOINTS

It makes sense for every player to have a simple system for regularly assessing the strength of their own grip. Use a marker pen to make some helpful checkpoints on a spare glove. Draw some dots on the first two knuckles of your left hand and an arrow on the heel of your left thumb at the angle shown. When you address the ball you should be able to see the very top of both dots, and the arrow should be pointing at your right shoulder, mirroring the line of the crease between the thumb and forefinger of the right hand. Use this glove whenever you practise, and it will clearly highlight any faults that creep into the way your hands sit on the club.

Aiming the Club and Body

Alignment is about more than just where your clubface is pointing at address. Your whole body needs be in the perfect position to give you the best possible chance of keeping the club on a good line throughout the swing.

❯ NEUTRAL ALIGNMENT

These two photographs show exactly what perfect alignment looks like. First, the clubface should be pointing directly at the target – whether that is a spot on the fairway off the tee or the pin on the green, the clubhead needs to be set perfectly straight.

Your body now needs to be set square to the target line. A way to picture this is to imagine that the greenkeeper has mown a narrow strip (indicated here with alignment sticks) that goes straight from your clubhead to the target. Your feet, hips and shoulders should all be parallel to that line. This is an essential point. Players are often careful to ensure the clubface is pointing in the right direction but are less strict with their body position. If your body is not set square your swing path will be sent off line, with disastrous results. If your body is open to (left of) your target line, you'll cut across the ball through impact, causing a slice. Conversely, if your body is closed to (right of) the ball-to-target line, the opposite rules apply, and you will hook.

TRAIN TRACKS

An excellent way to visualize the correct alignment is to imagine that you are hitting a shot off a set of train tracks. The track on which the ball sits relates to where your clubface should be pointing and the parallel track relates to the angle of your body.

⌃ DO NOT AIM YOUR BODY AT THE TARGET

There is a good reason why we say: 'Never aim your body at the target.' If you were to do this, with your feet and upper body in line with the pin (as shown above), your body would actually be closed at address. From this position you will block the ball to the right of the target or, if you manage to square the clubface at impact, you'll create too much sidespin, sending the ball left. This is why your body needs to be square to the straight line between the ball and the target.

If you are practising on a square mat (above right), you can use the top of the mat as a reference. Provided the tee part of the mat is aiming at your target, your body should be parallel to the line at the top. Simply by checking this you'll be able to use the mat to ensure you're in a good position.

USING ALIGNMENT STICKS

All golfers who are serious about making significant improvements to their game should check their alignment regularly (at least once a month). It might seem relatively basic but, as you compete on the course, small errors are bound to creep in. If these aren't quickly ironed out the detrimental effects will grow, eating into your confidence.

An effective way to check alignment is to lay some shafts on the ground – one for the clubface, pointing at the target, and the other parallel to this for your body. Alternatively, many golf shops now sell brightly coloured alignment sticks, which are a simple alternative to shafts, and as they are so clearly visible they will highlight any errors in your set-up. If your alignment consistently causes you problems, think about investing in a set of sticks and keeping them in your bag ready for when you practise.

Standing to the Ball

While the specifics related to the width of your stance and the position of the ball in relation to your feet will be addressed as we work our way through the different areas of the game, there are some simple rules relating to stance that are worth considering for all the full shots you play. Underpinning these rules is one simple premise that should never be forgotten: an athletic swing requires an athletic stance.

Right Golfers can learn much from observing other sports. Tennis player Rafael Nadal is perfectly balanced on the balls of his feet, ready to receive the serve and poised to move in any direction. An athletic stance is equally important in golf.

⌄ ❯ NEITHER FORWARD NOR BACK

First of all, it's worth knowing exactly where on your feet the weight should rest, both at address and through the swing. Think of yourself as a tennis player waiting for your opponent to serve. In order to react to the direction of the serve, you set your weight on the balls of your feet, which are around shoulder-width apart. Balanced but with enough poise to move quickly, this gives you the best chance of hitting a solid return.

Now, while admittedly you are not responding to a moving ball, the same rule applies in golf. If your weight is too far back on your heels or forward on your toes, you'll quickly lose balance as you take the club away. The only way to strike the ball cleanly is to make a series of compensations as you swing. Remember that all technically solid golf swings are simple, so – as shown below and right – set your weight on the balls of your feet at address and preserve the simplicity of the movement.

❯ LET YOUR THIGHS TAKE THE STRAIN

To understand how your lower body should be set at address, it is worth noting exactly where the power in a solid golf swing comes from. As you take the club back, your upper body will rotate and, provided your flexibility is good, at the top of the backswing your back will be towards the target. But while your upper body rotates through 90°, your hips will turn only a fraction of this amount (about 45°). It is the torque created between the angle of your hips and the full rotation of your back that generates genuine speed and power through the downswing. So, to ensure that your hips work correctly during the swing, your thighs need to feel strong, as if they are taking a small amount of strain in the address position.

The photograph (right) shows how far apart your knees should be at address: you should feel that your thighs are working to give you the correct posture. Importantly, the gap between your knees should remain the same through the swing (far right). Think of your thighs as the base from which you create both power and stability.

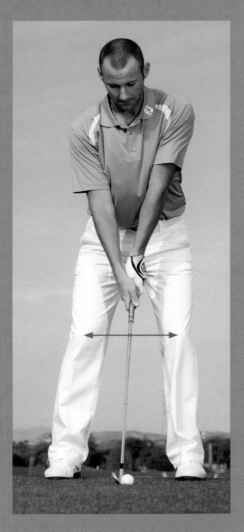

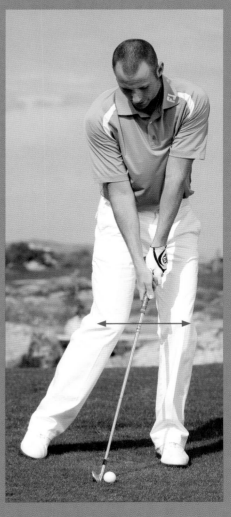

CHOOSING YOUR FOOTWEAR

When you are buying a pair of golf shoes there are three things you should take into consideration. The first – style – is obviously a matter of personal preference.

The second is stability, as your shoes need to offer enough grip to provide a stable hitting platform. Nothing kills the athleticism of your swing faster than the feeling that you might slip. Most golf shoes are now available with soft spikes as standard (these are made from plastic and have a number of small prongs),

and for the vast majority of golfers they offer plenty of traction. Metal cleats can also still be found, as some players prefer the feeling these provide. Be wary of wearing spikeless shoes in anything other than perfect conditions; even so, undulating ground can make walking the course difficult.

The third consideration is comfort. During a round of golf you will be walking for several hours, so it's crucial that your shoes are not going to make you feel tired.

Above Golf shoes such as these from Nike are designed to offer high levels of traction.

Essential Posture

You can often tell the difference between a professional golfer and a high-handicap amateur just by looking at how they stand to the ball. The pro will look athletic, setting clean angles between the upper and lower body. In contrast, the amateur will often look uncomfortable, slumping over the ball or standing too tall. Posture is a crucial part of the set-up, so use these tips to ensure that yours is spot on.

❯ CREATING THE RIGHT ANGLES

Take a close look at this photograph, as it represents the perfect posture.
1 There is a good amount of flex in the knees because, as we have seen, a strong lower body is required to support the rotation of the upper body.
2 Keeping his back straight, the player uses his hips as a hinge, setting his sternum over the ball. A 45° angle between the line of your spine and the ground is what you should be aiming for.
3 Crucially, as shown here, the arms should drop straight down. This will create clear space between your hands and the top of your thighs.
4 Finally, ensure that your chin does not drop onto your chest. Concentrate on maintaining your spine angle, from your lower back up into your neck (inset). In the ideal position, your abdomen and your legs should take the strain of supporting your upper body.

⌄ ELBOW FLEX

As you aim to set a solid posture, one trap that is easy to fall into is to become too tense. While your back should be straight, your arms should hang at a natural angle, as in the main photograph below. Do not allow excess tension to cause your elbows to lock (bottom right), because this can have a detrimental effect on the path of the club as you take it back. Allow a small amount of flex in your elbows. (Don't bend them too much – they should just feel soft and tension-free.) Not only is the club more likely to move on the right plane, but a more fluid swing will help you find good clubhead speed.

LEARN FROM THE PROS

Rory McIlroy

If you watch professional golf on television, observe how every player (including Rory McIlroy above) sets a good spine angle at address. In fact, studying how the best do it should help you follow suit. Ask a friend to take a photograph of you at address and compare your position with those of golfers who make a living from playing the game. This may seem a little ambitious, but there is no reason why you shouldn't get this static position spot on. Use a photograph to check your posture and you'll see if and where you are going wrong.

⌃ TEST YOUR POSTURE

If your posture has been set well you should feel incredibly solid at address, as if it would take a very strong force to push you over. To test your posture, hold your golf bag in both arms and take up your address position. Remember to set your spine angle and let your abdomen and legs take the strain of the extra weight. You should be able to hold your golf bag in this position without losing your balance. As you play your way through a competitive season it is easy to become sloppy with your posture, and this is an excellent drill that highlights exactly how you should be standing to the ball.

Starting Your Swing

Now you know what the correct static positions look and feel like, it's time to start your swing. The good news is that the best swings tend to be the simplest. A full turn without any unnecessary extra movements should send the club moving on a good path. The tips and drills here will make sure no unwanted errors creep in and become habitual.

⊻ ❯ SETTING THE RIGHT PATH

A technically sound golf swing begins with uncomplicated movement. Start the swing by taking the club straight back on the line along which you are aiming. Ensure that you are doing this by placing two alignment sticks on the target line, one in front and one behind the ball, to create a gate through which the clubhead should move.

As the club goes back through the gate the triangle created between your shoulders and the clubhead should remain intact. The clubface should still be pointing at the ball in this vital phase of the swing. Crucially, we are only talking about the first 60 cm/2 ft of the swing here. Once you have set the club on a good path, your body rotation will begin and the club will automatically move along the line inside the alignment sticks on the ground.

❯ KEEPING THE CLUB ON PLANE

The swing path is something that players can become very caught up with, constantly checking to ensure the club is moving correctly. This can cost you your feel for the game, but it is still a good idea to have an easy drill that will help you check your swing whenever you feel that excess sidespin is creating too much shape through the air on your shots.

In the sequence shown on the right we have used two alignment sticks to create a corridor, through which the club should move through the back- and downswing. Set the sticks carefully in the ground at the angle shown and start by making some slow swings, checking that the club doesn't hit either stick on the way back or down. Try to gain a sense of how the correct move feels and build up towards making some full-speed swings. This drill can be used at any point as a very simple way of checking the most fundamental of swing essentials.

CONSISTENCY IS KEY

The swing path illustrated on these pages will help you find a ball flight that is neutral, without excess side-spin causing it to shape too much from either right to left or left to right through the air. However, many top players have not swung the club on this textbook plane. What has enabled them to compete at the highest level is consistency: swinging the club the same way every time means they know where their shots are going and what type of flight to allow for.

While the rules for the address position apply to every player, when it comes to the swing, a movement that you can repeat time and time again is essential, even if the path of the swing is not from the pages of the coach's manual.

❯ ALIGNMENT, GRIP AND SWING PATH

One reason why a good grip is so important is that it has a direct impact on how your body is aligned at address; in turn this affects your swing path. If your hands are on the club in the correct way (below right), your forearms and shoulders should sit perfectly parallel to your ball-to-target line. If either hand is in the wrong position your forearms and shoulders will either open or close, depending on the fault. In turn, this will have a detrimental impact on your swing path (left), causing excess sidespin to be created at impact. A disastrous slice or hook is the likely outcome.

Swinging Through the Ball

The path along which the club moves through the downswing, in conjunction with the angle of the clubface at impact, will determine the consistent accuracy of your golf shots. If you keep it travelling on a good line, you will regularly hit your targets, and the game will start to feel quite easy. Here we look at the rules relating to the downswing and the line along which the club attacks the ball.

⊽ FINDING THE RIGHT PATH

If you take one piece of information from these pages, let it be this: the ideal swing path through impact will be from inside to outside your target line. We have used an alignment stick in this sequence to indicate the ideal direction of the clubhead through impact (think about marking this at the start of your practice routine – the clear visual direction will help to reinforce the message). As long as the face of your club is pointing at the target at the point of contact with the ball, you should find a very soft, right-to-left flight. The club moves in this direction because naturally it must move around your body. No player swings the club up and down on a straight line; instead we pivot around a central point.

Understanding this crucial fact and instilling the motion into your swing is the best way of finding consistency on the course. We will come on to how variations to this line cause different ball flights later, but for now, try to master this crucial path.

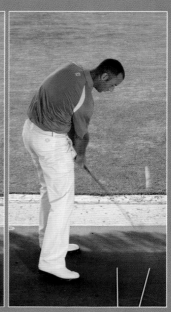

❯ START SHORT AND BUILD UP TO A FULL SWING

Now that you fully understand the laws relating to the swing path, it is time to groove the correct movement. First, lay the shaft of a mid-iron next to the ball, as shown, setting it at a slight angle – the shaft should aim slightly to the right of your target. Like the alignment stick used on the mat on the previous page, this will act as a very helpful reference for the ideal in-to-out swing path through impact. (It's also worth laying down a second club or stick to ensure that your alignment is perfectly square.)

Once you've done this, it's time to hit some shots. Start by making a very short (quarter-length), slow swing. Feel the correct move through the business part of the swing – you should be able to see if the club is moving along the right line. Gradually build up towards a full swing, hitting 20–30 balls in total. Once you are making a full, athletic, powerful swing (far right), the club should be moving on the correct route.

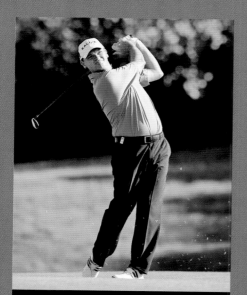

Paul Lawrie

❮ FOLLOW LAWRIE'S LEAD

We will come on to the importance of a smooth tempo, but at this stage it is worth pointing out that good clubhead speed and distance come from a gentle increase of pace through the swing. Don't snatch the club away as you start the swing. Not only is it likely that you will throw the club off line, your whole swing will have a stuttering rhythm.

Start the swing at a smooth pace and let the mechanics of a strong turn create speed and power through the downswing. If you get the chance, watch former Open Champion Paul Lawrie hit some balls. His technique perfectly sums up the notion of smooth power.

UNDERSTANDING SLICE

Easily the most common fault in the game is a slice. In this instance, the ball flight is itself evidence of a faulty swing path. When you slice, the ball starts to the left of the target and shapes aggressively right through the air. It is usually the swing path that causes the ball to start flying left, and because the clubface is pointing towards the target through impact (as it should be), excess sidespin is created, which sends the ball to the right. It is the combination of these two critical factors that lies behind golf's most common destructive fault.

Using Your Body

When you watch the best players in the world, the golf swing looks like a perfectly repeatable, almost unthinking movement. With the arms and body working together it is a motion that is incredibly efficient and controlled. Here we examine the simple mechanics behind a successful body turn.

❯ THE 'SPIKE' ANALOGY

This is an explanation that is sometimes used to give a golfer a clearer feeling for how the body works through the swing. You should imagine that a spike has been thrust into your back, running through your sternum, through the ball and into the ground. The 'spike' represents the axis around which your body should turn; staying 'centred' around it is the key to hitting shots that find the middle of the clubface as often as possible.

This photograph illustrates the line of the 'spike'. The centre of your chest should remain directly over the ball, swaying neither left nor right, throughout the swing. This underlines the simplicity of the golf swing: keeping your chest over the ball will improve the quality of the strikes you make.

CREATING POWER

As we have seen, your hips will rotate, but not to the same degree as your upper body. You'll achieve this naturally with a strong lower body, so there is no need to pay attention to it unless you feel yourself swaying off the ball. But it's important to understand that it is the extra rotation of the upper body in relation to the hips that creates torque. Think of this as stored-up energy waiting to be released through the downswing. Get it right and your shots will have impressive power without upsetting your balance or rhythm.

❯ TWO TURNS AND A HIT

In a bid to simplify the movement, coaches often describe the golf swing as 'two turns and a hit'. They are right, of course, even if most everyday golfers who regularly struggle to master such a 'simple' move would disagree.

Provided you have the flexibility to do it, your upper body should rotate so that your back is facing the target at the top of your backswing (right). As long as your left arm is straight at this point, this is a position of genuine power. Your body will uncoil with force, helping the clubhead to gain speed through the downswing. In the finish position (far right) your body should be facing the point at which you are aiming. Two simple turns – one back, the other through – lie at the heart of a powerful and athletic swing.

❮ NATURAL WEIGHT SHIFTS

Although the centre of your chest remains over the ball, you should feel your weight shifting naturally through the swing. When this is done correctly your weight should move to the right (away from the target) during the backswing and to the left (towards the target) through the downswing. This means that around 70 per cent of your weight is on your right foot at the top of the backswing. As you power through into the finish position, around 80 per cent of your weight should be on your left foot.

This is a simple concept, but for beginner golfers trying to get their shots airborne it can feel counterintuitive. Remember that it is the combination of loft on the clubface and your speed through impact (more speed equals more backspin and more backspin means lift and flight) that creates the desired trajectory. So, without swaying away from the ball, make a series of practice swings, feeling your weight moving onto your right foot as you go back and towards the target as you drive through.

Speed, Balance and Tempo

Speak to any sportsperson about the keys to success and they will often talk about the importance of rhythm. In cricket, both bowlers and batsmen need to move smoothly at key moments. In tennis a powerful serve requires rhythm, and the same applies to darts and snooker players as they search for repetition. Rhythm is that great unmeasurable quantity that lies at the heart of sporting accomplishment, and if you fail to find it, you'll be left looking to exert too much control. Here's how to find your ideal tempo for golfing success.

❯ FIND YOUR NATURAL RHYTHM

If you are a regular golf watcher you will know that some players seem to have a slow rhythm while others are fast. Take Ian Poulter and Fred Couples (right) for instance. These two men are at opposite ends of the tempo spectrum. Poulter looks as if he is in a rush to get the shot hit, while Couples has a relaxed, almost lazy tempo. The speed at which they swing the club, however, is a natural reflection of their characters. Whereas Couples is laid back, Poulter does most things with speed and intensity.

The point is that you should understand what sort of person you are, and this should determine the pace of your swing. If you are a naturally fast-paced person and you try to swing slowly, you will come unstuck.

Fred Couples

❯ GRADUAL SPEED

A good golf swing features a gradual build-up of speed. Always remember that hitting shots that travel a long way is about striking the ball from the sweet spot. You could have a ball speed of 150 mph/240 kph at impact (a rate that most professionals would be proud of), but if you hit the ball from the toe or heel of the club, the likely outcome will be a disappointing distance. So start the swing with a smooth takeaway and gradually pick the pace up. Not only will you reach optimum speed when you need it most, you'll also retain a good balance throughout the swing.

⌄ BALANCING ACT

Balance is a key attribute for any sportsman, and the reality is that rhythm and balance go hand in hand. There are many ways to check your balance through the swing, but this is one of the simplest and best. Take a wood – preferably your driver – and make a committed, powerful swing. As you hold your finish, you should feel solid in this position, as if a push by your playing partner would not upset your equilibrium. Make sure that your weight is fully on your left side and that your sternum is pointing in the direction of the ball. This represents the ideal finish and is the hallmark of any good golfer.

THE IMPACT OF PRESSURE

We'll talk about some of the mental challenges posed by competitive play later, but for now it is important to understand how pressure affects speed. Cast your mind back to the last exam you took. Remember the adrenaline coursing through your veins and your heart pounding in your chest. During that exam you probably wrote faster than usual.

The same happens under pressure in golf. Tension and adrenaline equate to a faster rhythm, which in turn can upset the harmony between the movements of your upper and lower body. So a good way to combat the effects of pressure is to walk a little more slowly than usual between shots and to control your breathing. This might seem to contradict the theory of natural rhythm, but this simple approach will help you restore fluidity to your swing.

Making the Right Contact

We have examined the ideal path of the club through impact, but what about the angle of descent into the ball? To a large extent it is determined by your ball position and, as this varies for different shots, we will cover it as we work through the techniques required for each area of the game. First, however, it is important to understand how trajectory responds to the type of strike you make.

❯ CONTACT DRILL

All the advice given so far has been geared towards one, over-riding aim: to be in the correct position as you make contact with the ball. You'll see top players with very different swings, but as they drive their bodies through the impact area, their positions will all be very similar. The photographs here illustrate what this position should look like:

1 The posture is similar to the ideal position shown on page 94, with the clubface pointing at the target.

2 The main difference is that the hips are slightly open, as the rotation of the body leads the arms through the downswing.

3 The arms are fully extended and the player's weight is moving in the direction of the target.

Take note of this position and try this drill. Start by assuming your impact position, making sure that all the key points above are in place. This can be as contrived and awkward as it needs to be, so long as when you swing the club you return to this position as you strike the ball. This is a simple way to focus your mind on what is comfortably the most important element of any golf shot.

STRIKE POINT

One of the rules of golf to which you should certainly pay close attention is the need to make a distinguishing mark on your ball. Dots, lines or drawings – it doesn't matter which you choose as long as, when you find a Titleist 2, you know that it is yours.

This can also help you when it comes to assessing your own ball striking. Every time you hit the ball, your drawing will leave a mark on the face of your club, which perfectly illustrates exactly how central the strike was. So if you are struggling with toe or heel contacts, marking the ball will reveal the problem and focus your mind on how to get back on track.

⌃ SWEEP OR HIT?

Broadly speaking, there are two different types of strike. When playing with your woods (above), you are looking for a flatter, sweeping action through impact, whereas with your irons (top) the angle of attack needs to be steeper. The reason for this difference relates, largely, to spin.

With woods you are looking to control the spin rate created. The extra length of the shaft, as well as the power and speed in the head, will deliver greater clubhead speed through impact, which translates into high levels of backspin that will get the ball airborne. Too much spin from a steep angle of attack will create a low initial launch angle followed by a rapidly rising flight: this might look impressive but it will lack power and penetration.

With irons, that backspin is what creates the flight and soft landing properties you want. Fortunately, only minor tweaks to your technique, plus a change of the position of your feet in relation to the ball, are required to do this. But for now it is important to understand that when playing an iron you are after a steeper angle into the ball, while with your woods, a flatter, sweeping action is crucial. The differences are subtle but will largely determine how successful you are with different clubs.

⌖ DOORWAY DRILL

An excellent way to gain a sense of what the correct impact position feels like is to pose it. Stand in a doorway and take your address position so that the clubface rests against the door frame. You do not need to make a swing, simply open your hips a fraction, move your weight towards your left side and feel the resistance of the door frame against the clubface. This simple drill is a good way to understand what the ideal impact position should look and feel like.

Driving Through to the Finish

Like a tennis player completing a topspin forehand, or a cricketer playing a flourishing cover drive, the way you follow through the ball and complete the swing should have both poise and style. You might think that a good finish is just a pose, but if it's wrong the swing will also have been littered with errors. Try to groove the key points highlighted here for a finish position that confirms your identity as a solid golfer.

❯ LAURA'S POWER MOVE

Take a close look at this photograph of Laura Davies as she drives through towards her finish position. Davies is famed for her unfettered style and powerful game, which few of her fellow competitors have been able to get close to matching. Her naturally strong physique has been key to her impressive distance stats, but equally important are the simple mechanics of her swing, which enable her to deliver incredible clubhead speed through the ball. Notice how there is no attempt to control the shot; instead she relies on her technique and commits to it entirely. Her right heel has lifted completely and this is a position you should try to replicate. But notice also how her weight is shifting so aggressively on to her left side that her left instep has started to lift a fraction.

While this extreme would not be advisable for every player, the lesson to be learnt is that of weight shift. Don't be afraid to let your weight drive towards the target through the ball. The speed and power this move engenders will create the trajectory for the shot that you're after.

Laura Davies

❯ ROTATION AND CONNECTION

The picture of Laura Davies also shows how her arms are working with the rotation of her body. Her arms are fully extended (like those of a javelin thrower at release) and the clubface points left.

To help you feel how the correct rotation through the ball works, take a mid-iron and set the butt end into your midriff (1 and 2). Turn your body back (3) and through (4), and the club will force your arms to work in connection with your body. Only once you have reached the full finish position should your body stop rotating. Completing this move is vital, as it is all part of your attempt to keep the club working on a good line through the whole of the swing.

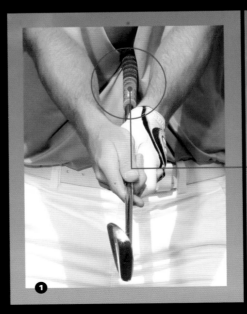

❶

❷

⊘ DO NOT KEEP YOUR HEAD DOWN

It is one of the oldest tips in the game. 'Keep your head down' is what we're all told when we start playing golf, but this simple and well-meaning tip can be misleading. Keeping your head down (as shown in a deliberately exaggerated way below) will actually only hamper the rotation and this can often lead to a slice. Once you have hit the ball (certainly not before) let your head rotate with your body. This will aid the rotation of your upper body and help you find that full finish position (right) that is so important to consistently good golf.

LEARN THE DRAW

On page 156 you will find some guidance on the keys to hitting a controlled draw. To understand how your hands, arms and body should drive through the ball, try some of the drills on this page designed to help you release the club more effectively. This move, described as the release, in conjunction with a few other adjustments to the normal address position, helps to deliver draw spin. For now, you need to understand that a fully extended release is essential for every swing you make. Without it you'll be unable to square the club at impact and you'll also be throwing away crucial clubhead speed.

Driving

AN OLD GOLFING ADAGE used to highlight the importance of putting goes: 'Drive for show, putt for dough.' However, without a solid driving game you will have nothing to putt for. The reality is that driving is your essential tone-setter. Do it well, positioning your ball in the best areas to attack the flags, and simple iron shots will yield plenty of birdie opportunities. Do it badly and you will be fighting against the tide, desperately hoping that your short game will salvage a respectable result. The importance of powerful, accurate driving should never be underestimated.

If you have ever been a spectator at a high-level tour event, you will know how exhilarating it is to watch star golfers smash towering 300-yard/275-m drives that split the fairway. Rhythm, balance and timing all combine to achieve these staggering results, so in many ways genuine power is the hallmark of a very solid technique. But power is a double-edged sword. While shorter hitters' wayward drives will find the rough, those of long hitters may carry into trees, water or any other hazard lying in wait. So it makes sense to remember that power is nothing without accuracy.

In this section we will take an in-depth look at the art of driving. We will examine the subtle but essential differences in the address position and swing, then look at the commonest faults that can creep in and suffocate your scoring potential. There will be advice on how to expand your armoury of shots on the tee to combat all conditions and situations. Finally, we will take a look at the strategy and practice drills that lie at the heart of thinking clearly and performing well.

Driving can be the most enjoyable part of the game, and when done well it can leave you with an advantage over the field, while removing pressure on other areas of your golf game. Let this section become your guide to 'driving for show' – the cornerstone of consistently impressive scoring.

Address Essentials

The first thing you will notice when you pick up a driver, along with the size of the head, is how much longer the shaft is. Many manufacturers offer 45-inch/114-cm driver shafts, and this extra length, in conjunction with the very small amount of loft on the face, requires a slightly different approach to the address position. Here, we explain the subtle differences that will enable you to hit long, straight tee shots.

> HITTING ON THE UP

With a driver in hand you are looking for a sweeping, shallow angle of attack. There are two factors that will help you achieve this: the height of your sternum and the tee, and the position of the ball in relation to your feet. Both factors, when set correctly, will help you hit on the 'up' swing, to make the most of the small amount of loft on the driver and to find a flight that does not carry excess spin.

Teeing the ball up with plenty of height will encourage you to make the ideal, sweeping motion. There are no hard and fast rules here, but the recommendation is to peg the ball up so that its middle is in line with the crown of the driver. Set the ball forward in your stance – in line with or just inside your left instep – but, crucially, make sure that your upper body does not lean to the left. Your sternum should still be over the middle of your stance and your hands should be directly below your sternum.

You should also notice the stance is slightly wider than for an iron shot. As the driver has a longer shaft than the rest of your clubs, the resulting swing tends to be a fraction longer as well. A wide stance provides a strong base from which to make a powerful upper body turn. This is the perfect position from which to hit a high but penetrating ball that eats up the distance.

‹ ANGLE YOUR SHOULDERS

This picture illustrates the perfect address position with a driver. If you refer back to the address shown in the previous section, you will notice the difference here: the player's shoulders are tilted, with the left higher than the right. This encourages you to get your body behind the ball through impact and helps find the ideal launch angle. From this position you will also be better placed to find the in-to-out swing path that is so important to accuracy. By tilting your shoulders a fraction you will set more weight on your right side than usual: again, this simple adjustment will encourage a shallower angle of attack into the ball.

PICKING THE PERFECT SHAFT

The shaft determines both the power and control of the golf club through impact. Picking the perfect one can be an incredibly technical process that involves analysing spin rates, swing speeds and launch angles. If you are thinking of buying a new driver you should also think seriously about getting it custom fitted. A professional will usually do this without extra cost (as long as you end up purchasing a club) and it can mean the difference between a driver you love and use for many years and one that quickly finds its way into the attic with other ill-performing clubs.

Remember that a player who has a fast swing speed needs a stiffer shaft than one with a slow speed, as the shaft needs to strike a balance between helping you find speed through impact and controlling the spin created.

Swing Essentials

Now that you have set yourself in the perfect position it is time to master the rhythmic move that will deliver both power and control from the tee. Above all, this is about finding the tempo and smoothness that will help your arms and body to work together through the swing.

∨ > SPEED THROUGH IMPACT

It almost goes without saying that the club should be moving at its fastest through impact. This requires a slow build-up of pace from the takeaway towards the top of the backswing and then down to the ball. An excellent drill designed to highlight whether you are actually doing this correctly is to make some swings holding the wrong end of the club. Listen for the big 'swoosh' made by the grip. This should come at the bottom of the downswing. The louder the 'swoosh', the faster you are moving through this key phase of the swing.

You can use this great drill any time, but many people use it as a warm-up exercise before going out to play.

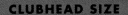

∧ EASY POWER

The most powerful golf swings are also the most graceful. This is because to generate plenty of carry you need two things: rapid clubhead speed through impact, and perfect timing. As you strive for as much distance as possible it can be surprisingly easy to forget the second point. Remember that you need to find a balance between speed and poise. If you lose your balance, a poor strike will kill your power.

To illustrate this, hit some practice drives, swinging at 60 per cent. You should notice that when you strike the ball perfectly, the distance you find is still good. The point is that while you need to achieve speed through impact you should never sacrifice a good quality contact.

∧ FLEXIBILITY IS KEY

The best way to ruin your rhythm is to let tension creep into your address position. Squeezing the grip with your hands will cause your forearms and elbows to tighten, with a knock-on effect on your flexibility. It doesn't matter whether you are a teenager or a pensioner, you need to make the most of your own flexibility.

To help you do this, make some practice swings with your hands moved to the very top of the grip, so the little finger of your left hand is not sitting on the club (see inset). You'll notice that this simple change will yield a much more fluid, lucid motion. When you return your hands to their normal position try to retain this fluidity, and the rhythm of your swing will be your biggest strength.

CLUBHEAD SIZE

Most modern drivers have heads that are 460 cc in size. Golf's ruling bodies have imposed a limit at 460 cc to prevent sweet spots becoming too large, making the game too easy.

A large sweet spot often masks an off-centre strike that offers plenty of distance, so if you are just starting out on your golfing journey it will provide plenty of forgiveness and playability. Better golfers, however, may wish to invest in a slightly smaller clubhead (around 420 cc). This can help reduce spin rates, improve overall control and help with shot shaping.

It is always worth doing some research before you buy, taking some time to find out which heads are aimed specifically at your level. A good custom-fitting session will then ensure the driver you opt for is set up perfectly for your swing.

Curing a Slice

It doesn't matter what level you play to, like every other golfer you will experience periods when finding the fairway off the tee feels almost impossible. Hooks, pushes and pulls will all make the target shrink in your mind's eye. At the top of the list of debilitating faults is the slice. Use the drills, tips and exercises shown here to iron out your killer problem.

∨ GO BACK TO BASICS

Every golfer knows how it feels to hit a perfectly struck shot, only to look up and see the ball slide farther and farther into trouble on the right-hand side. If you have been trying to build a score by allowing for your slice, you will undoubtedly have started to aim left with your body. A great way to restore your alignment without getting bogged down in the nitty-gritty of the position is to hit balls from the far left-hand side of the range. You will have no option but to start aiming more towards the right. This should straighten up the swing path and put an end to the destructive sidespin that is costing you so dearly.

∧ THINK BASEBALL

You might think that a straight up-and-down swing is the best way to keep the clubhead on a good line, but this is actually a major cause of a slice. As we have already stressed, your arms need to rotate with your body, creating a more circular swing.

If you're struggling to tame your slice, think of a baseball player smashing the ball out of the park: he simply swings the bat around his body. Use a baseball bat or a tennis racket to replicate this motion and feel your arms working with your body as it rotates. Now try to bring that feeling into your golf swing – it could be the key to straightening out your slice.

< ∨ HONE YOUR RELEASE

If you've tried the baseball drill opposite, the chances are that your release is improving. But if you need some extra encouragement try making some swings with an extremely wide stance, as shown here. A much wider base instigates the rounded movement and full release that you need. The great thing about this drill is that you shouldn't need to think about the right move – it should come very naturally. Try to filter it into your normal golf swing, driving your arms and your body powerfully through the ball.

SLOPE DRILL

Slices often come from an out-to-in swing path, which causes the club to cut across the ball through impact, causing destructive side-spin. If this is a persistent problem, try this drill. Find a slope from which to hit a series of shots where the ball is well above your feet. To strike it properly you have no option but to make the rounded (baseball-style) swing that is so important. You should notice a gentle right-to-left flight. Take some time to groove this motion and your slice will soon start to take the shape of a soft draw.

Finding the Fairway

With a longer shaft and a bigger head, the driver is the most difficult club in the bag to control. It's time to take a look at the other faults that will need immediate attention. Whether the problem is a hook, a lack of power or a consistent tendency to sky the ball, the advice on these pages should help you fix it.

< ∧ HOOK CHECKLIST

If you are suffering with a hook the first thing to check is your grip. It is easy to allow your right hand to become 'strong', meaning that it will have moved 'under' the shaft at address, encouraging an early release of the hands through the ball. If this is the case, weaken your right hand so the 'v' points at your right shoulder: this should have an immediate effect.

Now check your body alignment. If you are standing closed to the target line, your hands are likely to overtake the rotation of your body during the downswing, killing the synchronization that is so important and causing you to release your arms too early. There are two good ways to check your body alignment. You can either hold the shaft of your club across your shoulders to check if you are square (left), or get a friend to take a photo and analyse the evidence. Both work well to highlight this simple mistake if it has crept into play.

∧ LEFT FOOT ROTATION

As we have seen, your upper body needs to rotate with your arms through impact. If you are prone to letting your arms overtake your body, try this simple adjustment to your address position. Address the ball as usual, but turn your left foot out a fraction (towards the target). This will help you turn through the shot so that your arms and body work together.

> AVOID THE SKY

It may not be the most destructive fault in the game, but consistently skying your drives is certainly one of the most frustrating. Striking the ball with the very top of the clubface will send it looping high into the air without any real distance.

Skying is caused by an angle of attack into the ball that is too steep. Instead of hitting the ball on the up, you strike destructively down on it, as shown right: see how the player is set up with his weight too far towards his left side. To avoid skying, check your tee height, then your ball position to ensure it hasn't crept back in your stance. If these are not to blame, concentrate on your body action. Ensure that your sternum is over the ball as you start the downswing, and not moving towards the target. This will help you find a shallower angle of attack.

DON'T SNATCH AT THE BALL

You are standing on the tee with your driver in your hands, knowing that a powerful hit will set up a great birdie opportunity. Something that often happens in this scenario is that the usually smooth transition between backswing and downswing becomes too aggressive. You snatch at the shot and the results are disastrous.

Try to feel the flow of a smooth transition as you prepare to play the shot. Picture yourself throwing a ball, rotating your body back and through, building up to a strong release. Think of the flowing nature of this move and try to incorporate it into your golf swing.

This should help you to stop snatching at your drives and start swinging smoothly again. They will go farther and straighter as a result.

Adding Dimensions to Your Driving

If you have followed all the advice given so far, you should have all the basic keys in place to hit consistently straight, accurate drives. But what happens when the situation demands a slightly more creative approach? Here's how to adapt your technique to get the most from your game off the tee.

> FINDING EXTRA LENGTH

There will be the odd occasion when, as you look down a wide-open fairway, you might want to turn up the power. This should not be your stock shot but one you call on when you need to.

Start by setting your stance a fraction wider than usual: this will provide a stable base against which you can make a full, aggressive, upper body turn. Now tee the ball up a fraction higher than usual. This encourages you to get your body behind the shot and launch it high, with plenty of carry. Above all, do not try to swing your arms too quickly or throw your body at the ball. This may end up costing you a sweet strike, so maintain your normal rhythm but make these simple, subtle changes and you'll eke out a little crucial, extra length.

> ABSOLUTE CONTROL DRILL

For better, more consistent players who regularly compete on a variety of courses, it makes sense to learn how to control the flight. For instance, if you find yourself playing on links, it pays to be able to hit a low, chasing drive. Alternatively, resort courses reward those who can hit the ball long and high, taking out bunkers and bringing birdies into the equation.

The best way to control flight with your driver is to do it through your swing speed. Remember that the faster you swing the higher the ball flies, because of extra backspin. However, before you start trying to control flight through speed, you must put in some devoted time on the practice range. A superb way to develop this skill is to pick three targets – depending how far you hit with your driver, you need to pick one that is short, one medium and one long. Notice how the player (right) changes the length of his swing to control clubhead speed and thereby ball flight. This is the best way to manipulate flight and distance without upsetting the synchronization between arms and body.

Start by aiming at the shortest target. Move your hands down the grip and make a slower swing than usual. The only way to hit straight is to keep your arms working with your body, so if you slow down the arm speed you also need to slow down the rotation of the body. Hit a series of shots and you should notice the flight is lower than usual. Try to store the feeling of this swing in your mind.

Now hit towards the medium target and make a normal swing, concentrating on the synchronization of the movement. A faster swing will deliver a higher flight. Finally, take on the longest target. You need to swing harder, but don't sacrifice your balance to do so. Again, make sure that your arms and body work together and you should find soaring high flight that also offers a little extra distance.

ROTATION AND CONNECTION DRILL

As you work through the absolute control drill described above, it is easy to let the synchronization of the move become ragged. If you find yourself starting to hit wayward shots, you can simply perform the rotation and connection drill described on page 106. This should help you get back on track.

Plotting Your Route

Your tactics will play a crucial role in your success, and nowhere is this more important than at the tee. Good golf course designers will present you with more than one option off the tee. Mapping out how to play the hole so you avoid disaster and play to your strengths is key. Here's what to do.

> USE THE TEE MARKERS

One tactic employed by course designers is to position nearly all the grave danger down one side of the hole. For instance, the final hole at Sawgrass in Florida, used for the Players Championship, features water down the entire left side of the hole, with a couple of bunkers on the right. Left is dead, and if you watch the tournament on television you will see the vast majority of players peg up on the left side of the tee (see page 123). This allows them to aim away from the water.

(see page 123)

You should also employ this tactic regularly. As you look out over the hole ahead of you, identify where the key danger lies and tee up on the same side, so you can aim away from the trouble. This simple strategy should help you find a more positive mindset.

The danger zone on this hole is the out of bounds on the right, so it's best to peg up the ball on the right and aim left.

This is the short par-4 12th at Royal St George's, where a bunkered ridge is ready to swallow up the wayward drive. In this situation you should concentrate your aim on the very middle of the central tower.

PLAY YOUR OWN GAME

No matter what format of the game you are playing – match play or stroke play – it is easy to be swayed by the tactics of your opponents. But just because the other players in your group may be hitting a driver off a given tee, that does not mean you should follow suit.

It is a cliché, but one that you should certainly remember: play to your strengths. If you find it hard to hit a draw, don't let the tactics of your opponent push you into trying it. You are the only person who truly knows the best tactic for you, so be your own person and make choices unaffected by those around you.

∧ AIM POINT

A trap that amateur golfers regularly fall into when they practise is to bash a bucket of balls on a wide-open range without picking out a specific target. This lack of focus often follows them onto the course. When assessing the hole ahead you should always pick a target that is as specific as possible. If there is a building in the distance that stands on your line, choose a window to aim at. Likewise, if you are playing over a bunker, look for a spot you can easily identify, such as the corner of the trap. Never stand up and simply think, 'Somewhere up the right side will do.' This is a surefire recipe for disaster. Be as specific as possible and if you miss your exact target you are still likely to be on the fairway.

> LIGHTHOUSES

The legendary course designer Dave Jones once described the bunkers on one of his courses as 'lighthouses'. The sand is visible from the tee, acting as very clear pieces of danger to be avoided, but players can use these 'lighthouses' to their advantage.

Use a golf GPS device or course planner to calculate the distance to a bunker that is sitting in the middle or to left or right of the fairway. Now select a club that you know will not be able to reach that bunker. So, if the bunker lies at 260 yards/238 m and you know that your 3-wood goes 235 yards/215 m, take the 3-wood off the tee. Bunkers do not always have to be your enemy if you think clearly and use them as lighthouses.

Prepare Your Mind

One reason why a specific strategy is important is that it acts as a form of mental rehearsal. Your game plan will naturally involve an element of visualization, and in turn this will create a positive mindset. We will now look at how to perfect these mental skills and how best to use them on the tee.

⌄ POSITIVE RECALL

All golfers, no matter what standard, have some holes that they relish and others they hate. Not every hole is going to suit your eye – that's natural. The key, when playing a hole you don't like, is to ensure that you adopt a positive approach. A technique that players often use is to picture a hole they love to play. It might be the 5th at your local club, because its shape fits with your normal ball flight. Imagine yourself standing there and striking the perfect drive. Watch the ball shape gently towards the middle of the fairway. Now address the ball with this vision still in your mind and make a positive swing. This might seem a simple idea, but it's a great way of fooling yourself into feeling more comfortable with any situation that makes you feel nervous about your chances of finding the fairway.

∨ LINE UP YOUR BALL

This is a tactic used by some of the best players in the world, including Northern Ireland's Graeme McDowell. As they peg the ball up they point the straight line they have drawn on the ball directly towards their target. As they set up to the ball, they can use the line to ensure they set up square to the target line. It can also help with clubface alignment.

What this process does well is to help you feel confident in your position. If you know for a fact that you are well set and in the ideal position for a good swing, your chances quickly improve.

∧ FACE UP TO TROUBLE

Sometimes the tactic of trying to kill negativity with a positive image is simply not possible. When the danger facing you is severe, it is best to face up to it. Again, let's use the 18th hole at Sawgrass as an example. No matter how much you might want to block out the trouble on the left side, it will linger in your mind. Instead, look at the water and admit to yourself that it does represent a real danger. Now imagine what the best shot

Above On the 18th at Sawgrass, Tiger Woods tees up on the left side of the box so that he can naturally aim down the right side of the fairway.

you could possibly hit would look like. Visualize both the swing and the flight of the ball. Once you have done this, hit your shot. This technique will bring the danger to the forefront of your mind before pushing it to one side and replacing it with an image that is likely to induce a better shot.

MEANINGFUL PRACTICE SWINGS

Most golfers compete with a specific 'feel' in mind that they are looking to replicate in their swing. Use your practice swing to prepare yourself. If you can exaggerate the move you are trying to make in practice – for example, making a rounded, baseball-style swing as shown here – you're likely to achieve it when you swing for real.

Making Your Practice Count

As driving is such an important part of the game, you need to spend time focusing on it on the range. Hitting hundreds of balls without any clear structure, or without looking for any genuine results, will be a waste of time. Finding the odd hour here and there to spend working on your game can be hard, so here's how to make the most of your time.

> ⌄ USE ALIGNMENT STICKS

Alignment sticks are incredibly useful, and they can help with more than just your aiming. If you ever go to the practice ground at a high-profile tour event, you are likely to see a player using this drill.

By placing an alignment stick in the ground at the same angle as the shaft of the club at address, you will get a good idea of your swing path. Remember that the club shouldn't move drastically inside or outside this line. The alignment stick works as a simple visual aid, and will highlight mistakes in your swing path.

You can also use the alignment sticks to check where both your body and the clubface are aiming, which is one of the key elements to good golf that every player should try to nail down.

˅ SET YOUR GOAL

As we have already seen, taking care over your alignment is imperative when you practise. When it comes to hitting a drive, pick two targets at the end of the range, about 20 yards/18 m apart. These two points represent the edges of the fairway.

Now hit 20 drives. With the first ten, all you are trying to do is get the ball to finish somewhere between the two targets. Depending on how confident you feel, the next five shots should start to the right and shape back towards the middle of the gap between the two targets. With the last five balls, try to start the shot at the left-hand target and bend it back towards the middle. This is the sort of varied practice that, if you can do it with some level of control, will make you a far more rounded player.

˄ DRIVER OFF THE DECK

Another great drill that is designed to hone a shallower angle of attack into the ball is to try to hit some balls off the ground with your driver. As the ball is not pegged up, the only way to make a good contact and get the ball to fly up into the air is to attack it on a very shallow angle. Note that this is a very tricky drill, and you should only take it on if you are a fairly confident ball striker. When you revert to introducing a tee, the shot will feel far easier and your angle into the ball should be ideal.

DRIVER WEDGE PRACTICE

The trap that is easy to fall into when you are seeking to perfect your driving game is to start hitting the ball too hard. Playing shot after shot at full speed may also place unnecessary strain on your body.

An effective strategy to help you get the most from your practice time is to follow each driver shot with a wedge shot. As always, pick specific targets for both areas and you should be able to maintain your rhythm and, more importantly, your synchronization. This is good preparation for the course, as you will often follow a long shot with a short one.

Fairway Woods and Hybrids

THE RULES OF GOLF permit every player to carry 14 clubs; exactly what combination you choose is one of the most important decisions you will make before going out to play. Your fairway woods and hybrids, along with your wedges, are the clubs that provide you with options.

Fairway woods need to perform two roles. First, they should provide you with a second driving option, coming to the rescue when you are facing a tight fairway or hitting your driver poorly. Second, you need a wood you can hit consistently well, with distance, from the fairway. A high-flying shot that lands softly on the green is the key to playing par 5s and long par 4s.

Hybrid clubs are a relatively new addition to golf. For many golfers, they are far easier to hit than long irons, and they now feature in the bags of most players. As the length of the shaft is more like that of an iron, they should help you find even more control, but as the head is large they still offer impressive power through impact. However, hybrids come into their own from the rough. Easily cutting through the thicker grass, they can offer distance from long range even when your lie is not perfect.

The number of woods and hybrids you carry will depend on the type of golfer you are. While some players use two or three of each, others rely on just one, choosing instead to carry more lofted options at the bottom end of the bag. In this section we explain the keys to picking the right formula at the top end of the bag. Examination of the technique required for fairway woods and hybrids will be followed by some simple solutions for when things go wrong. Strategy tips and advice on the best ways to practise will offer further ways of ensuring that your fairway woods and hybrids are some of the most reliable and versatile clubs in your bag.

Fairway Wood Essentials

The set-up and swing required for a fairway wood is very similar to that of a driver. With the ball on the ground, however, the angle of the club into the ball needs to be even more precise. Here's how to hone your technique with your fairway woods specifically in mind.

▶ ⌄ SET-UP KEYS

The first and most important thing to note here is the ball position. When hitting a fairway wood it sits slightly further back than with a driver. The difference here is only small but when it comes to finding a clean, pure contact it is important. Crucially, you should still be aiming to strike the ball fractionally on the upswing.

Second, stand tall, as you would with a driver, setting a good posture with a straight back, bending over the ball at the hips. Let your arms hang down so that your hands are directly under your nose. One sloppy mistake that amateurs often make is to push their hands either towards or away from the target in the address position. This easily avoidable error will cause havoc to your fairway wood ball striking.

Above This photograph is a guide to the small but essential difference in ball position for a driver and a fairway wood. This will help you find the perfect sweeping strike through impact.

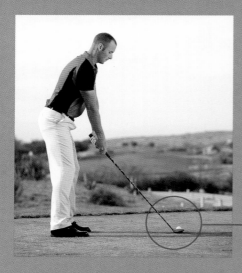

Traditionally, fairway woods have been numbered according to the amount of loft they offer, and players have chosen a range of usually odd-number woods. Nowadays, fairway woods are often marked with the actual degree of loft, so instead of a 3-wood, for example, you would carry a 15° wood. Whether you choose to carry two or three fairway woods, you must make sure the lofts are sufficiently different to hit key distance gaps.

The second thing to consider is that less loft does not always translate into extra distance. Those with slower swing speeds will often find they hit a 5-wood (with a loft of around 20°) farther than a 3-wood. There comes a point at which the slower swinger will not have the speed to create enough carry with less lofted clubs to make them worth including.

If you are about to buy new clubs, seek professional advice and get custom fitted first, to determine exactly the sort of composition you should be looking for at the top end of your bag.

◉ BRUSH THE CLUB AWAY

The picture opposite shows how the ideal address position should look. There is a triangle created between the clubhead and your shoulders that you should keep intact through the takeaway (above). Feel the club almost brushing the ground on the way back.

It is important that this movement stems from the rotation of the shoulders and not the hands. It is an incredibly easy move to get right but one that sets a wide arc and a sound swing path (benefiting both power and accuracy). Letting this become your key swing thought with your fairway woods is a good idea while you're out on the course.

◉ TEE HEIGHT

Take a close look at the face of your fairway wood. While the exact depth will differ from model to model you'll notice that it is nowhere near as tall from crown to sole as your driver.

This simple design difference makes your fairway wood much easier to use from off the ground. Although it might seem inviting and easier to hit when the ball is pegged up high, with a fairway wood in your hands the tee needs to be much lower. Tee it up so the ball is just above the level of the ground. As long as your spine angle remains solid through the swing, you should be able to find the sweet spot.

Hybrid Essentials

Hybrids have worked their way into the bags of many golfers over the last few years, becoming an invaluable new element of the set. More controllable than fairway woods, easier to hit than long irons and far more powerful than mid-irons, hybrids are an excellent choice in numerous on-course situations. But what technique should you adopt with your hybrid? Here are the basics behind successful hybrid play.

⊙ ⊙ ADDRESS POSITION

Some players struggle to hit their hybrids because they adopt the same approach as if they were using a fairway wood. You need to think of your hybrids as irons, and these two photographs illustrate where to set the ball at address. A position further towards the middle of the stance will automatically create a steeper angle of attack into the ball. Note also how the weight is split evenly between both feet. When using a driver or fairway wood, you will be looking to set a fraction more weight on your right side, but with a hybrid you should distribute your weight evenly. This is an essential element of sweet ball striking with your hybrids.

LOFT OPTIONS

To help you understand what sort of flight and distance you can expect from hybrids, manufacturers often label them by number (2, 3, 4, 5). The numbers refer to the equivalent loft in your irons, the idea being that if you carry a 4- and 5-hybrid there is no need to carry a 4- and 5-iron, as they cover similar distances.

For many golfers, hybrids – being more forgiving and offering just as much, if not more, power – become direct replacements for long irons. For others, their hybrids bridge the distance gap between fairway woods and irons.

If you prefer to carry a 3-wood and a 3-iron, consider a hybrid with little loft (around 18°) to plug the distance gap between the two clubs. Whatever your standard, your hybrids will come into their own when you are under pressure and looking for an option that offers control without compromising too much on power.

⊙ JUDGING THE LIE

Knowing when you can and cannot get a hybrid to the ball in a tough lie takes experience. We all bite off more than we can chew from time to time, attempting to hit the ball too far from a heavy lie in the rough. This will only leave you facing the same dilemma for your next shot. In practice, experiment by hitting your hybrid from a vast range of different lies, including shallow divots and thick rough. This simple process will highlight the dos and don'ts of hybrid strategy.

⊙ CHANGING YOUR SET-UP

One of the benefits of hybrids is their versatility. From the rough or a poor lie on the fairway, a hybrid can help you find a solid strike with good distance.

The key to success here is to force the angle of attack into the ball to be steeper than usual. For a normal hybrid shot your sternum will be directly over the ball (as shown above) but when the lie is poor, push the ball back in your stance a little; your sternum will then be ahead of the ball. You can also move your hands down the shaft a fraction to help improve the quality of contact. Keep your weight distributed evenly, but make sure that you are moving it onto your left foot through the downswing as usual. All these adjustments work to help you strike the ball before the ground, which is especially important when the lie is poor.

Thick rough *Shallow divot* *Fairway*

Problem Solving: Fairway Woods

The strike required with a fairway wood in hand is incredibly precise. The fundamentals that we have already looked at relating to this become even more important. So if you are having problems finding the right contact, or your fairway woods are proving destructively wayward, use these tips and drills to return to form.

◯ ◯ HONING THE STRIKE

As we have seen, your fairway wood needs to move on a shallow path through the contact area. If this move doesn't come naturally, you could be hitting a host of poor shots. A great drill to help you find the ideal angle of attack is to hit shots from different tee heights.

Place five balls on tees, pegging the first up high and gradually getting lower until the last ball is on the ground. Work your way down the line, concentrating on sweeping each ball off the tee. By the time you reach the ball on the ground, you should have grooved a shallower angle of attack.

⬣ FROM THE TEE

If you have opted for your fairway wood off the tee, the chances are that you have made this decision because the fairway ahead is particularly tight. It is essential, however, that you still make a normal swing, releasing the club (above left) towards the target as you would with any other shot. Trying to steer the ball (above right) down the fairway is a trap you must avoid. If you do this, your hands will not work effectively through the ball, and you will usually leave the face of the club slightly open and miss the shot to the right.

A good way to prepare for the shot is to imagine that there is a pane of glass about 5 feet/1.5 m away from you on your target line. Simply try to smash the glass with the clubhead after you've hit the ball.

⬣ SPINE ANGLE DRILL

When hitting a fairway wood, especially off the ground, one of the most common faults is topping the ball. Having set the correct address position, with your weight slightly back and the ball forward, you are attempting to hit the ball very fractionally on the up. If this becomes exaggerated, however, the bottom of the club will strike the top of the ball, sending it scurrying along the ground.

In this situation you need to attend to your spine angle, ensuring that your head isn't lifting through the downswing. But instead of concentrating on your technique, use the drill illustrated here. Place the ball on the ground and, about 6 inches/15 cm in front, stick a tee into the turf as shown. The aim is to hit a series of shots, grazing the tee after you have hit the ball. If it helps, try this drill without a ball at first. This will ensure your upper body stays over the shot and help you find a sweet strike.

Problem Solving: Hybrids

The reliability they offer means your hybrids will often be the long clubs you go for when the pressure is on, so errors in your game here need to be resolved without delay. Here we take a look at the hybrid mistakes most regularly seen and offer some advice on how to put them right.

Below Unless the ball is sitting down, when you may need to move the ball back in your stance to find the perfect strike, aim to bruise the turf through impact.

ⓥ ❯ BOTTOMING OUT

The term 'bottoming out' refers to the lowest point of the swing. With a hybrid you need to ensure the club isn't bottoming out too early, as this will mean you hit shots thin or even top the ball.

To gain a feel for where the club is bottoming out, set a solid address position and make a series of practice swings without hitting a ball. Look at the ground as you swing through the contact area and take note of where the club is coming into contact with the ground; place a tee in the turf in the key position. Now place a ball on the ground, just before the tee. (It is important that you do not place the ball on or ahead of the tee – don't forget you are trying to strike it on the downswing.) Set up in exactly the same way and hit the ball. This process will make your contact with the ball and then the ground far more precise and help you to drive through the ball for a far more powerful strike.

⌃ EXCESS BACKSPIN

The other most likely hybrid-related fault occurs if you generate too much backspin through the ball. If this is the case, your shots will rise quickly but lack any real penetration, and in strong winds they will be extremely hard to control.

The first thing to check is your ball position. Make sure it is no farther back in your stance than the mid-point between your feet. (It can even sit a little forward of the centre, but make sure that your sternum is still over the ball.) Now place an alignment stick on each side of your body at address, as shown above. Make some practice swings, ensuring that your upper body remains comfortably within these boundaries. Crucially, your left side should not come into contact with the left-hand stick during the downswing. Think of these sticks as the corridor within which you are making a complete upper body rotation.

SPINNING OUT

Good clubhead speed through the ball stems from a gradual increase of pace through the swing, as we have seen. One common mistake, which arises especially when using the longer, more powerful clubs, is to snatch at the shot from the top of the backswing (we have already examined this on page 117). What should be a silky smooth change of direction becomes hurried and jerky, and often causes players to spin out of the shot too early.

Look at the incorrect position shown in this photograph: the player's body has rotated too soon, leaving the clubhead behind. The outcome will be a devastating push or slice.

You need to know when to inject a little more speed through the downswing. Let the club drop as you start back down and then turn on the power. Getting the timing right will help you deliver the clubface square to the target through the ball.

Increasing Your Options

Both fairway woods and hybrids need to cover a whole variety of on-course circumstances. Being able to control the ball in different ways is the hallmark of a complete and confident golfer. No matter whether you feel ready to take these shots to the course or not, it is well worth trying them in practice. Understanding how to hit them will leave you with a better overall feel for the game.

Left Tiger Woods is the master of the low 'stinger' with a fairway wood. He manipulates his set-up and swing to drill the ball low through the air.

◀ ▶ **TIGER'S STINGER**

The 'stinger' is a shot made famous by Tiger Woods. Reaching for his fairway wood, he has hit fizzing drives that rose only around 15 feet/4.5 m off the ground. The shot's piercing nature makes it an ideal option when the wind is blowing.

Being able to play a punch with a fairway wood is helpful both off the tee and from the fairway, so it is well worth practising. At address, set your sternum a fraction ahead of the line of the ball. The swing you are looking for here is more akin to an iron shot, and this should be reflected in the ball position.

Now, there are two ways to keep the flight down. You can either reduce the pace of the swing (as explained on page 119) to impart less backspin on the ball, or you can reduce the length of the swing (which has a similar effect).

▲ As you can see here, the player has reduced the length of his swing both back and through, in a bid to reduce clubhead speed and also backspin. In this instance, by moving your hands down the grip and shortening the swing, you are treating your fairway wood more like an iron.

ARCING FLIGHTS

The design of a fairway wood makes it easier to shape shots from side to side than with a driver. For this reason, players often hit a fairway wood off the tee when the hole ahead demands a particular shape. We will discuss the basic techniques required to shape the ball on page 156, and they apply in exactly the same way here. For now, simply remember that shot-shaping with fairway woods is far easier off a tee than from the ground, so peg the ball up in practice to give yourself the best chance of a positive result.

◀ ▼ PLAYING SOFT-LANDING LONG SHOTS

One of the most impressive shots you'll see when you watch professional golf is the towering approach with a wood that flies high and lands softly on the green. Modern courses are making this an important shot for top players, so we are seeing it more and more often. It is a tactic that players adopt when ground conditions are hard and fast and the ball is likely to bounce through the green.

At address (1), set the ball a fraction further forward than usual: 1 inch/2.5 cm is probably enough – any more and you risk topping the ball. To find the flight you're after you need to get your body behind the shot and hit the ball on the up, even more than usual with your fairway woods. Widen your stance a little and set a touch more weight on your right side at address. Now make sure that you make a full upper body turn (2) and drive through the downswing into a full finish position (3).

This slightly longer than usual swing will help you generate more clubhead speed through impact, which should translate into extra spin and greater lift. Practise this shot at the range and you will gain a feel for the way that small changes to the finer details of the swing can deliver drastically different results.

Playing Par 5s

Today's most prolific and successful course designers often use par 5s to inject a little excitement into the round. If you can call on straight, long shots, you may well be able to reach the green in two and set up an easy birdie opportunity. But small mistakes will often face severe punishment. Your tactics on par 5s can play a huge part in your overall score, so here's how to think clearly when the prospect of making a birdie looms large.

CHOOSING WHICH CLUBS TO CARRY

Every hole on any course should demand your complete concentration, but there will inevitably be some holes that will have a greater say in your score. Dangerous par 5s fall into this category.

If the course you regularly play on has a par 5 that often leaves you with a 220-yard/200-m approach, it makes sense to carry a club – probably a fairway wood or a hybrid – that will allow you to hit that distance. If this means leaving out a 3-wood that usually travels 245 yards/ 224 m, or a 3-iron that goes only 205 yards/187 m, that may well be a compromise worth making.

The point is that you should select your clubs based, at least in part, on the specific challenges of the course you are about to play. Scoring well on those pivotal holes could be the secret to a good overall score.

◉ KNOW YOUR DISTANCES

It sounds like a simple enough thing to get right, but it is amazing how often golfers are guilty of over estimating how far they can hit the ball. When you play non-competitive golf, and especially when you are practising at the range, pay close attention to how far you hit the ball with every club in your bag. Be realistic about your distances and make a mental note of them. With your woods, you also need to know how far you carry the ball (the distance it flies before hitting the deck).

If there is water to carry from the tee or on the approach to the green, use your course planner or GPS device to calculate the distance. If it is on the limit of what you are capable of, play safe, as the extra pressure of having to make a sweet strike often results in disaster.

◗ PLAY TO YOUR STRENGTHS

This is by no means the most exciting part of playing golf, but laying up short of the green to attack with your wedges is often a shrewd decision. However, when plotting your lay up, play to your strengths. If your chipping and general feel around the greens are among the better parts of your game, get the ball as close as possible to the green. Your chances of getting the ball close even from a difficult position will be good. If your short game is not your biggest strength, lay up to a distance that you like to pitch from.

We will examine this concept in more detail on the next page, but for now simply note that when laying up on a par 5, you might be better off taking a mid-iron for your second shot and leaving yourself a comfortable distance of around 90 yards/82 m to the pin, or whatever distance you are confident from with one of your wedges.

Above If you have a particular pitching distance that you feel confident from, or if your short game is a weakness, lay up to a comfortable distance. For some, hitting a full shot is more likely to provide a good result than chipping from close range.

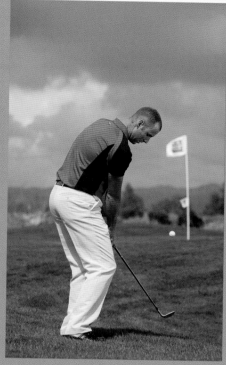

Above If your short game is strong, try to get the ball as close to the green as possible. Work out where it will be easiest to get your ball up and down from, and err on that side. Even if you don't find the putting surface, your chances of getting up and down will be good.

◗ RISKS WORTH TAKING

The art of selecting a strategy that allows you to attack and defend at the right moments is all about judging the risks that lie ahead of you. There are some instances when you have to trust that you are accurate enough and your ball striking is good enough to keep you out of trouble. But this should always depend on the nature of the trouble.

If your second shot to a par 5 is on the limit of carrying a greenside bunker, that will usually be a risk worth taking (depending on the quality of your bunker play). However, if instead of sand you have to carry extremely thick greenside rough or – worse still – water, such as this player (right) is facing, you may wish to lay up short of the green instead. Assess the nature of the risk before you decide whether it is worth taking it on.

Playing Long Par 4s

These are usually the hardest holes on the course, and the key to picking up shots on the field is to avoid making a big number. Here we will look specifically at the approach shot into the green, which will often be played with a hybrid or even a fairway wood. Creating a strategy that leaves you with a chance of making par and reduces your risk of a nightmare score is essential.

ⓥ WHERE TO MISS

It is golfing suicide to attack at all costs, oblivious to where the trouble lies. An important aspect of managing a round of golf is to know where to miss with your approach shots. So, before picking where to aim and which club to hit, study the green and its setting, and in particular think about where the pin is and where the majority of the trouble lies.

Look at the overhead view of the hole pictured below, the majestic par-4 2nd at Old Head Golf Links in Ireland. You can clearly see that there is no option to miss the green left – you'll be faced with a tough, downhill bunker shot (1) or, worse still, you may even lose your ball. It's better to disregard the pin, especially if it is sitting on the left side of the green. In fact, your best option may be to miss the

green short right (2), leaving you with a straight chip of around 20 yards/18 m. So if you find yourself in a scenario like this, as you stand over the ball, pick a club that will only reach the front half of the green and aim to the right of the pin. Opt to play a shot that you know will not leak left. If the shot drifts a little right, the chip you'll be left with will be relatively easy, offering a good chance of a par.

LONG GRASS SWINGS

Achieving success with your fairway woods requires good clubhead speed to help you get the ball away on a good flight. A shrewd way to prepare for a wood shot from distance is to make some swings in longer grass. The extra resistance from the grass forces you to swing a little more aggressively. So make a few practice swings in the rough, if there is any nearby, and then play your shot. You'll be ready for a committed, positive move through the ball.

IS BOGEY A BAD SCORE?

This is a question well worth asking yourself as you stand on the tee; the answer will obviously depend on your own expectations. For most amateurs, however, escaping a long par 4 with a bogey is no bad thing. So if your hybrid play is more reliable than your fairway wood game, think about attacking the green with the accuracy of your hybrid. Yes, you will almost certainly come up short, but a chip and two putts will leave your score intact.

USING CROSSWINDS TO YOUR ADVANTAGE

There are two ways of adjusting to the effects of crosswinds. You can either try to shape the ball into the wind, which has the effect of holding the shot straight, or you can allow the wind to take the ball. If you are attacking a long par 4 from distance, consider using the wind to your advantage. Let's say the wind is blowing from right to left. Aim right (as the player has done here, laying down an alignment stick to illustrate it) and allow for the wind to carry the ball. You will gain crucial extra length using this tactic rather than attempting to hold the ball straight in the breeze. Of course, your ball will be at the mercy of the wind, so if it is a particularly gusty day you'll need to devise a more conservative strategy.

Perfecting Your Long Game

If your fairway wood game needs some attention, it makes sense to head to the range with a well-structured workout plan. The tips, drills and advice on these pages are all designed to help you get the most from this precious time.

❯ NAIL THE BASICS

It doesn't matter whether you are practising your fairway wood or hybrid play or any other part of your game: it is always worth laying sticks or shafts down to help you check the fundamentals. However, as your ball position is so vital to the strike you find, it is particularly important here.

Start by fixing an alignment stick in the ground to act as a reference to your ball position, as shown here. Ensure the ball sits forward in your stance if you are using a fairway wood; your sternum will be fractionally behind the line of the top of the stick. Once you have set the stick for your ball position, lay another stick (or a shaft as we have done here, see inset) to act as a reference for your alignment.

As you lay down the shafts or sticks, be careful that they are all perfectly parallel or square to one another. If one gets knocked off line without you noticing, you'll end up grooving a technique that will ultimately cost you.

❯ TEST YOUR SKILLS

One of the reasons for carrying a fairway wood is the versatility it offers. Large, 460-cc head drivers are designed to be as stable as possible through impact, and even the top pros can find their driver hard to shape. But a fairway wood is a different story: its smaller head should make a soft shape easier to find.

The technique for shot shaping is explained on pages 156–57, but now it is time to test how well in control of the ball you really are. This simple three-step test is a great way to find out. First, pick a target on the range – a flag or a distance marker at the far end of the range would be ideal. Start by hitting five shots that commence their flight to the right and shape gently back. Next, try to hit five fade shots. Finally, attempt to play three punches that fly straight. Inevitably, not every shot will fly exactly the way you want it to, but this drill is about feel. The more you try it, the better your feel for the different shots will become.

PERFECT A SPECIFIC SHOT

Every golf course will have some tee shots that are relatively easy and some tighter ones that are tough. The pressure that builds as you prepare to hit a difficult drive makes it even harder. While you are on the practice ground perfecting your fairway wood game, think about the holes that you find hardest to play. Picture them in front of you and practise the drive that you would need, hit the shot and imagine where it would finish.

Without the tension of wanting to build a score for real and the visual impact of the danger itself, you should be able to hit some good shots. This extremely simple process acts as a form of mental preparation, building a positive outlook ready for when you face the real situation.

❮ ON-COURSE PRACTICE

Not every game of golf you'll play will be competitive. In fact, for many golfers, going for a 'knockabout' with friends or alone is an extremely enjoyable and relaxing form of the game. During these rounds, feel free to try different shots. Attempt a fairway wood out of the rough (left), or a fade off the tee. The knowledge you'll glean on the course, trying different shots with a clearly visible outcome, will teach you a lot about strategy and the shots you can and can't play.

Iron Play

IT IS COMFORTABLY one of the most impressive sights in golf. Standing behind Tiger Woods, watching from a distance as he works his way through the bag preparing for a tournament, is in itself a lesson in what pure ball striking really looks and – perhaps more importantly – sounds like. When Woods won the Open at Hoylake in 2006 he hit his driver only once, preferring instead to rely on his razor-like sharpness with his irons. His accuracy and absolute control in incredibly tricky links conditions blew the field away.

This no-driver strategy is unusual, and your own iron game will usually be the catalyst that transforms steady work with the driver into opportunities for good scoring. First and foremost, to succeed in this area of the game you need to rely on solid contacts every time. Striking an iron shot sweetly also happens to be one of the best feelings this game has to offer.

Regular competition, however, can take its toll on your technique. We all need to rededicate ourselves to the fundamental laws of the set-up and swing from time to time, and this section will show you how. And if you do regularly compete on the course in medals, Stablefords or match play, it can be easy to forget, as you desperately try to forge a respectable tally, that golf is supposed to be fun. Nowhere is this more apparent than when it comes to shot shaping and flight control with the irons. Whether you just try it at the range or you take it with you to the course, intentionally shaping your shots will leave you with a real sense of achievement.

From start to finish, this section will provide you with everything you need, from equipment advice and basic technique to strategy pointers and advice on how to develop your game. Digest all the information that follows and you'll gain a whole new level of appreciation for supreme performances like Tiger's at Hoylake.

Making Crisp Contact

Hitting every iron shot you face during a round sweetly should always be the goal. Without a pure contact, the rest of the technique is rather irrelevant, so here we will take a close look at the art of ball striking. The aim is simple: master the perfect angle of attack. Then you can move on to the more intricate elements of successful iron play.

◀ ⏶ PAPER CUT-OUT DRILL
Unlike with large-headed woods or hybrids that offer oversized sweet spots, ball striking with your irons needs to be as precise as possible. Your divots can tell you a lot about your swing, and making sure they are spot on is important. With your irons it is absolutely imperative that you strike the ball before the club drives into the turf. If you hit the ground first you'll lose all power in the strike.

To help you develop a better feel for where the divot should come, take a sheet of A4 paper and cut out a section in the shape shown above. Use tee pegs to attach the paper to the ground and place the ball towards the back edge of the hole in the paper. As you address the ball, remind yourself that the club should not come into contact with the paper through impact. This simple drill clearly highlights the sort of 'ball first, turf second' contact that you should be looking for. If you strike near the equator of the ball, with the club failing to touch the ground through impact, a 'thin' strike will wreak havoc with your flight and distance control – as has happened on the left.

⌃ TAKE SHALLOW DIVOTS

While the clubhead should take turf through impact, make sure that it doesn't dig too far into the ground. The ideal divot should be shallow (above right). If you have started taking dinner-plate sized chunks of turf (above left), it is a sure sign that you are getting too steep through the downswing. This often happens if you've been playing regularly in windy conditions. Far from helping you keep the flight down, an increase of backspin will only serve to send the ball shooting high into the air. If this is a problem for you, the next drill should help you solve it.

❱ CHECKING YOUR BALL POSITION

This drill might make you feel a little self-conscious as you practise, but it's the perfect way to check your address position. Tie a scarf around your neck and set up to the ball. The end of the scarf should be pointing directly at the ball. It is also important that the end of the scarf is in line with your hands. This is the neutral position you should be looking for, and if your divots have been getting too deep or you're not taking any turf at all, this should quickly get you back on track.

FORGIVING IRONS

Your choice of irons is a big one. Depending on the make-up of your set, you will probably have between eight and six irons in the bag. Ensuring they are well suited to your own specific game and aesthetic requirements is very important. Before you get custom fitted (which you should certainly do if you are thinking about spending a significant sum) you need an idea of what type of iron you should be playing.

Higher handicap golfers who need a forgiving model to inspire confidence should think about a deep cavity option (as shown below), with thick top-lines and wide soles. These irons are designed to optimize the size of the hitting area and to help ease the ball up in the air without forcing you to hit it too hard. There are two main downsides to irons like these – shot shaping is harder, and distance control can be slightly inconsistent (shots struck from the very centre may go a little farther than you expect). However, if improving the general quality of your ball striking is your main priority, this is the sector of the market to pay closest attention to.

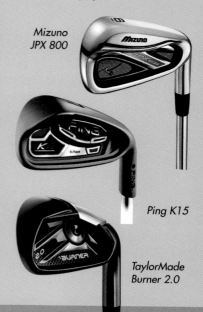

Mizuno JPX 800

Ping K15

TaylorMade Burner 2.0

Iron Game Essentials

As we emphasized in the first section, your posture dictates how consistently you strike the ball. It is time to concentrate on your spine angle more specifically, as mistakes here will be extremely costly, but they are easy to put right.

❯ STANCE AND SHOULDERS

We have already stressed the importance of a stable stance, which acts as the steady platform against which your upper body coils to create power. With your irons, however, your stance should be narrower, and your shoulders should be more nearly parallel to the ground than when hitting a wood. Angling your shoulders when the ball is pegged up and you are looking for a sweeping strike is ideal, but with your irons it can lead to disastrous thin or fat contacts. Narrow your feet and move the ball into the middle of your stance so that your shoulders feel parallel to the ground. Your stance should still offer enough stability for a powerful drive through the ball.

> WATCH YOUR OWN SWING SEQUENCE

Golf magazines often print top players' swing sequences, asking coaches to dissect every move. This sequence of photographs perfectly illustrates one of the most fundamental laws of golf: notice that, until the player has fully released the club, his head remains at the same level through the swing. If you are looking to hit shots consistently from the middle of the clubface (especially with your irons) this needs to be a feature of your game.

MID-CAVITY IRONS

If you are looking for irons that offer a significant level of forgiveness without giving up too much distance and flight control, mid-cavity models (as shown below) are ideal. These clubs look more like traditional irons than the oversized, ultra-forgiving alternatives, but the top-line should still be thick enough to inspire confidence in the consistency of the contact. With a set of mid-cavities your distance control should be a little more precise and the overall flights will be lower, as the spin created at impact is reduced. This category offers the balance between forgiveness and control that many mid-to-low handicappers enjoy.

Callaway Razr X

TaylorMade R9

⊗ DON'T COPY THE TIGER DIP!

Strangely, one player who does not follow the rule related to keeping your height through the swing is Tiger Woods (right). During his downswing he dips his head, losing height before rising up at the last minute to make a sweet contact with the ball. Of course, he has mastered the timing of this move and has fast enough reactions to make a pure contact, but for most golfers it is fair to say that this is not conducive to reliably solid striking. Focus on keeping your height the same through the swing, rotating around a static fulcrum – the middle of your chest.

TIMING THE RELEASE

While it is never a bad idea to concentrate on keeping a steady spine angle through the swing, you should also be conscious of the release. Once you have struck the ball and your arms have released towards the target, let your head turn to watch the flight of the ball. Your upper body should then be able to lift into the finish position. If you are consciously trying to keep your head at the same level through the swing, you may restrict the flow of your own rotation through the ball.

Tiger Woods

Problem Solving: Weight Movement

Knowing what the perfect positions look like is one thing; forcing yourself to replicate them, especially when your subconscious wants you to do something else, is quite different. An effective weight shift during the golf swing is imperative. If yours is not working, here's how to get back on track.

❯ ⌄ LOGO DRILL

If your weight is moving in the wrong direction through the swing, this drill will highlight any mistakes you might be making with your head position. Place a ball on the ground with the logo pointing towards the target so that, at address, you can just about see the edge of the writing. Now make a slower, more deliberate swing than normal, but stop just as you are coming into the ball and hold the position. Can you still see the edge of the logo? If the answer is 'No', an upper body sway away from the target is causing your head to move to the right.

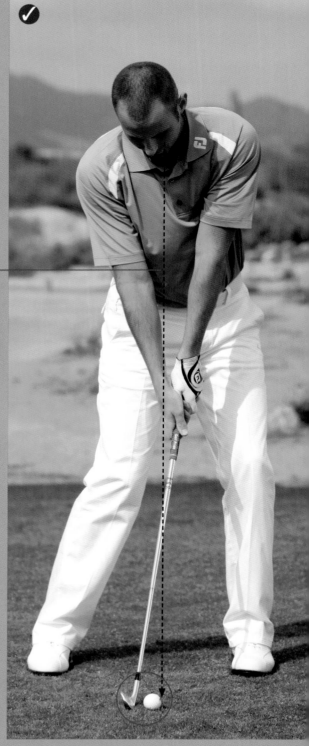

❤ WALK THROUGH THE SHOT

The great South African Gary Player used to incorporate a rather unusual move in the end of his golf swing that became his signature. Having struck the ball, he would often take a couple of steps towards where he was hitting, as if he were lending all his weight and power to the shot to get the ball as far up the fairway as he possibly could. Now, strictly speaking, you might say this revealed a lack of balance, but Player was one of the most accurate golfers of his age. Having nailed all the key mechanics, this move ensured he drove his weight powerfully through the shot.

If you fall into the trap of getting stuck on the back foot through impact, copy Gary Player's trademark move as a simple practice drill. As you strike the ball let your weight move onto your left side by taking a step towards the target: it's a good way to groove one of golf's most important fundamental moves.

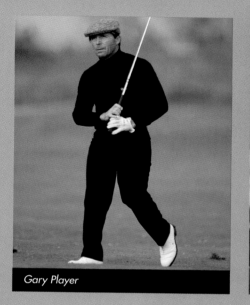

Gary Player

❮ THINK JAVELIN THROWER

When you think about it logically, the need to transfer your weight from the back foot to the front foot becomes obvious. If you want to propel a ball, or for that matter any other kind of object, it makes sense that your weight should move towards where you want the ball to go. Think of a javelin thrower (left): as they let go of the javelin, all of their weight is moving powerfully towards the target. This is the feeling you should be trying to replicate during the downswing. Trust the loft of the club to create the flight, because it makes no sense to move your weight away from the target as you make contact with the ball.

BLADES AND MUSCLE-BACK IRONS

For the most competent ball strikers, blades offer golfers the ultimate in control. Often forged, these provide the highest levels of feel, allowing players to dictate with greater ease the type of shot (trajectory, shape and distance) they are looking for.

Traditional blades or versions with a very small cavity (often known as muscle-backs) are what many professionals and good amateurs use. They are designed to help reduce spin through impact, but only those with better than average levels of clubhead speed will find a good flight easy to achieve. It is easy to be wooed into contemplating a set of blades by their stunning looks, but it doesn't matter how great they look in the bag – it's how they perform in your hands that really matters.

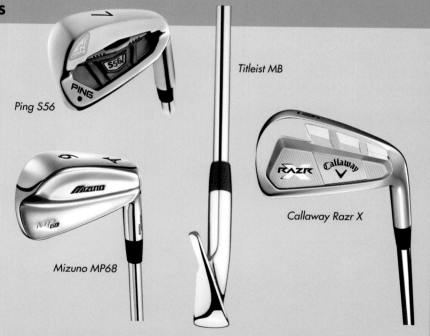

Ping S56

Titleist MB

Mizuno MP68

Callaway Razr X

Problem Solving: Identifying Errors

If you have checked your weight shift but you're still not able to find a silky smooth strike, do not despair. There are other errors that could be to blame. The tips, drills and advice here will help you home in on and then solve the main problem.

⊘ ⊗ RESOLVING TOE AND HEEL STRIKES

While striking the ball from the toe of the club will cost you distance, if you do the same from the heel you will suffer one of golf's most feared shots: the shank. Many golfers refer to it as 'the unmentionable', and it occurs when the ball strikes the hosel of the club and flies straight right.

Whether you are having problems with toe or heel contacts, try this drill. Place an empty ball box on the ground next to your ball, leaving you just enough room to make a clean strike (which side you place the box depends on whether you are suffering with toe or heel strikes). Now hit plenty of balls, simply aiming to avoid the box as you drive through the ball. The more shots you hit the better, as you will begin to groove a move that offers a more central strike. Start by swinging the club softly and, as your confidence grows, turn up the power.

⊘ LEARNING TO TRUST LOFT

We have already stressed the importance of trusting the loft of your clubs – it is the combination of this and your clubhead speed that will create the desired trajectory. This, however, is easier said than done, and for those who struggle to get the ball in the air, leaning back through the downswing can seem like the right thing to do.

This simple drill should teach you exactly how the loft of the club works. Take a 9-iron or pitching wedge and move the ball back in your stance at address. Lift your right heel so only your toe is in contact with the ground (this will force your weight to stay on your left side) and make a swing. Even though your angle into the ball is incredibly steep (as shown), effectively de-lofting the club, you should still be able to get the ball up in the air. Hopefully this will convince you that you do not need to lean back to create a decent flight.

⊘ SHAFT LEAN

We have discussed the importance of your sternum position at set-up and through the swing. Your hands should be directly under your sternum in these two key positions: if they aren't, your angle of attack will kill your consistency.

Start by checking your address position, making sure that your hands are in line with the middle of your chest and that the shaft is not leaning back from or forward to the ball. Now make a slow swing and hold your natural impact position, as shown. If the shaft is inclined forward a little more than at address, that is fine and is evidence of a good weight shift through the downswing. This should not be exaggerated however and the shaft should certainly never be leaning significantly forwards or backwards through impact. Check that you aren't making either of these mistakes and your angle of attack will be spot on.

BLENDED SETS

We have already looked at the three main iron options, but there is one other alternative. Many manufacturers offer players the opportunity to blend forgiving longer irons with short irons that are more feel-focused. The idea is that they provide confidence and forgiveness where you need it most – at the top end of the bag. In the shorter irons, where your striking should be more consistent, shallower cavities offer a greater level of control. It's a clever concept, and even some of those who make a living from playing the game like to look down at address on more forgiving long irons. As always, it makes sense to consult a professional who will explain how you can take advantage of blending different types of irons in one set.

Nike VR Pro Combo

Keeping the Flight Down

When discussing fairway woods we looked at the basic technique for keeping the flight of your shots down, so the ball penetrates farther through the wind. Those basic principles apply again here, but in this section we take a closer look at the finer details of playing a successful punch with your irons.

⊙ SOFT HANDS

If you have been fighting a strong wind all day, the natural inclination is to hit the ball harder and harder, forcing it towards your target. This, however, is a trap that simply must be avoided. Do not lose sight of the basic physics of the clubhead and ball through impact. The faster you swing, the more backspin you'll spark, and this translates to a higher ball flight. When playing the punch you need to strike a balance between enough speed to get the ball up with a reasonable amount of power and hitting it softly enough to keep the spin down.

Regularly trying this shot in practice is the best way to gain a feel for the kind of clubhead speed required. Before you play each shot, check your grip pressure (below). Feel your hands soften on the club and let the muscles in your forearms relax. A smooth, less aggressive action is what you are looking for.

⊗ CHECK THE CLUBFACE

As explained on page 136, when you want to hit a punch the ball needs to sit back in your stance (your sternum and hands should still be over the middle of your stance) and a fraction more weight should be set on your left side at address. These key alterations to your address position (shown above) will help you keep the flight down. However, as you set up with the ball farther back in your stance than usual, there is one very simple error you need to guard against: make sure the clubface is not pointing to the right of your target (above right). When you are concentrating on the many different areas of the punch, it can be surprisingly easy to let a simple mistake like this slip through the net. In practice, line up the logo with your target and use this as a handy reference point to set your body around.

◁ CLUBBING UP

When the wind starts to blow, your normal distance expectations are irrelevant. This is when your feel for the game will be put to the test, and a good imagination and plenty of creativity will serve you well. In a strong headwind, when you are trying to keep the ball down, take plenty of club. A softer swing will deliver the low, boring trajectory you need, so be prepared to take one, two or even three more clubs than you would for the same distance in calm conditions. Swing a little more softly and, despite the wind, you'll have absolute control over your ball.

PUNCHING FROM A DIVOT

There is no reason why you should rely on the punch shot only when it is windy. When the course conditions are hard and fast, keeping the ball running along the ground might be the best option to optimize your distance control.

Another situation when a punch comes in handy is when your ball is in a divot. By moving the ball farther back in your stance you will make your angle of attack steeper, and the club will drive farther into the turf than usual. Crucially, you should move your hands down the grip a fraction – this will shorten the overall swing arc to help you avoid hitting the ground before the ball.

When playing from a divot, this technique is the best way to find a solid strike. Adopt the same approach as you would for a punch and playing from a divot will not pose a problem to your score.

Shot Maker Tips

For the proficient ball striker, golf is largely a game of feel. Once you have nailed down all the basics, making significant and lasting improvements is about expanding your skill-set. The advice given here is designed to help those confident in their own ability to make the most of their instinctive feel for the game.

Take care to aim the clubface directly at your final target.

❯ GENTLE SHAPING

As you develop your game towards mid- or low-handicap territory, you'll find it helpful to learn how to hit a soft fade (left to right) and a gentle draw (right to left). These will help you in a variety of weather and course conditions. Learning how to hit these shots will also teach you important general lessons about how to control the clubface.

To hit a soft fade or draw (10 yards/ 9 m of drift through the air is what you should be looking for) you need to make some small adjustments to your address position. There are two different factors to consider as you set up – the line on which you intend the ball to start its journey and the final destination. For this reason, you need a clear picture in your mind of what the shot will look like.

Start by aiming the club at the point where you want the ball to finish. Once the club is in position it is time to aim your body: crucially, this needs to be in line with where you want the ball to set off: left of the final target for a fade (as shown here) and right for a draw. Once you are in the ideal address, do not think about the clubface position but instead just try to make a normal swing. The position of your body will manipulate the swing path for you.

Take time to practise this skill on the range. Vary your set-up position to see how this affects the flight of the ball. This sort of creative practice is the best way to improve your all-round golfing skills.

▶ ▼ USE PLASTIC BALLS

Instead of tinkering with the address position, some players like to feel the shape they're after in their swing. This requires a natural, in-built sense for what to do and how to control the flight. An excellent way to develop this feeling is to practise with plastic balls. Far lighter than the normal variety, they will accentuate the sidespin you generate. Also, as they don't go very far you don't have to worry about where they might finish.

If you understand the basic principles of swing path set out on page 98, you should be able to shape shots quite easily. As you improve, you could try hitting plastic balls around objects, like your golf bag as the player is doing here, forcing himself to hit fades and draws to avoid hitting the bag. The more you tinker with

your technique in search of different flights, the better your overall feel for the game will become, so use this practice to learn the feel behind shot shaping.

HOLDING SHOTS AGAINST THE WIND

The ability to shape shots can come into its own in a crosswind. The side-spin you apply through impact will counter the effect of the wind and hold the ball straight.

For right-handers this tends to be harder to do when the wind is off the left, and vice versa, but here's a great tip that can offer the control you need. Simply turn the clubface so that it points slightly to the left of the target before you set your grip at address, and then make a normal swing. This seemingly small adjustment will help the ball bore through the breeze, remaining straight throughout its flight.

Selecting Your Strategy

If you have followed all the advice in this section so far you should have a solid technique and be able to hit the ball where and how you want. Now it's time to select a plan that will let you putt from the ideal place for a birdie. Here are the basic factors you should be considering.

Opposite left The 17th at Kingsbarns is a perfect example of how course designers force you to think carefully about your strategy. Depending on the pin placement on such a vast, undulating green, you'll need to devise a plan that avoids the pot bunkers and leaves you with a straightforward putt.

❯ LOOK AT THE TOPOGRAPHY

There are many factors that come into play as you plan your approach, and one is the topography of the green. For instance, if it slopes from left to right you know that any shot landing on the left half of the green will bounce right. Likewise, if the pin is on a ledge it is important that the ball either pitches or runs up onto the correct level.

Hitting shots blindly at the pin without considering these factors will mean that your birdie putts will often be too tricky to be aggressive with. So pay attention to the topography, locate the optimum place to putt from and devise your strategy from there.

> LONG AND SHORT OF IT

If you have a golf course planner handy, try this exercise. Count how many bunkers there are short of the greens, then how many there are beyond the greens. You should notice a large number of traps short and a very small number long. Why do course designers place so much trouble in front of the green? Because most golfers miss greens short.

Of course, this is a slight generalization, but on most layouts you are better off playing long than short – the approach shot the player is facing here is a perfect case in point. Bring this theory into your strategic planning and make sure that if you are going to mis-club, you finish beyond the flag. You'll be surprised how few greens you miss.

⊻ WHEN TO ATTACK, WHEN TO DEFEND

Good golf course designers create greens that offer many options to those in charge of setting up the course. A perfect example of this is at Kingsbarns (below) in Fife, Scotland, where the architect, Kyle Phillips, has built large greens with many undulations. The placement of the pin can have a dramatic effect on the difficulty of each hole.

Rarely will you play a course set up with 18 difficult pin placements. Instead there will often be six hard, six medium and six easy pins. From the perfect spot on the fairway, playing to an easy pin, there is no reason not to take dead aim at it. A good shot will yield a very straightforward birdie chance. However, you need to know when to be conservative. Attacking tough pin placements might work from time to time, but if it goes wrong your score will take a hit. So devising a strategy based on which pins to attack and which ones to play towards conservatively is always a shrewd move.

⌂ FOCUSING ON THE PROCESS

The process of selecting a sound strategy offers a good mental preparation for the shot. If you are planning to hit a punch, stand behind the ball mapping out the exact flight of the shot. Make a few practice swings, 'feeling' the ideal move. Now set up over the ball and ensure all your fundamental positions are spot on. Many players then like to focus on one element of the swing – this allows you to concentrate on what you are trying to do without becoming too caught up in the mechanics. So in this scenario, you may wish to devote your mind simply to making a more compact swing than usual, curtailing your follow through as the player has done here. Committing to your strategy is essential, and this process will help you do that.

Combating Tough Scenarios

Every day on the golf course is different. A blustery afternoon on a tree-lined track will pose a whole different set of challenges from a dead calm day by the sea. Picking a clever game plan in a tricky scenario will give you an advantage over the field.

❯ ❯ ⌄ BLIND SHOTS

Undulations on courses mean that you will frequently have to hit a shot blind, over the brow of a hill. Often, especially off the tee, there will be a marker post for you to aim at, which will guide you towards the middle of the fairway. When hitting a blind approach, however, you need to be as precise as possible. Even if there is a marker post behind the green, it will not tell you where the pin is. In this instance, walk straight from your ball up to the brow of the hill, look at the green and pick a target. Now look towards the horizon and select something on your line that you will be able to see from where your ball is. This might be a telegraph pole, a pylon or a building, but whatever it is, it will become your target. It's easy to get this simple process slightly wrong, so stay focused.

⊙ PICKING THE WIND

One of the reasons the Open Championship is so cherished by golf fans is that it gives audiences the chance to see how the world's top players cope with windy conditions. This separates those with mechanically solid techniques from those with a natural feel and instinct for the game. No matter whether you are playing a windy links or a blustery parkland course, there are a number of wind-related factors you need to consider before you begin:

Direction Look at the flag or trees to gain a feel. If your playing partners are hitting before you, watch how the wind affects the flight of their golf balls. Try to get a general feel for where the prevailing wind is coming from because on tree-lined courses it swirls around and becomes hard to identify.

Strength This can differ between ground level and higher up, above the tree line. Just because there is no wind where you are does not mean the ball will not be affected. Again, look at the flag and the treetops for information.

Gusts A steady breeze is one thing, a gusting wind is quite another. Try to keep the flight a little lower than usual and don't start your swing if you feel the wind is about to gust. You may also wish to widen your stance a fraction at address to form a more stable base.

MANIPULATING PRESSURE

One of the principles of good match play involves the creation and passing on of pressure. For example, if both players hit the fairway and you have the honour for the second shot, you are automatically in the position of creating or diffusing pressure. Hit a beautiful approach and your opponent will need to follow suit; miss the green and all they have to do is play to the safe part of it.

With this in mind, you should always try to avoid unnecessarily diffusing the pressure. Fall back on your basic principles of when to attack and when to defend: they apply just as much in match play as they do in a medal. You'll create pressure by hitting a safe shot away from the pin without risking trouble. You'll also be surprised at how a simple approach to 20–30 feet/6–9 m can make your opponent sweat. You'll find that if you can develop a strategy that consistently yields pars, you'll win far more matches than you lose. If you are receiving shots, factor this into your approach and aim to make net pars to build pressure.

WET WEATHER

In the rain, the first thing you need to do is keep yourself and, more importantly, your grips dry. It is important to keep your towel dry, so it's a good idea to store it in the waterproof compartment of your golf bag. Use it to dry your grips and your hands before all your long shots. It is also worth buying a pair of wet-weather gloves (see below), as they will offer some crucial extra grip.

With regard to your swing, stability is key. Widen your stance slightly and keep the swing a fraction shorter than usual. You can do this by squeezing the grip of the club at address to create the tension that will restrict the swing arc. This will help you maintain a good balance for sweet striking.

Training Your Iron Game

Constructive practice does not have to feel like a chore. There are many ways to add a little interest to your training time while also making some significant improvements to your iron play. The drills described here are designed to do exactly that.

⩔ FLIGHT GAME

If you are practising on a grass driving range of the kind found at most golf clubs, you can use this game to improve your shot-shaping skills as well as honing your visualization.

Place three clusters of balls along the front of where you are hitting from. One cluster should sit directly on your target line, one to the right and one to the left, as shown. Now, the challenge is to hit the first ball over the left cluster and get it to shape right, back to the target line. Hit the next ball over the right cluster, trying to draw it back. Finally, try to hit one dead straight shot. Repeat the process five or six times and your control for each shape is bound to improve.

This game works excellently to establish a clear vision in your mind for each shot and to make you focus on the target as opposed to the technique.

> FROM SHORT TO LONG

As you have no doubt already picked up on, the technique required for a punch is very similar to that of a bump and run (see page 198). In fact, a
great way to develop the former is to practise the latter. Hit a few chip and runs, looking to hit each ball a fraction farther than the last. Without making any significant changes to the set-up or the essential technique, slowly build the length of the swing towards a fuller shot, as shown in this sequence.

As we have already explained, you should prevent yourself from swinging too hard, maintaining the smooth rhythm required for a deft chip. If you attempt this drill with a 7-iron you'll quickly work up towards and beyond 100 yards/90 m without sending the ball very high into the air at all. This drill works perfectly to illustrate just how much control you can generate when you need to.

WHEN NOT TO PRACTISE

Be wary of practising when the wind is blowing hard. If you head to the range and blast ball after ball into a left-to-right crosswind, for instance, you might unwittingly start to groove an ultimately damaging action. Fighting the wind to keep the ball on line can affect the neutral set-up and swing that you should be striving for. If the wind is really strong you may be better served practising your short game instead.

❯ SET YOUR AIM

As you work through all these drills, always have an alignment stick or shaft on the ground as a reference for your body alignment. Without having to concentrate meticulously on exactly where you are aiming, you should automatically be able to get into the perfect position.

Just be careful to ensure that when you change your target or are trying to manipulate the shape of the ball flight, you also move the stick or shaft. Forgetting to do this will only cause you to groove mistakes into your technique. Using shafts as a handy visual aid works to groove the basics throughout your practice session.

Pitching Essentials

You are nearing the green now, but you still need to make a positive, committed swing. Controlling your accuracy and distance will set you apart from the majority of your opponents, so read this section carefully and digest the advice. Devoting yourself to these core principles might just help you reach a new level of performance.

You may be carrying two, three or even four wedges in your bag but that doesn't mean you should always pitch with them. When conditions are poor, a softer swing with a 9- or 8-iron will offer more controlled flight. (Try the 'short to long' drill described on page 162 to help you create a controlled flight.)

The number of wedges you have to choose from will depend on how many fairway woods and hybrids you have in your bag. This is a delicate balancing act and only you can decide the composition of your bag. However, try to ensure that you don't have any significant gaps between the distances you are able to hit with your wedges. This will make life tough for you and will force you to play delicate half shots, which are notoriously difficult to control.

Robert Karlsson

⌃ ROTATION TECHNIQUE

If you get the opportunity, either on television or at a live event, take some time to watch Robert Karlsson play. At 6 feet 5 inches/1.95 m, he relies on incredibly strong fundamentals to ensure his move is as efficient as possible. At no time is this more visible than when he pitches. Notice the harmony between his arms and body. They work in complete unison, rotating back and through at exactly the same unhurried pace.

Try to replicate Karlsson's move by keeping your hands working with the turn of your abdomen, controlling distance with the amount of rotation you employ. This is the very basic secret behind consistently accurate pitching.

> SETTING A GOOD PACE

We have stressed time and again the importance of swing speed, but as you pitch – when distance control is that much more important – it is something you should think hard about. Speed is your way of controlling two crucial factors: distance and trajectory.

If you ever get to see the best players in the world practise their pitching, you'll notice that even though they have more loft in their hands, the flight of the shot they are hitting is usually relatively low. This is because they are able to gain maximum distance control by keeping their clubhead speed in check and using their full complement of wedges. When they need to call on a high shot they'll often take less club and hit the ball a fraction harder. When the wind is up, a smoother swing with a less lofted club keeps the flight down.

❯ PURE CONTACTS

When attacking the green with a wedge, some players like to move the ball a fraction farther back in their stance than usual. These photographs (top and bottom right) illustrate the small margin we are talking about in comparison to the ball position for your mid-irons. Be careful not to move the ball too far back. This will only make your angle of attack steeper and create more spin. You might feel more comfortable gaining a sweet strike from this position, but you'll lose control of the spin.

The other element to address here is your posture (far right). As the shaft of your wedge is shorter than any of your other irons it is easy to let yourself become hunched (top). Of course, you must avoid this by keeping your back straight (below); your abdomen and thighs should both feel solid as you prepare to take the club away.

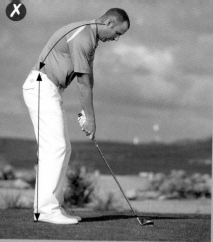

Pitching Distances

There are two ways to manipulate your technique to affect distance – either by changing the length of your swing or by directly altering its speed. By length we really mean the amount of upper body rotation you employ and the size of the swing arc. It is now time to take a close look at these two methods of control. Absorb this information and then determine, in practice, which works best for you.

Below Move your hands up or down the grip to help adjust your swing length. This will affect clubhead speed through impact and, ultimately, distance.

⬆ CHANGING SWING LENGTH

The first option for distance control is to try to maintain a constant rhythm for every pitch you play and use the length of the swing to produce different distances. To illustrate exactly how this works, let us presume you have just two wedges in the bag – a set pitching wedge and a 56° option. By making small changes to the length of the swing you will have different distances at your fingertips for each

wedge. To make a shorter swing (above left) simply move your hands down the grip and make a smaller upper body rotation. Always remember to keep your arms and body working together. For a longer shot (above right), go up the grip and make a bigger turn.

By keeping the speed of the swing constant, but changing the hand position and amount of body rotation, you will achieve very different results, and if you

practise enough you will know that a certain length of swing with a certain wedge will deliver the distance you are faced with. Now, this might at first look and feel like quite a mechanical process, but maintaining the same tempo requires real discipline, especially when there is adrenaline pumping through your body. This is a tactic that many top players employ to become as precise as possible with their distances.

⌄ ASSESSING THE LIE

A new rule restricting the depth and sharpness of grooves, phased in from 2010, was designed to place a greater emphasis on accuracy over distance off the tee. The grooves of new, conforming wedges will not offer quite the same levels of spin, especially from the rough.

If you are attacking the green from lush, thick grass, allow for more run when the ball hits the green. If this means playing away from the flag to a fatter, safer part of the green, then so be it: there is no real reason why you shouldn't be getting down in at most three with a wedge in your hands. If the ball is sitting down or on a bare lie, move it back in your stance more than usual. Above all, remember to take a close look at your lie if you aren't sure about how it is sitting, as the lie will affect your tactics.

⌃ ALTERING SWING SPEED

Your other option is to dictate distance through a deft feel for the pace of the swing. In this case, your address position will remain almost identical from wedge to wedge, distance to distance, but by altering the pace of the clubhead through the ball you'll reach different distances.

A player who does this properly knows that a three-quarter speed swing with a 56° wedge will go a certain number of yards/metres farther than a half-pace swing with the same club. So while the length of the swing may be similar, it is the subtle change to pace that alters distance.

No matter which approach you adopt, the key to success boils down to a very simple matter of practice. The more shots you hit, either on the range or during friendly rounds, the more your instincts will improve.

Pitching Problem Solving

You should relish your pitch shots, perhaps more than any other challenge you face. Nail the fundamental technique and deliver a pure contact, and a golden birdie opportunity will come your way. Get it wrong and you risk giving the field a two-shot swing against you. If you are struggling with this part of your game these tips should fix the problem.

⊻ LEAVING SHOTS OUT RIGHT

Do your pitch shots have a tendency to start straight and drift weakly towards the right? This is a common fault caused more by a defensive state of mind and a tentative approach than anything else.

As we have stressed throughout this section, pitching is all about control. The stricter you are, certainly with your distances, the more success you'll have. However, committing to the shot is just as important here as when you hit a full drive. Don't forget the basic mechanics of the swing and ensure that you release the clubhead towards the target as you would do normally.

If you have been leaving your pitch shots out right, it is most likely that you have been subconsciously trying to steer the ball onto the green, leaving the clubface open through impact. Simply concentrate on making a proper release and you should see an immediate improvement to the ball flight.

⊼ 'JUST A FLICK'

'I hit a great drive and left myself just a flick into 13.' The use of the word 'flick' in this commonly heard remark is misleading. If you take it too literally – and many people do – you'll start flicking your wrists at the ball, as shown above. Instead your wrists should be just as firm through impact here as if you were playing a full approach with a 7-iron. Flicking at the ball is the best way of killing your distance control.

❯ BALL STRIKING DRILL

If your ball striking is poor, any of the drills and tips on pages 146–47 will help. Alternatively, try this. Use two tees to peg some string into the ground just behind your ball, as shown. The aim is very simply to make a solid strike without catching the string.

This works well because the string becomes a very clear obstacle to be avoided. It will focus your mind on delivering the ideal downward strike and trusting the loft of the club to get the ball airborne. Hit 10 or even 15 shots without hitting the string before the ball, and the precision of your striking is guaranteed to improve. However, watch out for thin strikes. You still need to drive the club through the ball and into the ground.

❮ STABILITY DRILL

We have already stressed the importance of a firm lower body when you pitch. As this shot sits between a feel and a full shot, it is very easy to become a touch lazy with the core positions discussed in the first section. If you have been having problems with the quality of strike, or your accuracy is off, try this drill.

First set a wider stance than usual, and then angle your right toe in, as shown. This will feel uncomfortable, so when you swing do this drill slowly, but what it does well is stabilize the lower body. You should start to stay centred over the shot, and the simplicity of a good pitching action will quickly return.

Bunker Play

BUNKERS HAVE TWO FUNCTIONS. The first is that of protection. By strategically positioning traps either on the fairway or by the green, architects create clearly visible no-go zones. The intention is that a shot from sand is tougher than one from the rough. The second function for the course designer is aesthetic. Bunkers add a crucial element of definition to a layout, providing contrasts of textures and colours that increase the overall appeal of the landscape. Their visual quality can also have a strong impact on your mind. Knowing that a certain bunker must be avoided at all costs creates pressure and requires careful thinking from the golfer.

However, bunkers differ drastically in style from course to course. Those found on links layouts tend to be far smaller and deeper than most inland versions. Seaside traps pose a far greater threat, because often – owing to the severity of the lip or a difficult stance – your only option will be to splash out sideways. The ball will often be filtered towards these links traps, built as they usually are in naturally low-lying areas. Many of the bunkers on the Old Course at St Andrews, for instance, can't be seen from the tee, but as the ball scurries along the fairway they have a habit of drawing it in, costing you a shot. Inland traps, by contrast, are far less perilous. The lips are shallower and they are more spacious, providing the player with many more shot options. In fact, when the rough is particularly thick, players often prefer to find sand, where control is easier to come by.

Regardless of the type of course, a solid technique is essential in bunker play. But like all delicate shots, success is about feel, both for how the club will respond to the sand and for the strength required for the shot. The advice that follows should help you optimize your bunker game so that the danger posed by sand will not, in the end, result in a disastrous score.

Bunker Play Keys

For the best players in the world, finding their ball in a bunker is not a worry. With a carefully honed technique they are able to splash the ball out, leaving themselves with very little to do to make par. If you have the right approach there should be nothing to fear.

Below Gene Sarazen, seen here at Augusta during the 1930s, was the first player to use the modern-day bunker technique instead of chipping the ball out of sand. It was discovered that striking the sand before the ball provided far more reliable results.

∨ FUNDAMENTAL PRINCIPLE

It was Gene Sarazen who first adopted the modern bunker technique. Whereas players had previously chipped out of sand, Sarazen discovered that by using a club with the right amount of bounce (see box opposite) the shot could be played with far more control by striking the sand before the ball. Suddenly, the unpredictability of both strike and distance caused by trying to clip the ball off the surface was avoided by this far more reliable method.

Hitting the sand first allows the player to be more positive with the shot, knowing that a softer flight and landing will offer greater levels of control. So, unless you are playing a full shot from a fairway bunker, your aim should be to make contact with the sand before the ball. With enough loft on the club through impact, the ball will come out and land delicately on the green. This is the most important principle of bunker play; if you commit to it, driving the club powerfully through the sand, it could become one of your greatest strengths.

Take a look at the difference in sole design between these two clubs. This illustrates how the sand wedge (below right) is created to help you play the splash shot. You will notice from the inset picture on the opposite page that there is a significant amount of metal below the line of the leading edge. This is the bounce, and its role is to prevent the club from digging straight into the sand, allowing it to glide through instead. You will sometimes hear coaches talk about using the bounce for bunker shots: by this they mean that they want their pupils to concentrate on the point where the sole of the wedge comes into contact with the sand.

∧ ADDRESS CHECKLIST

The key to playing the splash shot is the angle at which the club works towards the ball. It needs to be shallow, allowing you to glide your wedge through the sand taking the ball as you go. So setting the ball forward in your stance is crucial. It needs to be ahead of your sternum at address, just inside your left heel (above left). Your hands should, as always, be under your sternum, so the shaft will lean back towards you by a small amount. The other element to consider is your alignment (above right). You may wish to stand slightly open, so that your body is pointing slightly left of your target. Don't overdo this, but opening yourself up a fraction will help you slip the club under the ball without causing too many directional difficulties.

< OPENING THE FACE

To maximize both the loft and the bounce of your sand wedge, think about opening the face. Whereas the leading edge for all your full shots from the fairway or rough should point directly at the target, when you open the face of your wedge it will aim slightly right. This will be offset by your open body position at address: with your body set to aim a fraction left, the leading edge of the club will be aiming at the target but you will have added loft.

Bunker Play Essentials

It is time now to look at the swing itself and point out some fundamental elements worth considering. This is about making the move as simple and reliable as possible, so that even when the pressure is on you can fall back on the basic principles of solid bunker play.

> SWING WITH CONVICTION

The great thing about a bunker shot is that you can be aggressive. Because you are aiming to strike the sand and not the ball directly, you can make a solid swing and the ball will not fly away out of control. For this reason, even though you may have less than 15 yards/14 m between you and the hole, you can make a fairly full swing (right). In fact, just as when you pitch, you can control distance through the amount of upper body rotation you adopt. Crucially, the through swing (far right) should be just as long, if not longer, than the backswing. This will help you find the steady build-up of speed through the contact area that is so important in all areas of the game.

< USING YOUR WRISTS

Opening the face of the club at address will offer extra loft, but you need to make sure that you maximize the effect of this adjustment. By purposefully hinging the wrists as you take the club back (inset), you'll be setting the ideal face angle for the downswing. As you release your wrists, sliding the club into the sand, the face position will provide the kind of dynamic loft you are looking for. A great way to illustrate how to use your wrist hinge to your advantage is to hit some one-handed shots (main image). With only your right hand on the grip your wrists will need to be more active to get the ball out. This drill also shows how forceful you need to be for a sand shot.

‹ WET SAND DRILL

A superb drill that will leave you with a deft feel for the amount of rotation you can employ is to stick some wet sand to the face of your wedge. Simply swing to the top and stop. If you committed to the swing and employed a good amount of upper body rotation, the sand will fly over your left shoulder. This will also help you check that your wrists are hinging in the correct way.

⌄ SAND VARIES

Sand can vary significantly from course to course. Other than taking some time to hit a few shots in a practice bunker before you head out to play (which is always a good idea but not always possible) there is no real way of knowing what it will be like. You can, however, deduce the consistency of the sand with your feet as you set up. You will no doubt have seen players shuffling their feet during the set-up. Not only does this offer a more stable stance, it also provides a feel for the sand in the bunker.

ALTERING THE BOUNCE

When you see your ball lying in a bunker it can be a natural response to reach, almost without thinking, for your sand wedge. You do, however, have a host of other clubs at your disposal, each of which can be manipulated to produce the results you are looking for.

On pages 180–81 we will examine in detail the technique for longer splash shots, but here it is worth pointing out that by opening the face of a short iron (9, 8 or even 7) you will create your own bounce. You can use this to your advantage to play to a whole range of distances.

Below This picture shows the Spaniard, Miguel Angel Jiménez, splashing out of a greenside bunker at one of his country's most recognizable courses, Valderrama. The sand that would be found here is very different to that found on many links courses. Practising from a range of different bunkers is the best way to gain a feel for how the club reacts.

Problem Solving: Perfecting the Strike

With the key to bunker play being the point at which the club strikes the sand, this is the area to focus on if things are going wrong. There is nothing to worry about if you find your ball in sand, unless you are unable to rely on the right contact. Here are four drills to help you.

∨ > PERCEPTION DRILL

When playing from a bunker you almost need to forget the ball. This may sound strange, but concentrating on a spot on the ball, as you might do with a shot from the fairway, will only cause you to catch your bunker shots thin, which often leads to disaster.

To help you lock your focus on the sand, place a paper cup over the ball. Aim to strike the sand just before the edge of the cup, gently accelerating through the contact, and the ball will spring out and onto the green. What this very simple drill does is teach you to trust the essential technique of striking the sand before the ball.

< ACCELERATION DRILL

We have already spoken of the importance of accelerating the club through the ball, but for some golfers the pressure of a bunker shot causes a timid, tentative approach. If you fall into this category, head to the practice bunker and play some shots without a ball.

The aim here is to strike the sand with enough force to make most of it land on the green. Imagine that someone is standing on the lip of the bunker and you are trying to cover them with sand.

When doing this ensure that you complete the swing so that, as you watch the sand fly, your chest is facing the target. This trains you to become more positive through the contact and to rotate your arms and body together. When you bring the ball back into play you'll start creating the forceful splash that is required for consistent escapes.

> BOTTOMING OUT DRILL

When playing a shot from the fairway, your divot offers a very clear visual guide to the way your club is working through impact. But sand doesn't offer the same precise feedback, so it is worth trying this drill to highlight how the club is – or should be – bottoming out.

Draw a box in the sand slightly bigger than a large banknote, as shown, and place your ball in the middle. Make the edges of the box fairly deep so they are clearly visible to you at address. As you stand over the ball, aim to strike the back of the box with the clubhead, then swing through to a finish.

If you have set the correct ball position at address and make the ideal, shallow swing, you will disrupt all of the sand within the box, as shown (far right). Not only does this train you to strike the sand before the ball, it also ensures that your angle of attack isn't too steep.

ON-COURSE FOCUS

Obviously you are not going to be allowed to draw boxes in the sand when you are playing for real, so you'll need a strong imagination to visualize the ideal move to make in this situation.

A good tactic is to select a spot in the sand to strike just behind your ball (this will be the equivalent of the back of the box). Simply concentrate on driving the club through this point.

Problem Solving: Spotting Your Mistakes

If you have tried all the drills on the previous pages and are still experiencing difficulty, there may be a problem with your set-up or technique. If this is the case, use the elements here to identify and then rectify the problem.

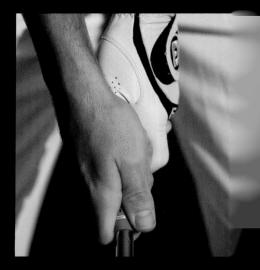

∨ > CHECK HAND POSITION

We will come on to the technique required for delicate chip shots around the green in more detail later, but one tactic many players use is to move their hands down the grip to gain a better level of control. This works from grass, and it can also be used from sand.

Now, this technique is fine if you have a good feel for what you are trying to do, but if you have been struggling with catching shots thin, it could be the cause. By moving your hands down the grip (right), you are raising the point at which the club bottoms out. Unless you have compensated for this at address (by widening your stance), it could be the reason for the problem.

So the advice here is simple: move your hands up into their normal position on the grip and the club will bottom out sooner, for more consistent contacts.

Below Make sure the club is bottoming out in the right place, otherwise you'll catch shots thin, as shown, or fat.

LEG SUPPORT DRILL

For successful bunker play you need a rock-solid lower half. This is where the stability that is so important comes from. Moving your lower body unnecessarily can lead to a whole host of poor strikes.

To resolve the problem, take your 9-iron, place its head in the sand and rest the top of the shaft firmly at the top of your hamstring in the address position (far left). You should be able to swing back and through to impact without the club falling down. But it's important to make sure that your upper body continues to rotate properly through the ball. The club will fall as you naturally move into the finish position, but as long as it hasn't moved before you've struck the ball, your technique will be spot on.

PRACTISING YOUR STROKE

One of the reasons that some amateurs find bunker play so tricky is that the rules prevent you from making a practice swing in the sand. Without a chance to train the mind and body immediately prior to the stroke, the results are often mixed at best. A great way to gain an element of feel for the stroke you are about to play is to find some thick grass next to the bunker and make some practice swings there. The grass will provide the sort of resistance you'll experience in the bunker and will give you a feel for how hard to swing.

TARGET PRACTICE DRILL

Head to the practice bunker taking 15–20 balls with you. Place four or five tee pegs in the green, all at different distances from the bunker. The aim of the game is to hit one shot after another, each to a different target. At first you may find distance control tricky, but as your feel improves with the shots you hit you'll start to develop a more natural appreciation for distance control. Perform this drill regularly and you'll soon become a dab hand from bunkers.

Long Bunker Shots

While a splash shot from near to the green is relatively straightforward and needn't pose any really significant threats to your score, sand shots from a little farther out – 30–50 yards/27–45 m – are without question some of the hardest you'll face. Designing a strategy to avoid this situation is important, but strategy and reality are two different things. The technique shown here should help you escape without damaging your score whenever this ugly scenario arises.

^ MANIPULATING THE CLUB
The club shown here is a 7-iron. You should notice, however, that the face has been opened to create bounce. With the bottom of the sole lower than the leading edge, the club will be better suited to maintaining its speed through the sand.

^ > LONG SPLASH KEYS
The first alteration you need to make is in your club selection. You can use anything up to a 7- or even 6-iron for this shot, depending on how far you want the ball to travel. Once you have selected your club, open the face (the importance of this is explained above right). Move your hands down the shaft and widen your stance a fraction, as shown right. The ball should still be positioned just inside your left heel.

All you need to do now is make a swing that strikes the sand about 1 inch/2.5 cm behind the ball, as you would for any greenside splash shot. As you don't have to rely on an extremely precise contact, the results when adopting this approach tend to be much more consistent. As with all other areas of the game, however, practice makes perfect. The more balls you hit in training, the better your feel for the shot will become.

⌃ WHAT TO EXPECT

When you are using a sand wedge, the ball comes out of the bunker with good height and lands softly. But with a 7-iron (above), the flight and roll are different. Even though you have opened the face and added loft, the trajectory will be lower than usual (if the lip is particularly steep, take a sand wedge and play a normal splash shot to safety). With a lower flight, you will also get more roll, so pick a landing spot well short of the flag to allow for it to run up. Practice is the best way to gain a feel for how this works.

COMMIT TO TECHNIQUE

One of the reasons amateurs tend to shy away from this approach is that, with a 7-iron in hand, they worry the ball will not clear the lip of the bunker. But unless the ball is close to a fairly steep face, you should be able to get it out.

Commit yourself to the technique. Do not compromise any of the essential elements in a bid to gain more control. What you may think will add control will only remove consistency.

❯ PLAY IT AS A SHORT PITCH

There is another way to play these long greenside shots. It involves adopting the same mentality and approach as you would for a short pitch. By moving the ball a little farther back than usual in your stance and placing more weight on your left side as the player has done here, you should be able to create a steeper angle of attack to clip the ball off the top of the sand.

This technique makes distance control extremely difficult, however. As you need to be so precise with the contact a consistent result is also hard to find, so we would always recommend playing a long splash shot, as the margin for error is much greater.

Escaping Dangerous Lies

When you hit your ball into a greenside bunker, the real danger arises when the lie is not what you were hoping for. Having to play from slopes, plug holes or wet sand requires a cautious approach. Here's how to adapt your approach when the lie is against you.

> ∨ PLUGGED LIES

The consistency of sand means that balls are often likely to plug. This happens more in soft sand than hard, but any high-flying approach that finds a trap is likely to plug. The key to getting the ball out is to blast it. Many coaches like their pupils to close the clubface at address to help force the ball out. Whether you close the face or keep it slightly open, the key point to focus on is the force of the shot. The club needs to strike aggressively down into the sand, blasting the ball and the sand onto the green. A steeper angle of attack will help you do this, so move the ball back in your stance at address. Aim at a spot in the sand just behind the ball and hit down. Remember the ball will have plenty of run when it hits the green, so aim for a safe area with lots of room for the roll.

< DOWNSLOPE BUNKER TACTICS

The opposite rules come into play if you find your ball on a downslope. In this scenario you need to prevent yourself taking too much sand and hitting the shot fat. At address, set a little more weight on your left side than usual. This picture illustrates how the ideal set-up looks. Again, focus on a spot just behind the ball – this will be the point at which the club should drive into the sand. The ball will naturally come out on a lower flight and will have more roll when it hits the green. Factor this into your thinking as you pick your strategy.

Whether you are playing from an upslope or a downslope, don't try to be too cute with the shot. Aim at the fat part of the green: getting down in three shots from here is a good effort.

∧ UPSLOPE BUNKER TACTICS

It is now time to take a look at the two trickiest lies you'll face in a bunker. Uphill and downhill lies automatically alter where the club bottoms out. If you haven't prepared for this, fat or thin strikes are likely. When the ball is on an upslope (above), place a fraction more weight on your right side at address. The angle of your shoulders should reflect the angle of the slope. Now concentrate on a spot at least 1 inch/2.5 cm behind the ball where you will strike the sand. The ball will pop up into the air so you may need to hit the shot a little harder to find the distance you need. These adjustments should help guard against striking the ball thin when it's on an upslope.

Right The left-handed Canadian player, Mike Weir, splashes out of a sodden greenside trap during the Open Championship at Royal Birkdale in 2008. A more aggressive approach is essential whenever the sand is wet.

WET SAND

What would have been a relatively simple splash shot in dry conditions becomes far trickier when the rain comes. Importantly, the sand is heavier, so the shot requires more speed than usual. Simply apply a little more upper body rotation and be positive through impact. The extra force is essential to help the club get through the wet sand.

More Bunker Options

The huge variety of lies and situations you can find yourself in when playing from sand will often require a creative approach. This is where your imagination and ability to manipulate your technique will come to the fore. Experimenting with different types of shot is an enjoyable way to practise, so don't be afraid to give yourself difficult lies in practise – the solutions you find may end up proving themselves invaluable when out on the course. Here are some common tricky situations with some escape techniques that you may wish to try.

> POT BUNKERS

Small with steep banks, these often represent the most fearsome danger a links course has to offer. The lie you draw will determine whether you can go for the flag or simply have to play out sideways. If you can go for the pin but need a particularly lofted escape to clear the lip, shift your aim point to the very top of the flag. Make some practice swings (without touching the sand with your club), looking at the top of the pin. This simple act of preparation leaves you with an instinctive feeling for how to generate loft. You will automatically retain the loft on the club through the hitting area if you 'feel' the shot. Without having to concentrate too much on the mechanics of the swing that you want to make (simply open up the club a little more at address to add loft) you'll develop an instinct for the shot.

> RUNNING BUNKER SHOT

If the pin is at the back of the green, the safest play would be to run the ball up to the flag instead of trying to fly it all the way back. In this scenario, all you need to do is square the face of your wedge a little at address. Play it as if you have a plugged lie, blasting hard down into the sand – this will de-loft the club, bringing the flight down and creating topspin that will force the ball to roll up the green to the flag at the back.

If you regularly watch high-level golf you'll notice professional players using this technique from time to time. Of course, you will need to practise this before using it in competition, but you'll soon find that a running bunker shot is not hard to pull off.

PRESSURE-PROOFING

When you're under the cosh, trying to build a score or beat a tough opponent, delicate greenside shots become more difficult and will pose a genuine test of nerve. Every golfer needs a way of committing to their strategy, playing short shots with positivity and not letting nerves create a tentative approach.

When your ball is in a bunker, you can use the resistance of the sand to help you become more aggressive. Simply open the face even more than usual, as shown here, and make a full, committed swing, aiming to make contact with the sand slightly farther from the ball than usual. This way you can funnel your nervous tension into a more aggressive pass at the ball without losing control of the shot.

Of course, you should never try out any new shots for the first time in competition, so test this and develop the technique during your practice. With extra speed and loft on the club, the ball will come out higher than usual but will still land softly enough to hold the ball close to the flag.

⌄ DON'T GET TOO CUTE

Every golfer has done it. You find yourself in a greenside trap with only a short distance to the pin. Your eagerness to save par leads you to get too cute: you don't hit the ball hard enough and it stops short of the green. It is one of the most frustrating mistakes you can make, so when faced with this scenario imagine the pin is 10 feet/3 m farther back on the green. Play to that point and take your chances with a mid-range par putt.

Splash Shot Game Plans

Now that you know the rules that lie at the heart of a successful bunker technique it is time to plan your escape. There are numerous factors to consider before you play, so take a look at the advice that follows and consider these elements when you find yourself in sand.

⌄ PICK THE SLOPES

An easy mistake to make when playing from sand is to concentrate too hard on the technique without thinking about what will happen when the ball hits the green. When playing onto a sloping putting surface, it is worth taking a moment to read the green. If you can, use the slopes to get the ball moving towards the hole and consider where would be the easiest place to putt from. This should be the same process you run through as you eye up a chip or a putt. Hitting a great bunker shot, only to see the undulations on the green take the ball away from the hole, is deeply frustrating. So take a quick look to see if there are any prominent slopes before you play.

⌃ READ THE LIE

On first inspection this lie might seem fine. However, if you've hit your ball into a recently raked area like this, the ball may be sitting on a slight slope. This will affect the way it responds to your splash shot, so take a good look, and if there is more sand behind the ball allow for a little more run than usual.

WIND CONDITIONS

When the wind blows, shots become more complicated, even bunker shots. Hitting into the wind, you'll be surprised at how aggressive you can be. The combination of breeze and backspin will stop the ball far more quickly than usual. Likewise downwind, the backspin you create will be almost nullified, and the ball will roll out more than usual. Be sure to allow for strong crosswinds, too, as you map out the shot you're about to play. Finally, if playing into the wind, prepare yourself for a face full of sand as you hit the shot – doing up the top button of your T-shirt is a useful ploy.

⌄ BLIND BUNKER SHOTS

One of Britain's finest inland golf courses is Woodhall Spa in Lincolnshire. Its fearsome reputation is largely based on the severity of its bunkers. When playing courses with particularly deep traps of this kind, you face the prospect of playing blind bunker shots – meaning you're so far down you are unable to see the top of the flag. In this scenario, take a moment to stand on the back lip of the bunker and rehearse the shot. Look at the flag as you make a practice swing to gain a feel for the distance required. Then pick a spot on the front lip in line with your target. As you step into the sand and address the ball, use this mark as your target. This pre-shot process will leave you well equipped to escape with ease.

Bottom Miss the green on Woodhall Spa's par-3 5th at your peril. The narrow green is surrounded by extraordinarily deep bunkers, more akin to the type you would find on one of Britain's coastal links.

Practising from Sand

So you have some precious moments to spare as you work on your game, and the practice bunker beckons. We have already offered plenty of drills for you to try that will hone all the different areas of your game. Here we will look at games and strategies to employ whenever you practise your bunker play.

> HIT IN, PLAY OUT

It's important to develop an interesting and varied practice routine. Here is a great game that will leave you with a deft feel from sand.

Take several golf balls and hit them from outside into the practice bunker. This part of the game forces you to visualize the flight and landing area of your chips – something we will come on to in the next section.

When you have hit all the balls into the bunker, every lie will be slightly different. Start with the easiest-looking shots and work towards the tough ones, playing out towards an easily accessible flag on the practice green. Take note of how many times you get up and down, then repeat the game. By the time you finish, your natural feel for how to play from sand will be greatly improved.

TEST THE REACTION

If you manage to find time to hit some greenside bunker shots before going out to compete, pay close attention to how the ball reacts once it hits the green. This will tell you a huge amount about the firmness of the putting surfaces and how the slopes will affect your shots. Also take note of the consistency of the sand, because sand differs from course to course, and this will arm you with some useful knowledge.

⌄ USE ALL YOUR WEDGES

Many players refer to one of their wedges as 'the sand wedge', but this is slightly misleading. You can use any of your wedges from sand and, as they all offer slightly different distance results, it pays to feel comfortable using all of them.

In practice, try playing the same shot (without aiming at a specific target) with all your wedges, keeping the rhythm of the shot the same. You'll notice how distances differ from wedge to wedge, and the knowledge you gain from this short exercise will be invaluable when you are battling for a score.

> DON'T GET SLOPPY

As you hit one shot after another, it's easy to let your normal standards for the address position drop. But if this happens you'll only be killing your own confidence by hitting poor shots. Pay close attention to all the fundamentals for every shot you hit. If it helps to concentrate your mind, draw some lines or lay down some sticks in the sand, as shown, as reference points for alignment and ball position. By the end of the session these will have become ingrained into your muscle memory for you to fall back on every time you are faced with a bunker shot.

Fairway Bunker Essentials

So now you know the keys to playing a successful greenside trap shot, but what about when your ball is in a fairway bunker? Being able to sweetly strike a full shot from sand will mean you can attack the target just as you would if your ball was sitting on a juicy lie in the middle of the fairway. This is about keeping the swing as simple as possible in search of a precise contact.

> BRINGING THE BOTTOM UP

If anything, you are looking to strike the ball fractionally thin from a fairway bunker, taking as little sand as possible. This may seem a risky strategy, as the ball still needs to clear the lip of the bunker, but a fractionally thin contact will come out with a great flight.

The most consistent way to achieve this is by reducing your swing arc. This will cause the swing to bottom out higher than usual, allowing you to clip the ball without driving the club into the sand.

First, move your hands down to the bottom of the grip and increase your grip pressure to tighten the muscles in your arms. Second, simply make a slightly shorter swing than usual, as shown right. The combination of these changes will have a profound effect on the way the club moves, bringing up the bottom of the swing for a clean contact.

ASSESS THE LIE

As with all bunker shots, take a close look at the lie. In sand the ball can often sit in small rake marks or depressions that make a clean strike hard to come by. So assess the danger posed by the lie before you select your strategy for the shot you are about to play.

< CLUB UP

The changes described opposite combine to reduce the length of your swing, but they will also restrict your speed through impact. There are few more infuriating scenarios than hitting a pure fairway bunker shot only to see the ball come up way short of the target.

In this instance your usual distances are irrelevant. As long as less loft will still get the ball out of the trap, take more club. If you would usually hit a wedge from the same distance, take a 6- or 7-iron and watch how the simple adjustments you have made will take distance from the shot.

> STAYING CENTRED

If swaying off the ball is detrimental from the fairway, it is fatal from sand. Cast your mind back to the spike analogy on page 100. Concentrating on keeping your sternum over the ball, as shown here, is a great swing thought to adopt when playing from sand. Make a couple of practice swings by the side of the bunker as you prepare for the shot, keeping this thought in the forefront of your mind. If you can do this during the actual swing the results will be good.

∨ YOUR CENTRE OF GRAVITY

We have already stressed that bunkers can differ almost beyond recognition from course to course. If you find yourself in a fairway bunker where there is plenty of sand, be careful not to shuffle your feet in too much at address. You need to create a stable footing (below left), but burying your feet in the sand (below right) will lower your centre of gravity, making a clean contact more difficult to find.

Fairway Bunker Drills and Tactics

If you are an accomplished ball striker you will already know that playing from sand or any difficult position will force you to rely on your feel for the game. If you know how to manipulate the swing to get what you want you'll know how to escape. Here we look at drills to improve your sand striking and the tactics you should consider before playing.

⌄ THINNING DRILL

A great drill designed to improve the quality of contacts you find from fairway traps is to practise catching shots fractionally thin from the fairway. If you know you are about to play a heavily bunkered, resort-style course, try this on the range before teeing off. Hit 5–10 shots, aiming to strike the ball without touching the grass. The margins involved are incredibly fine, as you still need to get the ball up and away with a reasonable flight. As always, the more you practise it the better you'll get.

LOOK OUT FOR SPIN

For the better player, one factor to consider is spin. A pure strike from sand can deliver significantly more spin than from the fairway. Throw in soft greens and a slight headwind, and the ball will probably fizz back once it hits the green. One way to counteract this (if the lip of the bunker permits) is to take one extra club and hit the shot a fraction softer. This will keep the spin down and offer you more control over the distance.

∨ SPLASHING OUT

There are occasions when a towering approach to the green simply won't be possible from a fairway bunker. A splash back out onto the short grass might seem like an incredibly simple thing to do, but you still need to consider your options.

Keep an eye out for any danger that might be lurking, including other fairway bunkers, and think about where you'd like to play your next shot from. Also, try to splash out towards a flat part of the fairway, as a sloping lie will only make the next shot harder.

∧ STRIKE AND POSTURE DRILL

Most golfers practise their fairway bunker play only on the course, when playing casually with friends or on their own. If, however, you have access to a practice bunker and can play full shots from it, this drill is a fantastic way to groove the mechanics required for a sweet contact.

Build up a small pile of sand and perch the ball on top. The aim is simple: to make a normal swing and find a clean strike. By building the sand up you are making the shot tougher, and if your posture isn't spot on throughout the swing you'll notice immediately.

MATCH-PLAY MOMENT

If you have hit your ball into a fairway bunker your original game plan for the hole is likely to change, especially in match play. Note that if your opponent is behind you on the fairway you can wait for him to play before deciding what to do. If he hits his approach close, you'll know you need to go for it. Alternatively, if he finds greenside trouble, your better option may be to splash out to safety.

When you are the one to play first, think about your situation. Weigh up the difficulty of the hole, the score in the match and the strengths of your opponent. Only once you have done this will you be in a position to make a sensible shot selection.

Short Game

SADLY FOR SOME, golf is not just a game played on a driving range. Indeed it is the combination of power and finesse that makes building a great score both a difficult challenge and richly rewarding. So now it's time to focus on the second half of golf's split personality and transform your ability with the long clubs into a score you can be truly proud of.

Imagination, creativity and a natural instinct for how to manipulate the flight and run of the ball all lie at the heart of a successful chipping game. To a certain extent this explains why children consistently surprise their elders with their proficiency around the greens. Spending hours on end challenging their friends to different chipping games leaves them with a crystal-clear feel for how to surmount any difficult situation. Young enough not to feel bothered by pressure, they simply see the shot and play it. If you can enjoy the short game, relish the challenge posed when the odds are stacked against you and feel comfortable manipulating the club, you too will have a short game that your opponents will envy and fear.

There are, of course, certain key technical elements that it pays to know. Just as with the long game, standing correctly to the ball allows you to hit the shot you want. We will explore this area in depth for all the different chips you can play, then offer some simple games and drills designed to leave you with a deft touch.

Even those players with deadly accurate long games can't ignore the importance of the ability to salvage pars from off the green. When conditions are tough, it is often the short game that separates the best from the rest. All the advice that follows is geared towards making you as confident as possible from short range. Success here often leads to success with the long clubs.

Short Game Essentials

For delicate 'touch' shots around the green you need an instinctive feel for a whole range of different shots. But before we explore the keys to natural control for flight and distance, it is worth paying attention to some of the basic principles of how to chip.

◀ EDGE OR BOUNCE

There are two commonly adopted approaches to chipping, featuring some subtle but important differences that you should be able to see from how the club sits behind the ball at address here.

The first (far left) involves driving the leading edge of the club into the very bottom of the ball, trapping it with a downward strike and a clean hit. The alternative method (left) uses the bounce to strike the ground through impact on a shallower path.

Different coaches advocate different techniques, so if you are new to the game try both in practice, then try to groove the principles into your muscle memory.

▶ GETTING INTO POSITION

The first approach (1), using the leading edge of the club, is the more traditional method and requires you to move the ball back in your stance at address, so your hands are ahead and the shaft leans forward from the ball. An open body position allows you to turn through, keeping the club moving on a good line.

The alternative method (2), using the bounce, requires a shallower angle of attack. Stand square to the target line and swing the club on a more neutral (less out-to-in) path. With the ball sitting slightly forward at address, the swing path is shallower and the bounce of the club strikes the ground through impact.

❯ NOT JUST HANDS AND ARMS

No matter which basic chipping method you employ, you still need to use your body just as you would with a full swing. Try this drill to illustrate the point.

Shut your eyes and make five practice swings without rotating your body, keeping the centre of your chest over the middle of your stance. Try to gain a sense for how much in control of the stroke you are. Now repeat the process, keeping your eyes shut but turning your body with the movement of your arms back and through (we are not talking about a huge coil here, just a gentle rotation). This drill should highlight how much more in control of the club you are when you use your body.

PERCENTAGE PLAYS

To become a good chipper you need to play the percentages. The more loft and flight you add, the harder it will often be to control where the ball ends up (unless the greens are particularly soft, in which case flying it all the way to the flag will be the most consistent play).

When the ground is firm, get the ball running as soon as possible. If there is no rough or sand between you and the pin, play for very little loft, allowing the ball to scurry to the hole like a putt. If you need to employ more loft, pick a spot to land the ball that gets you over the obstacle but is also as flat as possible, to allow the ball to run out.

Running Chips

Our next move is to nail down the key to the short game's percentage play – the bump and run. Particularly useful from tight links lies, this shot has essential putting elements to it. No matter what level you currently play to, the bump and run should be one of the most trusted shots in your locker.

⊙ ▶ BUMP AND RUN POSITION

The photograph below shows an ideal playing position for a bump and run. There is nothing in front of the player that requires loft on the shot, and the green has some tricky undulations. Landing a high shot on one of these slopes would take control away from the player, so a shot that runs more like a putt is more reliable.

The club you select for this will depend on two factors – where you want the ball to land and how much run you will need. There are a host of irons in your bag to choose from, and you can use any of them for a chip and run. So in this scenario, picture how the ideal shot would run out and choose a club that will give the flight and speed you want. Here, the player is using a 6-iron.

The bump and run is an incredibly simple shot, and this makes it your safest option around the green. By employing a solid putting motion you should be able to find a pure contact. There are, however, a couple of potential errors that you should be aware of.

First, make sure that your body remains solidly set over the ball. There is absolutely no reason for your upper body to jerk either towards or away from the target. Keep your sternum over the ball throughout and let the rocking of your shoulders create the speed.

The other fault to look out for relates to your wrists. They must remain solid through the stroke to keep a constant amount of loft on the club. If they flick at the ball the results will be hugely inconsistent. Focus on keeping them solid through impact – just as you would when putting.

⬥ TECHNICAL KEYS

Don't get too bogged down in the technique for a bump and run, as this is a feel shot that sits between being a chip and a long putt. To optimize their distance control, many players like to adopt their putting grip. Set the ball back in your stance as you would for a normal chip but employ a pendulum-like rocking of the shoulders to create momentum. These two pictures illustrate the simplicity of the motion. The hands remain set firm (albeit with a light hold of the club) and the shoulders simply rock back and through as they would for a putt.

◀ GOING UP BANKS

When the pin is perched at the top of a steep bank, a bump and run is usually your best option. There is a common misconception here, however. Many players like to pitch the ball into the hill in this situation, but this can kill the speed and cause the ball to roll back down to your feet. Moreover, aiming to pitch your ball into a bank means that there is an element of unpredictability about how it will bounce.

Whenever you are trying to get the ball up a bank land it in front of you on a flat area so that the ball is already rolling once it gets to the hill. This tactic should leave no room for any unwanted surprises. And above all, make sure you hit it hard enough to get the ball up the hill – there is nothing more frustrating than having to play the same shot again.

High-Flying Chips

Having covered the low shot, it's time to take a look at the most lofted of your chipping options. The lob or flop shot is often described as a 'parachute' shot, because the ball comes down from a huge height, landing softly and stopping quickly. Of course, it's a tactic you should employ only when you have to, but the situations that call for it are not uncommon, so use these tips to add the lob shot to your armoury.

⊻ ❯ THINK BUNKER SHOT

The technique required here is similar to that for a bunker shot. These photos illustrate what your address position should look like. First, sit a little lower at address than usual. This will lower your centre of gravity, anchoring you into the ground – you should feel that your thighs are supporting your upper body. As with a bunker shot, let the ball sit forward in your stance and open the face of the club to add both loft and bounce. Having set the face, let your body sit slightly open to your target line, as this alters the swing path, helping you to cut across the ball through impact, adding loft to the shot.

1   **2**   **3**

PICK THE LIE

Because this is played like a bunker shot you need a certain amount of grass under the ball. There are some lies that make a flop shot extremely dangerous. If the ball is sitting on a patch of hard ground with little grass (1), think about adopting a more conservative strategy – playing a flop shot will bring the bounce into play, which in turn can cause a thin strike that sends the ball flying a long way over the green. Having some fluffy grass under the ball (2) means that you have room to slip the club under for a good result.

The thickness of the grass under the ball will determine how precise you need to be with the strike. If there is plenty (3) you can aim to strike the ground about ½ inch/1 cm behind the ball (similar to a bunker shot) and use the bounce to keep the club moving. If the lie is tighter you need to nip the club in a lot closer behind the ball. The point here is very simple: the lie will determine your exact approach to the flop shot. Once you have decided how close to the ball to strike, concentrate on this spot as you swing.

◐ USING YOUR BODY

As with a bunker swing, the key to this shot is to be positive. Even though you are only looking to hit the ball a short distance, you need to employ good body rotation, being sure to keep the connection between the upper body and your arms through the shot. Notice how, even though this is only a short shot, the player's back has almost turned through to face the target at the top of the backswing. The grass underneath the ball will act like the sand in a bunker, taking some of the energy away from the shot, so don't be afraid to commit.

GENTLE APPROACH

A great phrase that encapsulates what the lob shot is all about is 'aggression without tension'. You need to be positive and commit to the tactic without your body becoming tense and the resulting stroke becoming too jerky.

Make sure that your knees and elbows are not rigid in the address and that your hands stay relaxed. This will help you find the flow that is so important here.

Problem Solving: Poor Strikes

If you are prone to fluffing or thinning your chip shots you can usually find the cause in one of two errors: technical mistakes or tension. The drills in this section are designed to get your chipping stroke back on track and alleviate tension when you are bidding to build a score for real.

❯ SOLID WRISTS DRILL

Perhaps the most common mistake made during all greenside shots relates to the way the wrists work. For a short chip, avoid introducing a flicking action, which can cause both poor contacts and erratic distance control. Your wrists should allow for a free-flowing stroke while also being solid enough to ensure a pure strike. This simple drill forces you to keep your wrists in a firmer position.

Get an empty golf ball box and lodge it between your forearms at address, as shown. If your wrists have a tendency to break through the swing, the box will fall to the ground, so the aim is to keep the box in the same position through the swing. Grooving this motion will create a solid, dependable chipping action.

❮ CONFIDENCE-BUILDER

For some players, poor chipping boils down to a simple lack of confidence in the strike. In this situation you need to make your practice a little easier so that you start to get a sensation for what a good strike feels like. To help, peg up four balls, starting high and gradually getting lower to the ground, then place a fifth ball on the grass. Work down the line – the drill starts easy and gets a little tougher as you work towards the ball on the ground. This simple process is a great confidence-builder.

❯ TWO BALLS AT ONCE

Poor strikes can come in many guises and produce a whole range of different results. If this is a problem for you, you simply need to refocus to become more precise than ever.

A great drill that is good fun and tests your precision is to hit two balls at once. Don't try to hit them towards any particular target, just concentrate on the contact. There is just enough room on your wedge to fit two balls, so aim at the line between the two and make a normal chipping stroke. If you are able to master this drill your ball striking from close range is guaranteed to become far more precise, eliminating the wayward strikes that have been costing you.

❮ LEG ACTION DRILL

You can use the same golf ball box to help your lower body action. Place it between your legs at address, as shown. As in the wrist action drill, you should be able to make a stroke without the box falling down. If your legs tend to move unnecessarily, this simple drill will iron out the problem. You should feel your thighs take the strain of a good posture and they should remain firm through the stroke.

RELAXING INTO THE SHOT

Tension is a short-game killer. Soft hands and a smooth rhythm are crucial when you chip, so you need to find a way of relaxing into the shot. This is where a good pre-shot routine comes into play, and we will look at this in more detail later (see page 214). However, a sensible method to employ when you chip is to make a whole series of practice swings.

As you stand next to the ball, mapping out in your mind how to play the shot, make 10–15 practice swings without stopping between each. Get a pendulum motion going and you should feel any tension fade.

Don't hesitate too long after you have finished your practice swings before playing the shot; just take a couple of seconds to set yourself and then play. You should be able to find the same tempo and fluidity that you created in practice.

Problem Solving: Lack of Feel

Your striking might be spot on every time but if you've lost your feel for pace control you'll fail to get up and down with depressing regularity. There are no hard and fast rules here, as feel comes from a very straightforward dedication to practice. The more balls you hit the better your natural instincts will become. Here's how to structure your practice so that it's enjoyable and you derive the greatest possible benefit from it.

❯ SPEED SKILLS

This drill, when completed successfully, will leave you with an invaluable feel for how to control your chipping distances. Place a group of balls (15 or so) in a pile next to the practice green and start by playing a shot to the far end of the green. The aim is to get as close as possible to the other collar without letting the ball leave the green. Every subsequent shot you play should stop a fraction shorter than the one before (use the same club for every shot). This might seem simple, but it is an incredibly tricky process that requires pristine striking as the speed through the ball slowly decreases.

Don't be put off if you struggle at first: you will probably need to try it a few times before you experience any real success. As each shot gets shorter, your swing will naturally become more compact. By the time you reach the end you should have a deft touch for distance control as well as the ability to make a clean, crisp strike for every chip you face. This will prove invaluable as you attempt to build a score on course for real.

❯ ONE SHOT, THREE OPTIONS

The greatest short-game exponents can play most shots in a range of different ways. The option they finally go for is based on the firmness of the green and the quality of the lie. To illustrate just how many options you have, and to give you a feel for manipulating the club, try this drill.

Pick a target on the practice green that sits about 10 yards/9 m away from you and play three shots using a wedge. First play a normal chip (1), making sure that you set up accurately for this at address. With the second ball (2), try to hit a lower chip that runs more than the previous shot. Visualize the shot before playing it and pick a spot to land the ball before rolling out. Once you've done this, play a third shot (3) adding more loft than usual: open the face of your wedge at address and adopt some more wrist hinge as you take the club away, for a higher flight.

This drill is a great way of showing how simple adjustments make huge differences. Importantly, you should also gain a genuine appreciation for how much easier the bump and run is than the more lofted shot, even if the latter is more satisfying when you pull it off!

RELYING ON FEEL

A simple drill that will leave you with a far better natural appreciation for chipping is to hit some shots with your eyes shut. Pick a target on the practice green and hit a normal chip with your eyes open. Then replay the shot with your eyes shut. Try to replicate the motion of the previous shot. Even though your eyes are shut you should have no real problems with the strike, and as you work your way around some different targets you'll gain a far sharper sense for how your body is working.

Problem Solving: Flight Control

In the last of these problem-solving sections we will focus on the finer details of the flight. Some golfers will stand over a shot and immediately see a way to play it. For others, however, this comes less naturally. Here we look at some simple techniques that will get you thinking the right way and seeing the shot with crystal-clear vision.

❯ LADDER DRILL

This is one of the oldest and most effective training drills for the ideal flight and landing spot. Place four or five shafts on the practice green, setting them up as shown here. The aim of the game is to hit a series of shots, trying to land the ball in a different section of the ladder with each shot.

Now there are two ways to do this – you can change the landing spot either through club selection or with the strength of your swing. If you are not sure which will provide you with the most consistent results, try both and settle on the tactic you feel most confident using. The reason this drill is so good is that it forces you to think more closely about the ideal landing area.

CONSIDER THE WIND

Conditions both on the ground and in the air will affect your shot. Even when you chip, the wind can play a big role in what happens to the ball during the flight. This is why the bump and run is such a valuable shot on windy links courses. Whether down, into or across, give a moment's thought to what the wind is doing and factor it into both your shot selection and your visualization.

⊘ BUMP AND RUN BAG DRILL

We have already mentioned that when playing a bump and run the stroke is more like a putt than a chip. The ideal flight is very low, so the ball returns to the ground quickly and rolls towards the pin. This excellent drill prevents you from adding unwanted loft, forcing you to play the shot properly. Set your golf bag about 5 feet/1.5 m in front of you, on line with the target. Play a series of shots, simply aiming to keep the ball between the bag and its legs, low to the ground through its flight. This forces you to introduce visualization into your chipping game and will give you a natural sense for how to keep the ball low.

⊙ THINK 'THROW'

The aim of many of the drills in this section is to leave you with a far more acute feel for the short game. There should be nothing unnatural about your approach. A great way to think about the short game is to stand next to your ball and imagine that you are not playing a golf shot but throwing the ball towards the target. You will quickly figure out how high to throw it and where to land it to get the ball close. Your golf shot should deliver exactly the same amount of flight and roll. If you have issues visualizing and mapping out your short game shots, think about employing this very simple technique.

Spinning Your Chips

Confident ball strikers should look to use backspin to offer extra control.
This is where the ability to rely on a sweet strike allows players to commit to
delicate shots with a fraction more aggression, knowing that backspin will
prevent the ball from getting away. This will add an extra dimension to the
play of those who are already competent around the greens.

❯ SPEED THROUGH IMPACT

We have repeatedly stressed the relationship
between speed and spin for long shots, and
here the same principles apply. Quite simply,
the more pace the club has through impact,
the more backspin you will create. Of course,
you need to strike a balance between being
positive and whacking the ball much too far.
It is essential, however, that you deliver good
speed through impact, so concentrate on
making a slightly more compact move than
usual and fizz the club through the ball.

For this shot you are looking to drive the
leading edge of the wedge into the bottom of
the ball on a steeper angle. This de-lofts the
club a fraction and will help you find that
low flight that bites on the second bounce.

❯ TECHNICAL KEY

If you are contemplating playing a spinning
chip, you'll want a fair amount of flight
before the ball hits and checks up on the
green. The technical key to playing this shot
is to set the wrists during the backswing and
retain this wrist angle for the rest of the shot.

In these pictures the player is using his left
hand only, to illustrate the way it should
work through the shot (the right hand should
remain passive, simply helping you set a
secure grip). In the finish position notice
how the sole of the clubface is still pointing
at the ground, the face looking at the target.

As long as you make the correct downward
strike (relying on the loft of the club to
provide flight) this technique will create the
high spin rate you are looking for.

⬆ WHAT TO EXPECT

We might be talking about backspin here, but there is no way the ball will actually bounce and then screw back when you chip – this is impossible for such a short shot, where a relatively small amount of clubhead speed is created. Instead the ball will bounce once and then grab, slowly trickling out towards the target. The technique that we have already laid down will deliver a low flight, the ball will jump forward once it hits the green and then quickly stop. As always it is essential that you allow for this flight and roll when you are contemplating how to play the shot. Of course, if the ball is sitting in longer grass, your chance of creating spin is reduced.

⊗ SHALLOW GROOVES

From the start of 2010, a rule that restricts the depth and sharpness of grooves came into play. While most amateurs will be allowed to continue playing with the old, higher spinning grooves until at least 2024, club manufacturers are no longer permitted to produce the old, non-conforming designs. The result is that control is taken away from the player when hitting from the rough. With shallower grooves you are more likely to get longer grass stuck between the face and ball at impact, and this will reduce spin. Even so, the skills on this page are well worth learning, and they apply equally to the fairway, where you shouldn't notice any real drop-off in spin rates.

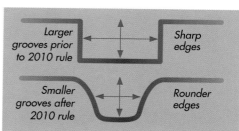

BALL SELECTION

There are many varieties of golf ball to choose from, and it is around the greens that the differences are felt most readily. Premium, multi-layer balls help players create a higher degree of spin and enjoy a greater level of feel, both as they putt and when chipping.

Other Chip Shots

Creativity and imagination around the greens are the hallmarks of a complete player. Having the self-belief to adopt a different approach to a given scenario may give you the edge over your opponent. Here are some alternative short game options to consider.

❯ ⌄ TOE CHIP

This is a shot that some of the world's best players discovered over time, as a solution when the greens are incredibly fast and a 'dead' contact is the only way of gaining any real control. The address position you need is much the same as you would adopt for a bump and run but, crucially, you should line up the ball with the toe area of the clubface (see close-up picture, top right). Make a positive swing, simply aiming to strike the ball from the toe. When you do it correctly you'll find the 'dead' contact you are looking for, which bumps the ball onto the green before the slopes take it down to the hole.

You must still accelerate through the ball, because if you don't you'll be in danger of a double hit. When the pin is close to you and the greens are fast, this shot will often be your best option.

⊙ USING YOUR SPLASH SHOT

There are certain occasions when your best option is to employ the technique discussed in the previous section (see page 173). When the ball is buried in thick grass or lying on a muddy patch, the percentage play is to treat it like a bunker shot. So widen your stance, set the ball forward (below) and make a longer swing. It is absolutely vital that you strike the ground before the ball, using the bounce to allow the speed of the clubhead to continue.

It is worth stressing how important it is to practise this shot, as this is by far the best way to gain a feel for how the club interacts with the turf. Figuring out how close to the ball you need to strike the ground is the key to success.

⊙ ⊙ CHIPPING WITH YOUR WOODS

Your other option around the green is to use your woods. This tactic has become more and more popular in recent years, due to the consistency of strike it offers the player. When the ball is sitting down a little or on a bare lie, a wood will give you a greater margin for error with the strike. Ensure you stand tall to the ball and take your normal putting grip and set-up. Make sure that your wrists are firm through the stroke, so that you are not adding any loft. A sweet contact will jump the ball forward before allowing it to roll out steadily towards the target.

⊙ PUTTING FROM OFF THE GREEN

Just because your ball is not on the green doesn't mean you can't use your putter. When the grass around the green is particularly short, your putter, like your woods, will be a safer, more predictable option than hitting a lofted chip with a wedge. Whenever you are putting from off the green make sure that there are no areas of thicker grass or other obstacles between you and the start of the green. These will kill the momentum of the shot and leave your ball well short of the target. If there is a divot or a sprinkler head, for instance, between you and the hole, you'll have little option but to go for a more lofted wedge shot. If there is nothing in the way, however, choosing to putt is the sensible, percentage play.

Short Game Shot Selection

Now that you have a whole host of different short game shots at your disposal, it is time to take a closer look at some of the elements that come into play. Successfully mapping out the shot is a great way to prepare yourself for a positive outcome, so consider the following factors as you devise your strategy.

⊻ GROUND CONDITIONS

The firmness of the greens should have a huge bearing on your shot selection. During the winter you'll generally play more lofted shots because you will know that the ball will stop just as soon as it hits the ground. Trying to run it up to the hole will be harder to judge. Likewise, if it has been raining, and especially if there is any water on the putting surface, take the unknown elements out of the shot by going through the air. Conversely, when the ground is particularly hard under foot, a clean strike with your wedges is slightly harder to come by. Keeping the ball down and running it towards the target may be the safest play. If you know the conditions will favour a certain type of shot, hone this on the practice green (below) before you head out to play.

❯ LEAVE YOURSELF EASY PUTTS

You stand behind your ball and eye up your shot, knowing that getting the ball within 5 feet/1.5 m will be a great shot. You then step up and play a beautiful chip that runs a few feet past. The problem, however, is that by running the ball past the hole you have left yourself a very tricky downhill, left-to-right putt.

The point is that you need to know where to leave your ball to give yourself the easiest short putt possible. Giving yourself a longer but straighter uphill putt is often far better than leaving the ball closer but with a heavy break and speed to deal with. Let this small but crucial element become a part of your pre-shot planning and your short game statistics will improve rapidly.

◆ WATCH THE ROLL

Your chip will often give you an idea how the next shot – your putt – will roll. Once you have hit your chip, watch it carefully as it runs towards the pin. This will give you a general sense of how the slopes on the green will affect the run of the ball, and if your chip goes past the hole you'll see how the putt back will break. Study the roll of the ball and you'll be able to make a confident stroke, knowing exactly how the putt will move. Turning away too soon is a simple mistake that makes the next shot unnecessarily uncertain.

◆ PIN OUT?

Some players like to take the pin out when they chip from close range. This is really a confidence thing: they like to feel as if there is nothing that will get in the way of the ball rolling into the centre of the hole. It is worth remembering, however, that a chip that is on line and running a fraction too fast will often hit the pin and stop dead. If you've taken the flag out, you will be left with a long return putt. Also, from longer range, if you keep the flag in you will have a far better feel for the length of the shot.

Before You Play

Very few golf shots are played without the possibility of a disastrous result. Whether it's a tight drive, a pitch to a heavily guarded green or a delicate close-range chip, there is a huge amount of skill attached to blocking out the negatives to focus on a successful outcome. The tips on this page are tailored specifically to chipping, but the basic underlying principles can, and indeed should, be employed in every area of the game.

INTERRUPTIONS

It is a situation you see all too often. A player is preparing to hit when a gust of wind or a loud noise upsets his rhythm. Instead of stopping and starting again, he continues, only to hit a bad shot. The lesson to be drawn is this: your pre-shot routine should flow just as much as your swing. If anything interferes, refocus and start again.

⊻ SELECTING THE SHOT

Selecting the type of shot you are going to play before you have even seen the lie is a mistake that many players make. Your first move should be to scrutinize the lie, see how much green you have to work with and visualize how the ideal shot will pitch and roll out. Think of this as part one of your preparation sequence prior to playing a shot.

Below Here, the Australian Robert Allenby closely scrutinizes his lie. Before he selects exactly what shot to play he wants to be sure about how the grass behind his ball will affect the shot.

Robert Allenby

⌃ 'FEEL' THE SHOT

Now that you know what the ideal shot will look like, it is time to focus on the simple mechanics of the shot that you are about to make. Don't get too bogged down in the details of the swing; instead, try to feel the right shot as you make a practice swing. If you need to play a high shot try to make sure that you are delivering the club through the impact area with plenty of loft. Try to find a patch of grass near your ball that is similar to your lie, as this will give you a feel for how the club will react. By making three or even four practice swings without stopping between each, you will set a smooth, relaxed rhythm in preparation for the shot. This represents part two of your preparation sequence.

⌄ HONE IN ON THE TARGET

You now know what shot you are about to play and how it should feel, so it's time to take your address position. Having gone through this process you should automatically stand to the ball correctly without the need to tinker with your set-up.

As you stand over the ball, take one last look at the hole and then glance at where you are trying to land the ball. This will make sure that you are target-focused at this critical phase of the sequence and will also prevent any destructive thoughts from creeping in. As you look towards the hole, you'll start to develop a natural feel for how to play the shot.

⌃ TRIGGER MOVE

Many players like to rely on a trigger move before they start the swing. This is another element of making a given situation feel normal, part of an everyday occurrence. Graeme McDowell, for instance, has spoken of taking a deep breath and then exhaling just before he begins his putting stroke. A good alternative would be to loosen your hands on the grip a fraction. This simple move relaxes the forearms to create a greater level of freedom in the chipping stroke. Once you have made your trigger move, take the club back without hesitation – don't linger in the address position giving tension enough time to reappear.

Practising Your Short Game

There is no reason why practising your short game should not be great fun. The time you spend on the practice green is invaluable, and while we have already covered some specific drills designed to cement key moves, your routine should also have an element of competition and enjoyment. Here's what to do.

⊻ NINE HOLES, 18 SHOTS

This very simple game offers you a quantifiable way of judging the strength of your short game over a period of time. Place nine balls around the green in different places – create a variety of lies for yourself to test your ability from a range of different positions around the green. The aim is to get each ball up and down. This is not easy, of course, but the very best players will score less than 18 by holing a couple of their chips and getting the rest dead.

Set yourself this challenge at the start of the season and then, as you develop your game through the year, try it again and again. Keep a mental note of your score and you'll be able to judge your improvement on the green. As you try to beat your previous score, you'll also be adding a small element of pressure to your practice routine, preparing yourself for the heat of competition.

⌃ CHIPPING INTO A BASKET

We have stressed the importance of visualization when you chip, and this drill helps you develop that crucial element perfectly. Take 20 balls and from around 10 yards/9 m chip towards either a basket, such as you would get on the range, or an open umbrella. When you've hit all the balls, count how many finished inside the target. This drill forces you to focus on your landing spot, and as you try to reach a respectable score it will generate a crucial element of pressure. As with the previous drill, as your technique and short-game ball striking improve through the year you should see quantifiable improvements every time you try this game, giving you a genuine confidence boost.

PRACTICE BALLS

Golf balls vary greatly with regard to the feel they offer. For this reason, if you play with softer, premium balls you should also practise with them. However, the hefty price tag on premium balls makes it tempting to practise with slightly cheaper, harder alternatives.

Here's a good tip. Whenever you play for real, put any old premium balls that have been scuffed to one side, ready to go into the practice bag. Likewise, if you find an abandoned premium ball in the trees or deep rough, do the same. This way you'll quickly assemble a collection of good quality practice balls that will give you the same feel you'd get when playing for real.

⌃ HOLING OUT GAME

While it is always a good idea to vary your shots regularly when you practise, in order to gain a more comprehensive feel, this drill is about generating pressure. At the very end of your practice time, pick a relatively easy 10-yard/9-m chip. Set yourself the challenge of not leaving the practice green until you have holed the chip. You will be surprised how soon pressure starts to build, especially if it is starting to get dark. It is games and drills of this kind that will help you cope with tension out on the course.

Warming Up Before a Round

The practice putting green is usually a busy place on the morning of a tournament day. It is here that players are looking to hone their feel for the pace and firmness of the greens. Giving yourself enough time to hit a few warm-up shots is the most professional way of preparing for the challenge ahead. There are, however, certain traps to avoid and techniques to employ. Here's what to look out for.

⊽ ⊙ DON'T PRACTICE

A warm-up routine is very different to a practice routine. While in practice (right) you should be trying either to cement some key technical moves or to gain a better feel for how to manipulate the club, when you warm up (below) your sole aim is to arrive on the first tee ready to compete. Around the greens, this means getting a feel for how the ball reacts when it hits the putting surface. Hit shots to different targets and make a mental note as to whether the ground feels firm or soft to chip onto. Also see whether the greens are receptive to spin and how much the ball is rolling. You should not be trying to achieve anything beyond gaining a sense for the ground conditions, so there will be no nasty surprises when you get to the course.

MAKE IT EASIER

One of the worst mistakes you can make in practice is to lose your confidence. If you try to play tricky shots from tough lies there is every chance that poor strikes will come into play and lead to some doubts in your own mind when you get to the course. When you warm up, give yourself good lies (below) by the side of the green to get a feel for the ball on the clubface. The more sweet shots you hit, the more confident you will become.

PREPARING FOR THE COURSE

It is always a sensible idea to prepare yourself for the challenge of a particular type of course. If you are warming up before a hot summer round or you are about to compete on a links, develop a feel for your bump-and-run shots before you go out to play. Also hit plenty of putts from off the green (left). In both instances, your aim should be to get the strike spot on and then watch how the ball reacts once it starts rolling on the green. You will see how the combination of speed and slope of the green affects the ball, and once you're out grinding your way to a good score, this information could prove absolutely invaluable.

CHIPPING AWAY FROM THE GREEN

There will be occasions when you play courses that offer a very different set of challenges around the green. For instance, you might be playing somewhere like Wentworth or the Belfry just after they have hosted a big tournament. In this case, the rough around the green is likely to be far thicker than you are used to. A great way to gain a feel for how this affects the club through impact, without leaving you with any fear for the scenario, is to find a patch of rough away from the green and warm up there. Don't try to hit the ball towards any specific target – just aim to get the club on the ball and feel how to play shots from this position.

Putting

NO OTHER AREA of the game is quite so quantifiable. By the time your round finishes you can add up the number of putts you have hit and there, written in front of you, will be a tally that does not lie. For the world's top players, breaking the barrier of 30 putts per round is the general goal. A solid short game that yields simple, single-putt pars will help, but there is also another side to this figure. Putting well often means doing the unspectacular things with skill. Regularly hitting putts from over 30–40 feet/9–12 m to within 'gimme' range will do a lot for your scoring potential, taking a huge amount of stress off your shoulders.

Then there are the mid-range putts. Hole one or two of these for confidence-boosting birdies or unlikely pars, and you'll be bouncing to the next tee with renewed vigour. Again, the world's best players would expect to see a couple of these go in during 18 holes. The closer you get to the hole, however, the greater the pressure. When you reach the nervous zone inside 5 feet/1.5 m, you will expect to hole out every time. Having the mental and physical skills to ensure that you do so is one of golf's great challenges. You can be sure that as soon as you miss one short putt, the hole will shrink and the next one will be even harder.

So, what should the average amateur be aiming for on the greens? The answer is to keep three-putts off the card and to become as solid as possible from close range. Nothing saps confidence and morale quite like an avoidable three-putt, and the feeling of unfulfilled potential that abides is demoralizing. From close to the hole, your ability to block out the situation and focus on the process will ensure that your technique remains solid. In this situation it helps to fall back on certain mechanical keys that, if grooved into your game, will help the precision of your putting. These will become the foundations to all solid putting, so we will take a close look at how they can be developed without costing you the natural feel that is equally important on the greens.

Putting Essentials

The putting action is an incredibly simple move that many people overcomplicate as they search for accuracy and ultimate precision. But, just as with so many other areas of the game, the more relaxed you are the better the move will be. As we take our first look at the art of putting, we will consider how to get the basics nailed down with natural ease.

❯ SOUND FOUNDATIONS

This is how the address position should look. Notice (far right) how the player is set square to the target line (1), as he would be for a full shot. A square stance is required to keep the putter working on a good path, just as with any other club. He has set a secure base, with a stance that is around shoulder width (right). A strong lower half is required to prevent unnecessary swaying during the stroke. Again, as with a full shot, the posture is athletic, allowing the hands to drop down into a natural position. It is important that you find a grip you are comfortable with (2) and that your set-up is relaxed, with a good amount of flex in the knees (3) and elbows (4) – if your body is rigid, you'll lose feel for the stroke. If you are struggling with your putting, revert to this simple, crucial position.

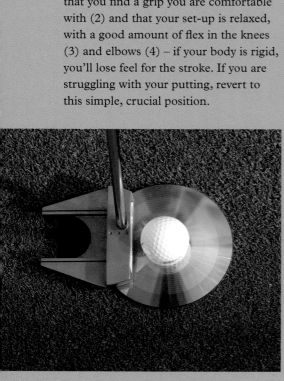

❮ GET YOUR EYES IN LINE

One of the core principles of putting revolves around the position of your eyes in relation to the ball. To check if you are set up correctly, place a compact disc on the ground and rest the ball in the hole in the middle. As you address the ball you should be able to tell if your eyes are directly above the ball by checking that it appears centred on the CD. This means your perception both for your stroke and the line of the putt will not be distorted. This is one of the key principles to nail down early on, so that it feels familiar and natural.

⌃ ANGLE OF ATTACK

Putts that keep running smoothly, holding their line, are usually the result of impeccable strikes. Some simple striking drills appear on page 238, but for now it is worth pointing out the importance of the angle of attack. The fundamental rule is that the putter should move on a very shallow arc. Feel the putter moving in a pendulum-like motion, with the head remaining low to the ground throughout the stroke. The perfect angle of attack, as shown above, will get the ball rolling quickly without it popping up into the air. The sooner it starts rolling off the face without jumping or skidding, the stronger the overall stroke will be.

⌃ ⌲ KEEP YOUR FOREARMS IN LINE

Remember that, when you are putting, a very small amount of hinge in your wrists is fine but too much will cause major problems with both accuracy and distance control. To find a solid stroke with little wrist action, make sure that the shaft of the putter is in line with your forearms, as shown here (right). If your hands are too far forward or back (above), you'll have a tendency to employ too much hinge during the stroke.

A solid position will promote a more solid, reliable action, where the momentum for the stroke is created as you rock your shoulders.

⌲ SHOULDER ANGLE

For those with an orthodox left-hand-above-right grip, the tendency is to let the left shoulder sit a fraction higher than the right at address (as you would with a driver, though not quite so extreme). The problem is that, with such a short stroke, this shoulder angle may cause you to cut across your putts from outside to inside the target line.

As you concentrate on your fundamentals, try to ensure that your shoulders are square to the ground at address. This very simple but often overlooked element of the stroke often lies at the heart of keeping the putter head moving on a good line.

Swing Arc and Path

Just as with the long game, the very simple aim on the greens is to return the putter square to the target through impact. If you can do this often and from both long and short range, your accuracy will make you a deadly competitor. The theory behind the swing path is detailed here and might just become the secret to your success on the greens. There are two commonly used techniques to choose from.

⌄ ARCING STROKE

If your putting stroke follows the natural path around your body, it is inevitable that you will have a gently arcing action. The putter head will move inside the target line on the way back, returning to square through the contact before moving inside the line on the way through. Your body acts as the axle around which your arms move.

The photograph below left illustrates the point. First, note the gentle nature of this

shape; if it becomes exaggerated, trying to find a square face through impact is almost a matter of chance. If this is your preferred technique, think about using a classic 'Anser'-shaped putter (inset). The heel-and-toe weighting will encourage the correct movement of this swing arc. Also note that at address the arms are tucked in a fraction, working closer to the body and promoting the arc of the stroke.

Ping Anser putter

⌄ ALONG-THE-LINE STROKE

The alternative technique is to keep the putter moving along a straight line so that the face is pointing at the target all the way through the stroke (below right). Choosing a face-balance putter (inset) is your best option here, as it is designed to work back and through on the same line.

For a straighter stroke, move your elbows away from your body a fraction more at address, but don't allow tension to build up in your forearms, as this will kill the overall fluidity of the stroke.

Mizuno Line 90 mallet putter

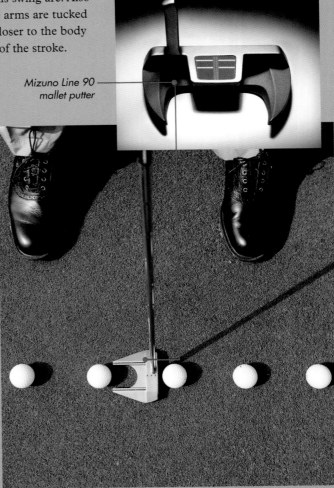

> LONGER PUTTS

Even if you like to keep the putter head moving along a straight line, it is inevitable that for longer putts there will be a small amount of natural arcing. As you take the putter back and through with a longer swing, your arms work around your body, causing a curved motion.

The point here is that you should not try to dictate the path of your stroke when putting from long range. Let the putter head move back and through on a natural arc because, from distance, the flow of the stroke and subsequent speed of the ball are the two most important factors.

Billy Mayfair

◄ SQUARE FACE

Neither of the approaches described on the opposite page is right or wrong, and the only truly important consideration should be to ensure that the putter face is pointing at your target as you make the strike. With the putter in hand you might think this is a given, but you would be surprised at how easy it is to open or close the face through contact.

The American golfer Billy Mayfair is famed for his unusual out-to-in stroke. Through the ball, however, the face is always square to his target, and since he is able to repeat the same move every time his statistics have always been impressive.

INSIDE EYELINE

On page 222 we talked about the importance of getting your eyes over the ball at address for the best possible perception of stroke and line. If you use an arcing stroke, however, your eyes may sit slightly inside the ball-to-target line, encouraging the gently shaping move you are looking for. However, if you adopt this approach it is important that you pick your line very carefully before addressing the ball – do not second-guess yourself once you are in the set-up position.

If your eyes are not directly over the line of your putt, you may see a slightly different break at address. This is likely to be wrong and will result in a very simple and avoidable alignment mistake.

Stroking Your Putts Smoothly

It is time to look in more depth at the less scientific essence of a successful stroke: rhythm. As with the long game, your tempo and fluidity of motion are important for both accuracy and distance control. We will break the putting stroke down into its crucial components to arm you with all the knowledge necessary for a simple, effective and free-flowing movement.

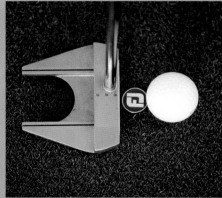

⊗ AVOID THE STOP-START STROKE

We all know that putting is a game of precision, but if you try to exert too much control you'll only end up stifling your own potential. A trap that you should avoid is that of a stop-start rhythm. From backswing to downswing, let the putter head flow without stopping. If you can keep your hands moving at a uniform pace (perhaps increasing the

speed a fraction through the ball to ensure a committed strike) your natural rhythm will arm you with a deadly feel for pace control. As you can see (below), the player has stopped at the top of the backswing. From there the only way to deliver the putter is by making a jabbing movement, which kills the flow of a good stroke.

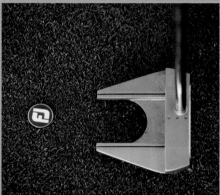

⊗ STAYING STILL

There is no reason why your head should move at all during the putting stroke. Indeed, if it does, the face angle through impact is unlikely to be exactly where you want it. A great drill designed to help you check this most important fundamental is to place a marker down and sit your ball on top of it. Make a normal stroke, looking at the marker until long after you have struck the ball (above right).

This extremely simple method teaches you to keep an ultra-still upper body. In fact, keeping your head down long after the ball has gone is a good way of introducing stability to the stroke if you start struggling on the course when competing for real.

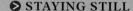

⊗ ALIGNMENT

Your alignment sticks will come in handy on the green. The basic principles concerning the effect of alignment on your swing path, discussed in the first section of this chapter, apply just as much here. Quite simply, you should not expect to hit your putts on line if you do not stand square to the correct ball-to-target path. If you open or close your body the putter will work across the ball through impact, sending it off in the wrong direction and also creating unwanted sidespin. So try to keep your set-up as simple as possible by using some alignment sticks or shafts to set the best, most effective lines at address, as shown here.

❯ FEEL THE FLOW

We have already looked at the relationship between grip pressure and rhythm, but this becomes more critical on the greens. As with a full swing, if your grip gets too tense, your stroke will lack freedom.

An excellent drill to get you feeling a good tempo is to make a series of practice strokes without a putter. Place your hands together as if they were on the grip and deliver the same pendulum-like movement you would on the greens. With your hands hanging down naturally, without a putter, you'll notice how free the move feels. You should aim to recreate this when you bring the putter back into play.

If you notice that the putter is not allowing your hands to hang naturally, it might be the wrong length. In this case, seek some focused professional advice.

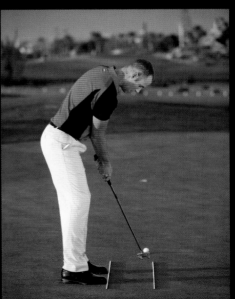

Problem Solving: Short Putts

Most bad shots can be dismissed with an excuse – the wind, the lie or even unsettling noises can help you put poor shots out of your mind and look more positively to the future. When it comes to short putting, however, there are only so many times you can blame spike marks on your line before you need to take a long, hard look at your approach. Short putting should be easy, but with the pressure mounting mistakes can quickly creep in. The tips and drills shown here will highlight the issues you may be having and offer simple solutions.

> BODY MOVEMENT

If your putting has been letting you down, your first check should be your body movement. If your legs slide or your upper body sways, the path of the putter head will be compromised, sending the ball rolling along way off line. You can use alignment sticks for this, planting them either side of you as shown. If your body is moving unnecessarily, you'll bump into the sticks, clearly drawing your attention to the problem.

This drill simply works to help focus your mind on the importance of keeping your body solid through the stroke – an essential element of accurate putting.

◄ HOW HARD TO HIT?

Golfers tend to fall into two categories on the greens: those who like to see the ball dying into the hole and those who like to hit it firmly into the back. Both approaches have pluses and minuses.

Hitting the ball firmly means that you can take out the break but, of course, if you miss you'll be left with a tricky putt back. Also, if the ball catches the lip it will usually spin out. If you die the ball into the hole you have to allow for a lot more break, which, as it is dependent on speed, can be hard to get spot on.

Padraig Harrington is a player who likes to die the ball into the hole, allowing for plenty of break. Tiger Woods falls into the other category, often hitting the ball hard into the back. One of the great bonuses of adopting Tiger's approach is that it forces you to be positive, driving the ball towards the target. This is often the best tactic if you are not sure exactly what the break is going to do. Find out which method you feel most comfortable using and if you rely on that when under pressure you'll relax and hole out with greater consistency.

❯ LISTEN OUT

An excellent tip that helps many players from close range is to purposefully not look at how the ball rolls. From close in, simply listen out for it dropping into the hole. The body movement issues that we have already looked at often come as players lift the upper body too soon, anxious about the result. If you fall into this trap, keep your eyes down until you hear the ball go in.

TENSION

Nowhere will you feel tension on the golf course more than on the greens. Short putts will test your nerve. It doesn't matter whether you are playing for a living or just competing against friends: you need to find a way to remain calm. We have already examined the importance of pre-shot routines and how they can help you relax. It makes sense to have a routine for when you putt, too, and part of that should be to cheat your senses by controlling your breathing. Before you draw the putter head back, take a deep breath and exhale slowly. This will relax your body, ready for a far more relaxed, free-flowing stroke.

Problem Solving: Yips

Golf is one of the few sports where players can experience the yips. The feeling through impact is akin to a small electric shot being sent through your hands; the involuntary twitch that follows sends the putter off line and the ball goes in the wrong direction. The yips needn't send you into despair, however. As long as you change your approach to the game on the greens you should be able to get through the problem.

Stewart Cink

❯ LONG PUTTERS

Over the years debate has raged over whether long and belly putters should be banned. Many golfers feel that players who anchor the putter into their midriff gain an unfair advantage by removing an element of the unpredictability of the hand movement. But as the relevant rules look set not to change for the foreseeable future, long and belly putters remain a perfectly acceptable part of the game, and they have helped thousands of players get through the yips. Stewart Cink (pictured right) is one top-level golfer who has kept the putter head stable by using a belly putter to deadly effect during his career.

By separating the hands or using the belly to anchor the stroke, players are able to find a pendulum-like action. If you are having problems with your putting, there is no need to stick to the short putter. Change your approach and all the bad memories you have on the greens will be reset, giving your scoring potential a new lease of life.

❮ ALTERNATIVE GRIPS

For many golfers the destructive element of the yips stems from the right hand. As the putter drives through the ball it is the right hand that takes control of the stroke, and a jagged move sends the ball off line. To combat the problem, some big-name players have turned to using different grips, as shown here.

The key to both is that the palm of the right hand is off the club. In the version on the left you should notice that the left-hand grip is normal, with the right hand holding the club more like a pencil. In this instance, the right hand is simply there for stability, with the left more in control of the club through the stroke. The claw grip in the right-hand picture, by similarly taking the palm of the right hand off the club, has transformed the fortunes of many good players. So if you are struggling why not give it a go?

◁ BERNHARD LANGER

Bernhard Langer is one high-profile player who found a new technique to overcome the yips. He has used strange grips and long putters, as shown here, to remain competitive throughout his career, winning two Masters on the lightning-fast greens at Augusta and picking up close to 100 further tournament victories around the world since turning professional in 1976.

The different approaches Langer adopted enabled him to rediscover a smooth stroke, and his case bears out the point made opposite: if you are suffering with the yips, try a whole new approach. Holding the club differently will reset the feelings you have in your hands and keep any involuntary twitches at bay.

⊙ LEFT BELOW RIGHT

Another alternative grip option is to set your left hand below your right at address. This is widely used at all levels of the game to address the point made at the start of this section about getting your shoulders square to the ground: with the left hand below the right, this is far more likely. If you are struggling with the yips but don't want the drastic change of moving to a long putter or a claw grip, try this approach first. Keep both thumbs running down the middle of the shaft and try to keep the tempo of the stroke as smooth as possible.

It pays to practise any of these new methods long and hard before you play, as anything unusual will feel hugely uncomfortable under pressure. However, once you have chosen to make a major change, stick with it – swapping back and forth will do your game no good.

Problem Solving: Distance Control

Great distance control is about having an instinctive feel for the speed of the greens. When you have that feel at your fingertips you'll be able to take a look at the target and naturally know how hard to hit the putt. But when things aren't working quite so well, it all starts to become too mechanical as you search for a greater level of control. If your pace settings are off, use these simple drills to rediscover a delicate feel.

▶ TIGHT GROUPING

A great way to develop your appreciation of speed before heading out to play is to hit 10–15 balls to a spot on the opposite side of the green. Don't aim at the hole but at a point a good distance away from you. The aim is to make your grouping of the balls as tight as you possibly can. Your first attempt is likely to produce mixed results, so repeat the process three or four times. The good thing about this drill is that you will readily notice your own improvement as you hit more balls.

If you are playing a course with big greens and know that you will face many long putts, this simple pre-round routine will develop your feel so you are ready for the challenge.

◀ CHECK YOUR RHYTHM

Rhythm and distance control go hand in hand, so if you are struggling with the pace of the greens, it makes sense to spend a little time ensuring the speed of your stroke is as smooth as possible.

A good drill is to place two tees in the ground to act as markers for the length of your stroke. Notice how the player here is set up very slightly nearer the tee to his right. Without aiming at anything specific, swing back and through at a constant pace, using the two tees to guide the length of the stroke. If your rhythm is disrupted by any juddering moves, the balls you hit will travel different distances despite the strokes being the same length. Try to keep the speed of the putter head working evenly; the more balls you hit with the tees as references, the closer the resulting grouping of balls will be.

This drill will also help you guard against decelerating the putter head through impact – one of the most common mistakes in the game.

◀ ▼ FLOW INTO THE BALL

As you scrutinize your putt, studying the line and stalking the prospective path of the ball into the hole, it is easy to let excess tension come into play. Stress will only hamper the flow of the putter, so if distance control is a regular issue for you, incorporate an element into your pre-shot routine that reminds you of fluidity. Stand behind the ball and make some one-handed swings (left). It doesn't matter which hand you use, as the most important thing is to feel the putter almost creating its own rhythm. Feel the flow while looking at the target and you'll gain a more instinctive appreciation of pace.

Tiger Woods (below) often hits putts one-handed on the practice green to improve his feel before going out to play. This simple technique is a great way of removing control to gain a tempo that will ultimately improve your feel for distance and green speed.

Tiger Woods

Picking Your Line

The vast majority of putts you'll face will slide from one direction to another with the natural contours of the green. Getting the pace spot on and picking the right line are the two key ingredients, so now it is time to turn our attention to the latter. Picturing how the ball will track towards its target is an essential element to your pre-shot routine. Here's what to look out for.

⊙ GET LOW DOWN

You will have noticed how golfers stalk their putts, getting as low as possible to read the slopes. From here you are in a better position to see how the shape of the green will affect the roll of the ball. Camilo Villegas, the Colombian PGA

Tour player, takes this approach to the extreme, as you can see here, employing his 'Spiderman' stance to get his eyes as close to the ground as possible. But the simple point to remember is that the lower you get the easier it is to pick up on any contours.

LINES OR CURVES

Golfers tend to fall into one of two categories. First, there are those who like to think of every putt as straight. The idea is that you pick your target based on the point where you expect the ball to break. You hit the ball straight to that spot and let the slopes do the rest of the work. Many players like the simplicity of this approach and, by concentrating on hitting a specific spot, can keep the mechanics of the stroke in check.

The second mindset is to think not in straight lines but in curves. Padraig Harrington has said that when he putts his best he doesn't pick a precise target. Instead, he sees the general gradient of the green and combines that with his natural feel for pace to get the whole equation right. This second approach is less aim-specific and more feel-based, requiring an instinctive visualization of what the putt will do. Both, however, prepare the mind and body perfectly for the stroke.

Camilo Villegas

◁ LOOK AROUND THE HOLE

If you regularly watch top-level golf you will notice how players often walk up towards the hole and make a practice swing from there. This simple process allows them to gain a feel for how the putt will break at this stage of the putt, as the ball decelerates. From here you can pick up on crucial but subtle slopes and also see whether uphill or downhill gradients will come into play. Remember that this is the key area of any putt, so always pay close attention to what the ball will do as it homes in on the hole.

◁ PLUMB BOBBING

One of the oldest green-reading techniques is plumb bobbing. The technique involves standing behind your ball, directly down the line of your putt so that your chest is square to the hole, and letting the putter hang straight down, as shown here. With just your dominant eye open, line up the bottom of the shaft with the centre of the ball and then look towards the hole. If the shaft also dissects the middle of the hole, your putt will be flat. If the hole is to the right of the line created by the shaft, the putt will break to the left. If the hole is left of the shaft, the putt will break right.

This technique is less commonly seen in the modern game, but it is still very useful if you are not sure how the putt you are facing will roll.

⌃ ADOPT A DIFFERENT APPROACH

If you are struggling to read a particular putt, why not try this slightly different approach. Imagine that you have taken dead aim at the hole. Now try to judge how much the putt would miss by. If, in your mind's eye, the ball has come to rest 2 feet/60 cm right of the hole, that tells you how far to the left you need to aim. On occasions you will struggle to see the line, and this tactic might well be of use then.

Tackling Tough Putts

No matter how much you might want to play to a certain area of the green to leave you with an easy putt, there are some occasions when you will be left facing an incredibly tough scenario. The complexities of a normal putt suddenly increase, and unless you adapt your approach your score will take a hit. Here are four common difficult positions and some sensible suggestions for how to respond.

▶ TWO-TIERED GREENS

One feature that course designers use to protect their layouts against consistently low scores is to build a tier into a green. This creates two levels, offering the greenkeepers good choices for pin placements. If you find yourself on the wrong level, the key to success is getting the pace right, so walk the length of the putt to get a feel for the distance. Stand on the brow of the hill and make some practice swings, looking at the hole – this will give you a feel for how the putt will run once it's on the correct level. Next, pick a spot on the brow of the hill to aim at and try to run the ball over this point. Finally, as you are standing next to the ball making practice swings, picture the roll of the putt, seeing the ball roll down towards the hole. This will give you a feel for the pace.

SPIKE MARKS

Bernhard Langer

When Bernhard Langer was left with a relatively short putt to retain the Ryder Cup for Europe at Kiawah Island in 1991, he was conscious of a spike mark on his line. Golfers are not allowed to tap down spike marks, and so – with the eyes of the whole golfing world looking on – he tried to find the bottom of the cup by steering the ball around the blemish. He narrowly missed, and this moment has come to encapsulate the tension and pressure of the Ryder Cup.

Since there is nothing you can do about spike marks on your line, our advice would be to hit the putt a fraction harder to try to take out some of the break. If you attempt to drop the ball into the hole at dead weight it is more likely to be knocked off line by the mark. Try to be as positive as possible and your chances of success will improve.

❯ SHORT LEFT-TO-RIGHT BREAKERS

If you are a right-handed golfer, these are some of the toughest putts you'll face, especially when they also happen to be downhill. The common mistake is to be slightly tentative and leave the face open, missing the putt to the right. If you find yourself falling into this trap, making one small change to your set-up will help. Take your address position with your eyes farther over the ball than usual, so that they are a fraction to the right of the target line. This should be only a small adjustment, but by setting your body farther over the ball than usual you guard against pushing the putt and letting it trickle off to the right.

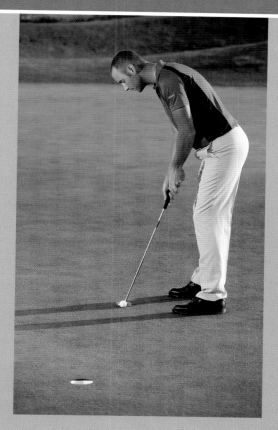

⌄ DOUBLE-BREAKERS

Putts that break more than once add an extra element of difficulty and will need some extra attention. Remember that the slopes nearer the hole will have a greater effect, because the ball decelerates towards the hole.

The key to getting the line right is to have a clear image in your mind for how you expect the ball to roll. Once you have achieved this, commit yourself to the line. Just because you know it is going to break twice does not mean you should be any less precise about your alignment. If you devise an image for the putt and then dedicate yourself to your alignment, you should be able to survive this potentially problematic situation.

Perfecting Your Stroke

Now that you understand all the key principles behind a solid stroke, it is time to focus on grooving it so that the whole move becomes ingrained into your putting memory. It doesn't matter whether you play every week for a living or just occasionally with friends – every so often you need to rededicate yourself to the process of putting. Here's how.

In the previous section we looked at the best way to prepare your short game for the challenge of competition, and the same rules apply here. There is no point in hitting a series of tricky but holeable mid-range putts, as all you'll do is see the ball miss regularly, sapping your confidence.

So before you head out to play, start by hitting some long putts to no target in particular, but trying to get the grouping of balls as tight as possible. Make sure that the putt you are hitting is relatively flat so that you are able to get a feel for the true pace of the greens.

Once you have a good feel for the speed of the greens, focus on short putting. Hit a series of putts from no more than 3 feet/1 m to develop a solid action and get used to seeing the ball going into the hole. This two-stage pre-match routine will train your mind and body for positive results out on the course.

⬥ HONING THE STRIKE

We have already touched on the importance of consistently sweet striking on the greens for a good roll of the ball. If you focus on this in practice you won't need to think about it while trying to grind out a score on the course.

A great drill to groove a more central contact is to place two pieces of adhesive putty on the face of your putter, leaving just enough room for the ball, so that any wayward contact will be clearly highlighted. This is one of those drills that you may find incredibly difficult at first, but as your focus on the purity of the strike slowly sharpens you'll make sweet contacts more often than not. Use it for just five minutes every time you practise and your ball will always have a strong roll, threatening the hole every time.

▷ KEEP YOUR HANDS WORKING TOGETHER

As we have seen, it's important to keep your wrists firm. A fantastic drill to highlight any errors that may have crept in is to place the palms of both hands down the side of the grip, as shown. Do not put any pressure on the club with your fingers, as the key here is to remove control to see if the essential mechanics of your stroke are working. Simply swing back and through, checking that your wrists are not hinging unnecessarily at any point through the stroke. This drill will also work to square your shoulders up, so that the putter moves along a good path.

◁ ⌃ STRIKE AND PATH

Here is another great drill that will keep your strike in check while ensuring the ball is leaving the putter face on the right line. Find a dead flat part of the green and start by placing two tees in the ground, just wider than your putter. Then place two more tees in the green, on your line, closer to the target, creating a space just wider than the ball. The aim here is to avoid hitting any of the tees – either the first set with your putter head, or the second set with the ball. This is a great way to check that the ball is being struck sweetly and on the correct line.

Pressure-Proofing

Some players have a stronger mental aptitude than others, but the good news is that no matter what your strengths are you can learn to stay calm when the heat is on. The more pressure you face, the more your mind will relax if you see the situation as nothing unusual. Even if you do not compete regularly on the course, you can still prepare yourself for the challenge.

⊻ ❯ SNAKE DRILL

The concept behind this drill is to gradually turn up the tension and the difficulty of the putts, so that by the time you reach the end, your stroke will need to stay strong under pressure. Set eight balls around the hole as shown, starting 2 feet/60 cm out and gradually spiralling farther from the hole so that every putt has a different break. The challenge is to hole all of the balls – if you miss one at any point you must return to the beginning. As you make your way to the last couple of balls you'll need to concentrate on the process and keep the basic mechanics of your stroke strong.

< PHIL MICKELSON'S PREPARATION

There is a variation of the snake drill that forces you to hole a succession of putts, this time from the same length all the way around the hole. It is a drill favoured by Phil Mickelson, and when he faces short putts on the course, you can see that he visualizes himself completing this drill. He'll make a couple of practice strokes from different angles, as if he were running through the round-the-world drill he does in practice. As he comes to hit the one that matters, his brain is seeing the situation just as it does in practice. This simple process helps Mickelson feel comfortable under pressure. If you can add similar elements of your practice routine to your on-course preparation, your stroke should remain strong under pressure.

❯ ADDED SIGNIFICANCE

In every round of golf you play, some putts will be more significant than others. It might be a short curling downhill putt to save par on a tricky par-3, or a makeable birdie putt to kick-start your back nine – both are common scenarios that require a calm approach as you realize the importance of the situation.

When you desperately want to make a certain putt, don't change your pre-shot routine. Stalking the line for longer than usual will only take you out of your comfort zone, emphasizing the pressure of the situation. It will also upset the rhythm of the routine, which may have a knock-on effect for the tempo of the stroke.

So stick to what you always do and try to keep moving so that you maintain a good flow right through to the stroke itself. Changing your approach when the situation is critical will only make you even more acutely aware of the pressure you are facing.

⌄ SIXTEEN PUTTS OR BETTER

Most practice putting greens have nine holes cut in them, and you can use these to test your skills. Start by standing next to hole No. 9 and putt towards No. 1, working your way around the green. Try to complete the course in no more than 16 putts.

Depending on how large the putting green is, and thus how long the gaps are between the holes, this can be a tough challenge. The only way to do it is by developing an instinctive feel for the pace of the green. If you don't allow yourself to leave the putting green until you have finished the game, you'll also have to keep your stroke working well under pressure.

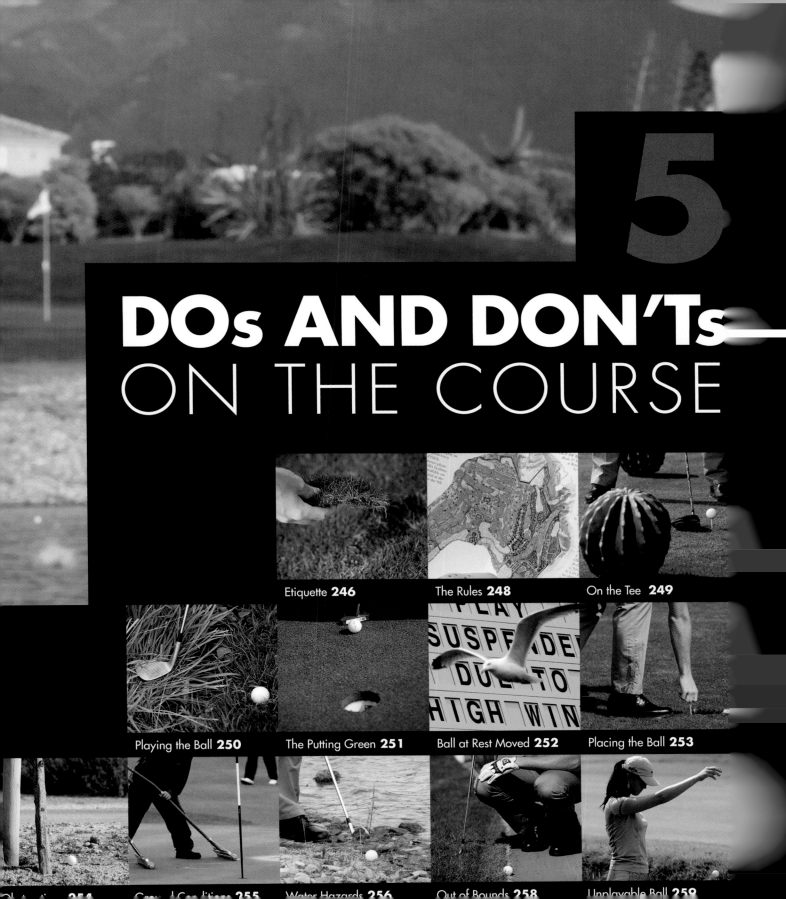

DOs AND DON'Ts
ON THE COURSE

5

Etiquette **246**

The Rules **248**

On the Tee **249**

Playing the Ball **250**

The Putting Green **251**

Ball at Rest Moved **252**

Placing the Ball **253**

Obstructions **254**

Ground Conditions **255**

Water Hazards **256**

Out of Bounds **258**

Unplayable Ball **259**

Introduction

Thirty-four rules govern the game of golf, covering a wide range of scenarios, from what to do if your ball is sitting in a rabbit scrape to where to drop when you have hit your ball into water. It is each player's responsibility to develop a sound understanding of the rules of play. Equally important is the manner in which the game is played: with courtesy, care for the course and consideration for other players.

The rule book is a substantial volume, because it needs to cover a vast array of different problems that can arise on courses that have been moulded from the natural landscape. Don't worry: you are not expected to know all the intricacies of every rule (very few players do – even those at the top of the game), but a sound understanding of the key principles will hold you in good stead. In this chapter we will run through some of the most common rules-related scenarios and offer simple tips for how to proceed, as well as detailing some of the key rules.

Golfers should also follow a less formal code of behaviour based on common sense and the sporting spirit of the game. Covering aspects that range from repairing damage you have made on the landscape of the course to keeping up a good pace, these points of etiquette are, in many respects, no less important than the rules that provide the framework of the game. Understanding the difference between good and bad etiquette, and sticking to the principles set out on the following pages, will make you a golfer that others will want to play with.

Etiquette

For non-golfers, one of the most impressive aspects of the game is the respect competitors show each other. Unlike more combative sports, in golf players have a responsibility to ensure they are not disturbing their opponents. Golf etiquette covers all those — mostly — common-sense elements that combine to ensure that everyone has a fair chance of scoring as well as possible. Here's what to look out for.

⊗ REPAIRING DIVOTS

Every golfer deserves a fair chance of finding a good lie on the fairway, and for this reason you should always repair divots. For the most part this

involves simply replacing the piece of turf the club has removed through impact, as shown. However, some courses prefer players to repair divots by placing seed in the blemish. This is intended to speed up the repair of the grass, so the fairway gets back to normal as quickly as possible. On the tee, keep a look out for a box of seed, which many greenkeepers will make available to you. Instead of replacing your divot simply spread some seed in the blemish and the grass will quickly grow back. Whether you are on the fairway or on the tee, if there is no seed available, always replace your divot.

⊘ WHERE TO STAND

Consideration for your fellow players is essential, so be careful about where you stand when others are hitting. Don't stand directly behind another player who is hitting (as shown here), as any small move you make is likely to be visible, disrupting his or her concentration. The best approach is to stand quietly off to the side and behind the player, in a position to see where the ball goes without causing a disturbance.

ON THE GREEN

It's especially important to be aware of what others are doing when on the greens. You should always avoid standing on or walking across another player's line. Doing this is infuriating, as the footprints you leave are likely to bump a putt off line and it shows a general lack of consideration. Remember to be especially careful if you are tapping your ball in from close range. Either take a stance that avoids your playing partner's line or mark the ball, let your partner putt and come back later.

❯ RAKING BUNKERS

It is one of the most frustrating sights in the game. You've just hit your ball into a bunker and you walk up to find that an inconsiderate player from an earlier group has failed to rake the sand, and your ball is sitting in a footprint. Never forget that every player deserves a fair lie, so always be sure to rake your footprints and marks in bunkers.

⌄ MARKING YOUR CARD

If you are playing in a competition you will need to take a few moments regularly during the round to mark down your scores and those of your playing partner. It's essential to find a time and place to do this that doesn't hold up play. This player (below) has got it wrong: don't mark your card on the green immediately after you have finished a hole. The group behind is likely to be waiting for you to clear the green. Instead, walk to the next tee and record the scores while your opponents are preparing to play.

⌃ WHERE TO LEAVE YOUR BAG

This is a factor that often exposes an inexperienced golfer. Having just putted out, a group is making its way to the next tee, but one of the players has left his bag on the wrong side of the green. The group behind are ready to play but have to wait for the player to scurry over to the other side, pick up his bag and make his way back across. When you reach a green, always leave your bag on the side nearer to the next tee, as the player has correctly done here. This is one of those small but essential elements that help to guard against slow play.

SLOW PLAY

If there is one persistent problem that all golf clubs face, it is slow play. The time it takes to play different courses can vary greatly: resort courses, for example, tend to have much longer walks between greens and tees. But whether you are waiting for another player in your own group to deliberate endlessly over a shot or pausing for the group ahead to finish the hole, delays are likely to kill your rhythm and leave you desperate to finish the round. Golfers can quickly develop a reputation for slow play that makes others avoid playing with them.

If there is no group in front of yours, try to make sure you aren't holding up the players behind. If you are waiting for a playing partner to hit, spend the time thinking about your own shot and devising your strategy, so that when your turn comes you know exactly what you are going to do and are ready to play – this will help your pace of play immensely.

If you do find that your group is holding up the players behind, simply let them play through. A good way to do this is to hit your tee shots on a hole, then call them through.

Understanding the Rules

For the most part golf is a self-policing sport, so it requires an immense amount of honesty and integrity from the participants. Whereas in sports such as football players often try to influence the decision of the referee, in golf the reality is that you are often your own referee. Every player is expected to act in accordance with the rules, and anyone who fails to do so will develop an unwanted reputation. Read and digest the information that follows, whether you are new to the game or have been playing for some time. In fact the rules can often be used to your advantage, which could make all the difference to your scores.

R&A AND USGA

The rules of golf are jointly composed by the R&A and the United States Golf Association (USGA). They have evolved over time to reflect the changing nature of the game. For instance, with golf club manufacturers pushing the technological capabilities of their products, it has fallen on the shoulders of the R&A and USGA to act as guardians of the game, revising the rules to protect treasured golf courses and ensure that the nature of the challenge remains the same.

Revisions to the rules of golf are made regularly (every four years). You can send off for your own copy of the rules via the R&A website or, alternatively, if you are a member of a golf club, it may have copies.

DEFINITIONS

A part of the rule book that you should definitely read is the section on definitions. This explains what is meant by all manner of terms such as 'abnormal ground conditions', 'loose impediments', 'hazards' and 'obstructions'. Only if you know what each is describing will you truly understand how to proceed under the rules. Confusing loose impediments with movable obstructions, for instance, could mean that you incur penalty shots.

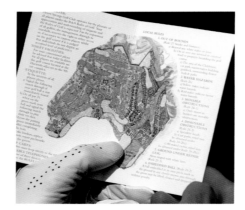

Left and below Always check the local rules, as they might just offer you a free drop from cart paths. Likewise, if you familiarize yourself with the definitions of key terms within the rules you will avoid confusion over how to proceed in any given rules-related scenario.

< LOCAL RULES

A list of local rules will usually be printed on the back of your scorecard. These are laws that apply specifically to the course you are playing, under a provision that allows each club to set rules to suit the unique environment of its course. How to proceed when your ball finishes on a cart path, or what to do when you hit your ball into an environmentally sensitive area, are two of the most common questions covered by local rules. If you are playing a competition on a course you don't know very well, take a moment to familiarize yourself with the local rules. Knowing them may well benefit you during the round, as you will know what to look out for while out on the course.

On the Tee

Rule 11 deals with the various dos and don'ts on the teeing ground, and here we offer a quick breeze through the essential laws – from where you can tee up and stand to the penalties for breaking the rules.

◖ WHERE TO PEG UP

On page 120 we saw the importance of using the width of the teeing ground to help you aim away from danger. For example, if there is water down the left-hand side of the hole, you should tee off on the left side of the box to aim slightly away from the trouble. It's a simple concept but one that can help you set a positive strategy for the hole. The good news is that the rules can help you here. As long as the ball is pegged up within the area of the tee, you can stand outside it, as shown here. Just be careful that you are in no danger of striking the tee marker as you drive through the ball.

◔ PENALTIES

The penalties for teeing up outside the allowed area are different for stroke play and match play. In the former, you receive a penalty of two strokes and are required to play another drive from within the correct area. If you continue without addressing the mistake, you will be disqualified once you tee off on the next hole or (on the final hole) on departing the 18th green.

In match play there is no penalty, but your opponent has the right to force you to cancel the shot and play another one from the correct area, which is very frustrating if you've just hit a great shot.

◗ THE TEEING GROUND

So where can you tee up from? And where can't you? These are questions well worth asking, and the important fact to remember is that the teeing ground is rectangular. The rules allow you to peg up between the markers (no nearer the hole than the line between them), anywhere within two club lengths away from the direction you are hitting. This photograph shows the player measuring this out. You can use this element of the rule to your advantage in two ways: to find a perfectly flat area to stand that is not being interfered with by any divots, or to add a small amount of crucial length on a par 3 when the club you are hitting might be a little too much.

Playing the Ball

Rules 12–15 deal with all aspects of playing the golf ball. Above all, remember that you should play the ball as it lies without making the shot any easier for yourself. Here we look at some of the specific rules that are often unwittingly broken.

STANCE AND ADDRESS

This is a rule that amateurs often break unintentionally. There is a profound difference between 'taking' and 'building' a stance. These terms refer to the way you find a firm footing for your shot. A player is always entitled to take a secure stance but should not shuffle the feet unnecessarily or use them to clear the area around the ball. If you do this you will often be improving the area of your swing, making the shot slightly easier.

The same principles apply to the way you address the ball with your club. It can be frustrating to have a tuft of grass, or a thicker shoot, sitting behind the ball, but you are not allowed to use your club to flatten it down. You are allowed to ground the club fairly behind the ball, but pressing down grass deliberately will cost you a two-shot penalty in stroke play and loss of hole in match play.

PRACTICE SWINGS

So you have hit your ball into the trees and it's sitting up, but you are not sure whether you can get the club properly to the ball. As you make a few practice swings to test the line of the swing, you knock off a branch. This is a scenario that has caught out many players in the past, because, by breaking off a branch or a leaf, you are deemed to be improving the line of your swing. So be careful when you are preparing to play and make sure that you don't accidentally improve your chances of a clean strike – it will cost you two shots in stroke play and loss of hole in match play.

Above left and left Remember that, while you are entitled to take your stance fairly, it is against the rules to use either your club or your feet to improve the area of your swing.

DOUBLE HIT

It has become one of the most infamous shots in the game. In the 1985 US Open at Oakland Hills, T.C. Chen, the leader during the final round, hit the ball twice in one stroke. This might sound like a trick shot, but the dreaded 'double hit' happens sometimes around the greens, especially to those with less confident short games. In this situation the shot played counts as one, but the player must add another penalty stroke to his score. Chen's double hit was his fourth shot on a par 4. He took a further three to get down, wiping out his four-stroke lead.

T.C. Chen

The Putting Green

The laws relating to the putting green are covered by Rule 16. From marking your ball and touching the line of your putt to repairing marks on the surface, here is your essential guide to avoiding debilitating penalty shots on the green.

◢ REPAIRING PITCH MARKS

When you hit an approach that lands directly on the green, it is likely to leave a pitch mark. In wet conditions pitch marks can resemble little craters and as such are very easily detectable, but no matter how deep they are you should always keep an eye out for them and be ready to make repairs. Use a tee peg or a pitch mark repairer, shown above, to fill in the hole – you can do this even if it lies on the line of your own putt. Once you have eased the turf in around the mark, use the bottom of your putter to pat it down; the green will be as good as new, so anyone who putts over your pitch mark will not be affected by the damage.

◢ YOUR SHADOW

On a sunny day, shadows cast across the green can make focusing on a precise task that little bit harder. With this in mind you should take care over the position of your own shadow. Make sure it is not on another player's line, or anywhere near the ball as the player prepares to putt, as any small movement you make will move the shadow and be distracting. When you are attending the flag (as the player above is doing) make sure your shadow is not being cast over the hole. This is an element of etiquette as opposed to a rules pointer, but you should always try to avoid disturbing another player's putt.

◢ ILLEGAL STANCES

When putting, it is illegal to stand on, astride or on an extension of your line. This rule was introduced to prevent players from adopting croquet-style stances on the green.

There are, however, exceptions to the rule that are well worth knowing. If you are standing in an illegal position accidentally, or because you are trying to avoid standing on your playing partner's line (as the player is doing in this photograph), you will escape penalty. But generally you should try to avoid standing on or astride the extension of the line of your putt to be safe.

◢ MARKING YOUR BALL

Golfers are allowed to mark their balls on the greens. This rule allows you to wipe any mud off the ball before putting. Many players also like to place the ball down with their alignment mark pointing at the target, to help them set up to the ball.

The correct marking process involves placing a 'coin, marker or similar object' directly behind the ball. If you accidentally move your ball in the process of marking it, you will avoid a penalty as long as you replace the ball.

Padraig Harrington

Above Padraig Harrington was caught out at the 2011 Abu Dhabi Championship when he unwittingly nudged his ball and failed to replace it. As the incident came to light only after his round was completed, the Irishman was disqualified.

Ball at Rest Moved

One factor that distinguishes golf from most other ball sports is that on every shot you are the one creating the momentum. You are not relying on your reflexes and instincts to respond to a moving ball but striking a ball at rest. Of course, this is what makes golf such a captivating test of nerve. Here we look at some aspects of Rule 18, which comes into play when a ball at rest moves.

Padraig Harrington

BALL FALLING OFF THE TEE

It's a common scenario. You're standing on the tee, eyeing up the fairway ahead, and just before you begin your swing, you nudge the ball off its tee because your hands are shaking with cold or nerves. You needn't worry: under Rule 11-3 you can simply peg the ball back up and start again without penalty.

Likewise, under Rule 18 you won't be penalized if you move your ball while removing a loose impediment on the green, or while searching for it in a hazard (where loose impediments are blocking your view), in an obstruction, in an abnormal ground condition or in water in a water hazard.

⊙ HIGH WINDS

At the Open Championship you will occasionally see a strong wind cause a ball to roll away from where it came to rest, especially on the greens, where the grass is shortest. The competition committee can choose to stop play in these circumstances, but this doesn't always happen.

As long as you haven't addressed the ball you need not worry: simply play it from where it comes to rest. However, if the ball moves once you have taken your stance and laid the club down behind it,

Above Padraig Harrington struggles in the wind at the 2008 Open Championship, an event he went on to win. When the breeze is this strong be careful not to ground your club at address, because if the ball moves you will be hit with a penalty stroke.

you will incur a one-stroke penalty and will need to replace the ball. For this reason, players often do not ground their club on the green when the wind is particularly strong. Hovering the putter behind the ball as you prepare to play will help you avoid a penalty if the ball moves.

DEFLECTIONS

You hit your ball onto the green and, as it runs out, it strikes your playing partner's ball. In this scenario – which happens more often than you might think – no penalty is incurred, but the ball that was originally at rest must be replaced. If, however, you are playing in a stroke-play competition and you hit a putt that strikes another player's ball at rest, you will receive a two-stroke penalty. (In match play there is no such penalty.) This is why it is usual to mark your ball on the green when you are waiting to putt.

Lifting, Dropping and Placing

There are many on-course scenarios that will require you to take a drop. Developing your confidence about what you can and can't do under Rule 20 will help you make smart choices and also speed up your play. Of course, whenever you believe you are entitled to a free drop, you should call over one or all of your fellow players to discuss the situation. Here we run through the basics of lifting, dropping and placing the ball.

⌄ HOW TO DROP

Before lifting your ball to take a drop you must always mark its position (1). Place a tee peg, a marker or a coin in the ground to signal where the ball was originally sitting. Failing to do this will cost you a one-shot penalty, and you'll need to replace the ball before beginning the dropping process all over again. Once you have marked the position of the ball and measured out the area on which you are allowed to drop (2), stand upright with your arm stretched out horizontally, as shown here (3). Again, if you fail to adopt the right position you'll be hit with a one-shot penalty.

One final point worth making is that when you are taking relief from abnormal ground conditions or immovable obstructions on the green, you should drop the ball at the nearest point of relief.

RE-DROPPING AND PLACING

A host of circumstances will require a re-drop (such as if the ball comes to rest more than two club lengths away from the point at which it was dropped) and it is well worth checking the details of Rule 20-2c to familiarize yourself with them. If your ball does come to rest in the wrong place, just run through the dropping process as before.

Of course, there must be a provision for when the ball simply will not come to rest in the correct area. If you have dropped the ball twice without success, carefully locate the spot where it landed on the second drop and place it there.

If the ball is successfully placed but subsequently moves, avoid picking it up and replacing it – the rules state that you should play it as it lies. Alternatively, if the ball will not come to rest on the

determined spot, you need to find the nearest area to place it where it will remain unmoved (that is not in a bunker, water hazard or nearer the hole). If you are taking a drop in a hazard and the ball will not come to rest, the nearest spot to place it should be within the hazard.

NEAREST POINT OF RELIEF

You'll hear this term regularly, and it's used when you have the option of a free drop away from immovable obstructions, abnormal ground conditions or wrong putting greens. Knowing this definition is essential as you will often face such scenarios.

There are a couple of crucial points to remember. First, as with any drop, the position you choose should not be nearer the hole. Second, the position should be as near as possible to where the ball was originally sitting while offering total relief from the obstruction, ground condition or wrong green.

Having established the nearest point of relief, you need to drop your ball within one club length of it.

Loose Impediments and Obstructions

The basic principle is that you should play the ball as you find it. There are, however, certain things you can remove to help you find a fair lie. Knowing what counts as loose impediments and obstructions under Rules 23 and 24 will play to your advantage. Here are the basics.

Twigs are treated as loose impediments and can be removed from around the position of your ball.

You are not permitted to remove loose impediments from a bunker. However, courses often use a local rule allowing you to remove stones from sand.

◀ WHAT ARE LOOSE IMPEDIMENTS?

This rule refers to all natural objects that are not fixed or growing, embedded or stuck to the ball. The most common loose impediments are stones, twigs and leaves. Worms and insects, and the casts and heaps they make in the ground, are also treated as loose impediments.

You are allowed to remove loose impediments, but not when both your ball and the impediment lie in a bunker or a water hazard. As always, it is also worth checking the local rules, as courses sometimes permit players to remove stones from bunkers.

▼ SPRINKLER HEADS

These are treated as immovable obstructions on the course, and you are entitled to relief without penalty whenever one represents an interference. If your ball is lying on the sprinkler head, or it is affecting your stance or swing, find the nearest point of relief and drop within one club length. However, you will not receive a free drop if your ball is off the green and the sprinkler head is sitting on the line of your shot (as shown left), unless the local rules state otherwise: at certain courses you will get relief if the obstruction sits within two club lengths of both your ball and the green. It can be frustrating if you are planning to putt from off the green and your line to the hole is obstructed, but unless the local rules come to your aid you will simply have to come up with a different strategy.

Above Young trees are often staked to help their growth. If you find your ball in this position you will usually be allowed to take a free drop. However, you should consult the local rules first.

▲ WHAT ARE OBSTRUCTIONS?

An obstruction is anything artificial that may impact on your lie, stance or swing (or the line of your putt if you are on the green). Cart paths, roads, golf-ball cleaners and course signs all come under this heading. If the obstruction can be moved 'without unreasonable effort, without unduly delaying play and without causing damage', you can simply take it away and carry on with the shot. If the obstruction can't be moved you'll gain a free drop.

There are a couple of things to keep in mind. You do not get relief from an immovable obstruction that is out of bounds – indeed, out-of-bounds markers themselves are deemed to be fixed, may not be removed and are not treated as obstructions. Also, the local rules may declare that certain areas (such as paths or roads) are integral parts of the course, and if this is the case you will not be entitled to relief.

Abnormal Ground Conditions

You will gain relief without incurring penalty shots from abnormal ground conditions, which are defined as 'casual water, ground under repair or hole, cast or runway on the course made by a burrowing animal, a reptile or a bird'. Here are some typical scenarios.

⬤ ANIMAL SCRAPES

These, like other abnormal ground conditions, come under the remit of Rule 25. You get relief when your ball lies in the scrape or it affects your stance or the line of your swing. In this scenario, you'll need to find the nearest point of relief, from where you will have one club length to drop your ball without penalty. If the ball lies on the green you will also gain relief from an animal scrape that sits on the line of your putt.

If you encounter animal scrapes, the chances are you will also find animal droppings. You can treat these as loose impediments and remove them from around your ball before you play without penalty.

⬤ CASUAL WATER

If it has been raining hard, puddles are likely to build on a golf course, as was seen frequently during the 2010 Ryder Cup. You are entitled to relief without penalty if your ball is sitting in casual water or your stance or line of swing is affected. If you are in a bunker, however, remember that the nearest point of relief must be in that same hazard. If the whole bunker is filled with water and you don't have the option of playing the ball as it lies, you'll have to drop it outside – unfortunately under a penalty of one stroke. On the greens, even if your ball is not sitting in casual water, if there is water on the line of your putt you are entitled to take relief without any penalty.

Below Standing water such as was seen at the 2010 Ryder Cup at Celtic Manor is treated as casual water. Take a moment to familiarize yourself with your options, especially on the green, as casual water on the line of your putt should always be avoided.

Water Hazards

One of the most attractive aspects of golf is the way courses incorporate natural features to provide unique playing environments. Of course, this creates diverse rules scenarios. Lakes and ditches are common features, and it is well worth knowing how to proceed under Rule 26 when your ball makes its way into one of these hazards.

LOSING YOUR BALL

If your ball flies into a lake, it is likely that you won't be able to retrieve it. The good news is that you don't have to be able to retrieve your ball to proceed with the options described here. However, it must be certain or virtually certain that your ball is lost within the water hazard.

For instance, let's assume you have blasted your drive over a hill into an area where both dense undergrowth and a water hazard are lurking. Nobody in your group has seen the ball go into the water, so you can't be sure that it isn't in the undergrowth. In this scenario, you need to go back and play your previous shot again.

❯ DROPPING OPTIONS

If your ball goes into a water hazard and there is no way of playing it, you have to take a penalty drop. In this situation you have two options. The first is to play the shot again from the same position. If you are on a par 3, for instance, and would prefer a full shot into the green, this option might well be preferable. It is also worth remembering that if it was your tee shot that found a watery grave, and you want to play it again under a penalty of one stroke, you can tee the ball up.

Your second option is to drop behind the water, on a line between where the ball last crossed the hazard and the pin. There is no limit to how far back you can go, so this is worth considering if you want a full shot to the green.

◉ LATERAL WATER HAZARDS

Slightly less common, lateral water hazards are marked out by red stakes, which are employed by those setting up the course when there is no way a player could drop his ball behind the hazard. When you hit your ball into water marked out by red posts or lines, the rules give you two extra options beyond the two explained above. Keeping the point at which the ball last crossed the hazard, the player can drop either within two club lengths of this spot or on the opposite margin of the water hazard, the same distance from the hole.

∧ PLAYING FROM INSIDE A WATER HAZARD

There is nothing in the rules to stop you playing a ball that is lying within a water hazard. Simply remember that you are not allowed to ground your club, so at address make sure that it is hovering clear of the ground. Bear in mind that while it can be tempting to play a ball that is sitting in water, if this goes wrong it will leave your score in tatters. Water slows the club down drastically through impact, and if you don't get enough power to force the ball out, you will be faced with the same situation all over again. So before you decide to take on the shot, have a very close look at the lie. If you decide to go for it, hover your club well clear of the ground at address and then make a committed swing. A tentative approach will cost you dear.

❯ BEWARE LOOSE IMPEDIMENTS

We have already covered on page 254 the dos and don'ts related to removing loose impediments, but it is worth underlining here that you are not allowed to touch or remove loose impediments when both the ball and the objects (such as stones, twigs or leaves) lie within the boundary of a water hazard. This often catches golfers out, because you are allowed to remove loose impediments in other areas of the course. Doing so in a water hazard, however, will cost you two penalty strokes or loss of hole in match play.

Out of Bounds

Every golf course has a boundary, which is usually marked by white stakes or lines, fences or walls. If your ball crosses the out-of-bounds line you'll have to add a penalty stroke to your score and play another shot from the same position as the previous, offending, shot. We'll look at the laws associated with out of bounds (Rule 27), so that unnecessary mistakes do not end up costing you in competition.

PLAYING A PROVISIONAL BALL

To help the pace of play, golf's ruling bodies allow players to hit a provisional ball if they think – but are not sure – that their original ball is lost. So, if you have smashed your ball into trees and fear it is lost, clearly tell your fellow players that you intend to hit a provisional ball (failure to do this will mean that your second ball is automatically in play, under penalty of one stroke).

Once you reach the area where the first ball landed, you have five minutes to search for it. If it does not come to light, your provisional ball will become the ball in play, under a penalty of one stroke. If,

however, you find the first one, you can play that and pick up the second ball. But you cannot find your first ball in a bad spot in bounds (such as in a bush) and choose to play the second ball instead.

❯ TAKING YOUR STANCE

There is nothing wrong with standing outside the boundary of the course to play a ball that lies inside. As you can see here, the player's ball is clearly in bounds, and there is nothing to stop him addressing the ball as he normally would. Remember, however, that you do not get relief from obstructions, such as roads, that are out of bounds.

> WHEN IS THE BALL OUT OF BOUNDS?

Your ball has come to rest perilously close to the out-of-bounds line, but is it in play or not? In this scenario, the line drawn on the ground is out of bounds, but the whole of the ball must be on the line or over it to be out of bounds. It is also worth pointing out that the stakes used to define out of bounds are deemed not to be obstructions and are fixed. If you remove one, as the player pictured here is considering doing, you'll get a two-shot penalty in stroke play or lose the hole in match play.

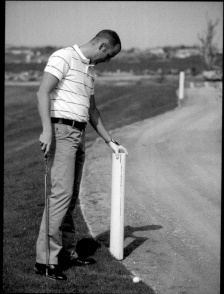

Unplayable Ball

There will be occasions when, despite the fact that you can see your ball, you simply cannot play it. Instead of attempting to chop your ball back towards the fairway (a risky tactic, especially if your ball is stuck in a very difficult place), Rule 28 gives you the the option to take a drop under a penalty of one stroke.

Michelle Wie

⊻ DROPPING OPTIONS

If you have deemed your ball unplayable, you have three dropping options:

1 First, you can go back and play another ball from where you hit the last shot. If you do this, beware of not holding up the group behind. If they are already waiting for your group, it is a sensible idea to let them play through as you make your way back. Remember that if you have played a provisional ball, that does not become the ball in play if you have found your original in an unplayable position.

2 Alternatively, you can mark the position of the ball and drop somewhere back on a line keeping the position of the original ball between you and the pin. If you take this option there is no limit to how far back you can go. It is always worth familiarizing yourself with this option as it may prove invaluable.

3 Your final option is to mark out two club lengths from where the ball is lying, not nearer the hole. When doing this it makes sense to use the longest club in your bag, to give the clearance you need to find a clean lie and a reasonable shot back into play.

Right If you need to take a drop in a bunker under the unplayable ball rule, remember that you still need to drop the ball inside the trap, unless you opt to play the previous shot again.

⊼ BUNKER OPTIONS

There will be rare occasions when you find your ball nestling in a particularly nasty spot in a bunker. If it is resting under the lip and there is no way that you can find a stable stance, your best option might be to declare it unplayable. In this scenario you will have to drop the ball in the bunker, unless you opt to play the previous shot again. If you do choose to drop your ball in the bunker it is likely to plug, leaving you with a difficult shot.

Above and right Phil Mickelson runs through the correct dropping procedure on two different occasions during a troubled first round at the 2010 US Open at Pebble Beach. Note that he is using the longest club in the bag, his driver, to mark out the dropping zone; and that his arm is held out at right angles to his body.

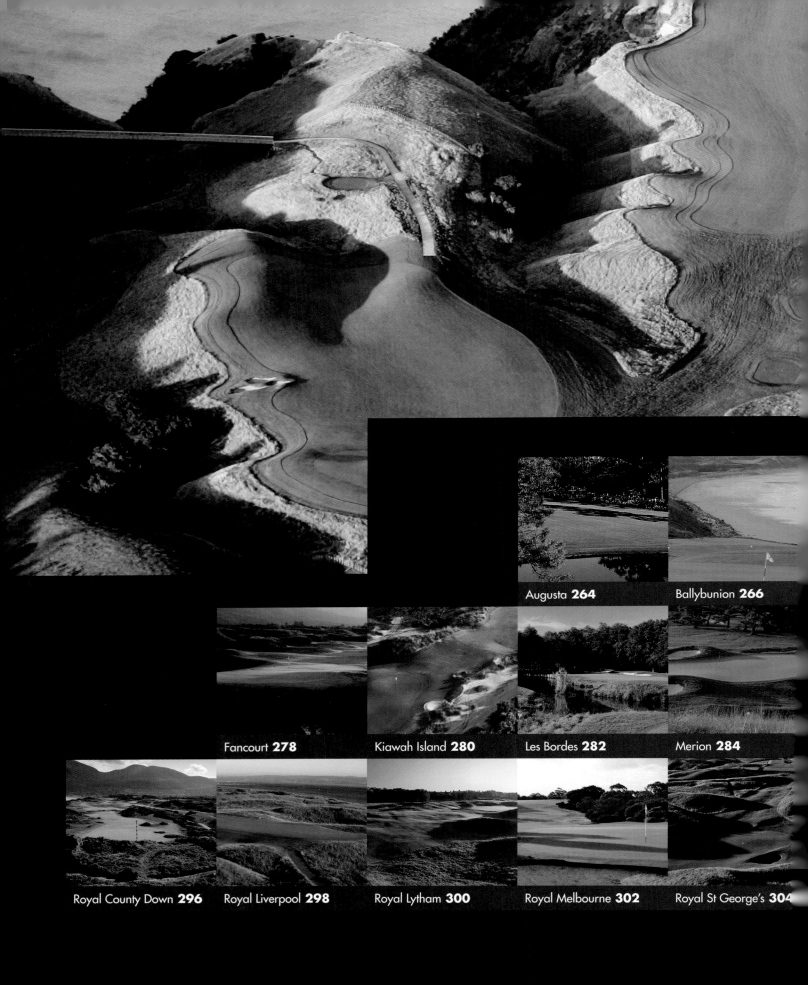

Augusta **264**

Ballybunion **266**

Fancourt **278**

Kiawah Island **280**

Les Bordes **282**

Merion **284**

Royal County Down **296**

Royal Liverpool **298**

Royal Lytham **300**

Royal Melbourne **302**

Royal St George's **304**

6
COURSES

Banff Springs **268**

Barnbougle Dunes **270**

Blue Canyon **272**

Cape Kidnappers **274**

Carnoustie **276**

Muirfield **286**

Oakmont **288**

Pebble Beach **290**

Pinehurst **292**

Royal Birkdale **294**

Shinnecock Hills **306**

St Andrews **308**

TPC Sawgrass **310**

Turnberry **312**

Valderrama **314**

Introduction

The great designer Robert Trent Jones wrote: 'The first golf course architect, of course, was the Lord, and he was the best there has ever been.' The early golfers of Scotland and the Netherlands played on relatively undefined patches of ground wherever they happened to live. There was no such thing as a typical golf course. And while a few elements have become standardized, there is still no standard golf course.

The Scots became the defining influence on golf in the mid-eighteenth century, when the Honourable Company of Edinburgh Golfers laid down the first set of rules in 1744 and, ten years later, 22 'noblemen and gentlemen' gathered to form the Royal and Ancient Golf Club of St Andrews (R&A). But there was no set number of holes per course, and they continued to vary until 1858, when St Andrews, which had reduced its course to 18 holes, standardized this number for a round of golf.

Golf course 'design' was born at around this time, as the great players of the day were called upon to lay out the 'links' of newly formed golf clubs. These great players were all Scottish, and they had all played on the links courses of Scotland – those strips of infertile, sandy soil between the beach and the town or fields. Inevitably they tried to recreate the features that gave their home courses distinction. They looked for green sites in dewy hollows, or on humps or hillocks, to test technique. Sandy holes where sheep sheltered from the wind were replicated by early bunkers.

Today's golf course designers are master craftsmen. They have the benefit of computer-aided design, sophisticated earth-moving machinery, real-estate lawyers, civil engineers and environmentalists. But, in essence, they are still doing just what Allan Robertson, Tom Morris and Willie Park did more than 150 years ago.

Augusta

Augusta National Golf Club, Georgia, USA

Tennis at Wimbledon or Flushing Meadow, motor racing at Le Mans or Indianapolis, racing at Longchamp or Churchill Downs, golf at St Andrews or…? Most people, even those who have little knowledge of golf, would probably answer, 'Augusta National'. Its modern-day fame comes from its hosting of the Masters, the first major of the professional golfing year, and the only one held annually on the same course. But that fame would not have arisen had it not been for Bobby Jones, and his desire to establish the ideal course on which he and his friends might play away from the glare of publicity.

Jones was the greatest amateur golfer of all time, but he was also good enough to take on and beat the best professionals of his day. After he retired from competitive golf in 1930, the adulation of the public made it hard for him to play in peace, and he sought out a site for his own private course. He had some novel ideas about how it might be set up, seriously testing the best players while allowing the high-handicapper to get round in 100 or so without completely losing heart.

JONES'S DESIGN PARTNER

It was an accident that led Jones to find the perfect architect to help realize this concept. In 1929 he had been knocked out of the US Amateur Championship unexpectedly early. That year the event was held at Pebble Beach, California, so he took the opportunity to play two nearby courses, Cypress Point and Pasatiempo. Both had been designed by Alister MacKenzie, a Leeds physician turned golf course architect – one of the very best

Below The 15th hole presents the classic golfing dilemma: whether to lay up safely for a likely par or risk the water for the chance of a birdie. In the 1935 Masters, Gene Sarazen went one better and holed his 4-wood second shot for an albatross two.

CARD OF THE COURSE

Hole	Yards	Par	Hole	Yards	Par
1	445	4	10	495	4
2	575	5	11	505	4
3	350	4	12	155	3
4	240	3	13	510	5
5	455	4	14	440	4
6	180	3	15	530	5
7	450	4	16	170	3
8	570	5	17	440	4
9	460	4	18	465	4
Out	3,725	36	In	3,710	36
			Total	7,435	72

'I've never been to heaven and, thinking back on my life, I probably won't get a chance to go. I guess the Masters is as close as I'm going to get.'

FUZZY ZOELLER, 1979 WINNER

in the world in fact. Jones knew immediately that he had found the right man for the job. The course they jointly designed opened in 1933.

Although today's course is little altered from the original (with a new 16th hole and revisions to the bunkering) it is set up for the Masters in a manner far removed from what Jones or MacKenzie could have anticipated. The greens are maintained at frighteningly fast speeds, and trees and rough have been planted where previously there were neither. It provides a spectacle for television and it prevents scores becoming ridiculously low, but these days no high-handicapper would survive a single hole, let alone 18.

Yet Augusta remains a fabulous (and fabulously beautiful) course. How often we viewers are on tenterhooks as the leaders pass through the treacherous Amen Corner (the 11th, 12th and 13th holes) with Rae's Creek awaiting just the tiniest slip up. Will they risk all and try to get on the 13th and 15th greens in two? And there are – to us – impossible putts on the 16th and 17th greens. Or how about that slick, long, downhill putt on the last green that must go in to avoid a play-off? The Masters is always dramatic. It is also unique among the majors for its invited field of under 100 competitors. The spectators, too, are a select group, returning year after year, and their considerate support upholds the traditions of sportsmanship embodied by Bobby Jones.

● Augusta is ablaze with azaleas during the Masters. Before the site became a golf course it was a plant nursery, Fruitlands, owned by Baron Louis Berckmans, a Belgian horticulturist who popularized the azalea in America.

Ballybunion

The Old Course, Ballybunion, County Kerry, Republic of Ireland

A round of golf on the Old Course at Ballybunion is a unique experience. None other than Tom Watson would agree. He was very much responsible for alerting the world to the existence of this place, which was largely unknown outside Ireland when he first visited in 1981. It is now acknowledged as one of the world's greatest courses, and many a star golfer has made the pilgrimage to play it.

Ballybunion is a long-established club, founded in 1893 in the far west of Ireland on a stretch of quite incomparable dunes overlooking the Atlantic Ocean. There are many golf courses in the west of Ireland set on dunes overlooking the Atlantic, but what sets Ballybunion apart is the way the course is routed over, through, across and along the dunes. So the golfer is asked to play a huge catalogue of different shots throughout the round to adapt to the constantly changing topography.

NATURAL HAZARDS

The Old Course excites golfers of all abilities. The round starts ominously, for there is a graveyard awaiting the merest slice from the 1st tee, and from here to the corner of the dogleg on the 6th the course slides into gear rather as an Irish morning slowly gathers momentum. At this point the adrenaline kicks in, with a delicious pitch up to a green on top of the dunes, the first of a series of greens that seriously tests every aspect of the

Below The full might, majesty, dominion and power of Ballybunion is encapsulated in the conjunction of the wonderfully sited 10th green and, beyond it, the magical 11th fairway.

approach game. This hole has no need of a bunker and, once away from the opening (inland) holes, there are remarkably few bunkers on the course as a whole. Such is the brilliance of the green sites that grassy swales and fall-aways protect the holes even more strongly than sand would.

One of the finest holes on the course – one of the world's great holes – has no bunker, either. It is the unforgettable 11th, a gorgeous hole tumbling down through the sand hills alongside the Atlantic, with a green cleverly defended by encircling dunes. There are great holes still to come, but it was the short 8th that particularly appealed to Watson on his first visit, with an all-or-nothing shot to a tiny green and desperate recovery work required should the tee shot fail to hold the putting surface.

Ballybunion boasts back-to-back par 3s on the inward half: the 14th and 15th. Like every hole on this course, they were dictated naturally by the exciting coastal land forms, and the 15th is a great short hole, played to a marvellous green backed by the Atlantic Ocean. Following this, the excellent 16th and 17th both make excursions to the oceanside. Ballybunion should be on every golfer's must-play list.

● *Ballybunion was enlarged into an 18-hole course in 1926. The designer was Fred Smith. His layout was so good that when Tom Simpson was engaged to upgrade it in 1937 he suggested only three minor changes to the course.*

COASTAL EROSION

It is the stuff of nightmares: seeing your course washed away by the unstoppable power of the sea. Ballybunion faced the prospect of losing some of its finest holes to the Atlantic Ocean in the 1970s. An appeal was launched, and that was when Ballybunion found that it had friends – and generous ones – all over the world. With the threat of global warming raising sea levels, erosion is now on the agendas of many golf clubs throughout the world.

CARD OF THE COURSE

Hole	Yards	Par	Hole	Yards	Par
1	392	4	10	359	4
2	445	4	11	449	4
3	220	3	12	192	3
4	498	5	13	484	5
5	508	5	14	131	3
6	364	4	15	216	3
7	423	4	16	490	5
8	153	3	17	385	4
9	454	4	18	379	4
Out	3,457	36	In	3,085	35
			Total	6,542	71

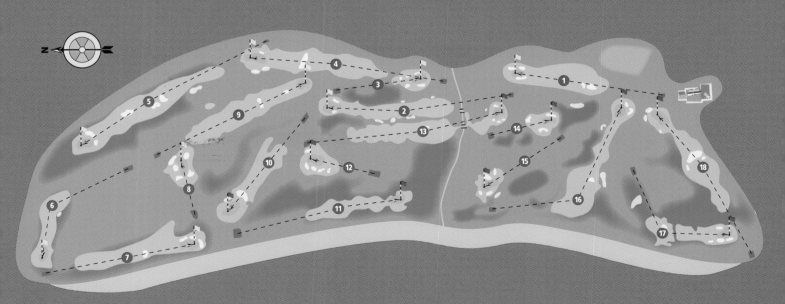

Banff Springs

Stanley Thompson 18, Fairmont Banff Springs Hotel, Banff, Alberta, Canada

Early golf courses simply evolved. Golfers found a route through whatever natural obstacles existed where they had chosen to play. There was minimal earth moving. The emergence of the earliest course architects, such as Old Tom Morris, towards the end of the nineteenth century was accompanied by earth moving on a very small scale – as much as a couple of men with shovels, or possibly with a horse and scraper, could move. Enter the steam shovel. It could not exactly move mountains, but it could shift a large amount of dirt in a day. Throw in dynamite and almost anything became possible – or it did if you had a huge budget at your disposal.

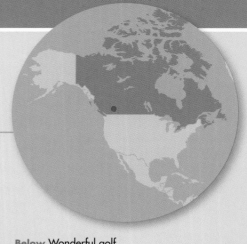

Below Wonderful golf in an exquisite setting. Stanley Thompson's course at Banff Springs is exceptional – the 4th hole is, quite simply, one of the greatest holes in golf.

The enormous Banff Springs Hotel belonged to the Canadian Pacific Railway (CPR). It was the jewel in their crown, standing proudly overlooking the Spray and Bow rivers and surrounded by the stunning scenery of the Rocky Mountains. It had had a golf course of sorts since 1911, but it hardly matched up to the rest of the facilities on offer at this world-class hotel. The CPR had money and they also had railway trucks – trainloads of them. They had seen what Canadian architect Stanley Thompson had achieved at Jasper Park, the resort of their rival railway Canadian National, so they hired Thompson themselves.

LUCKY ACCIDENT

Banff's most famous hole, the 4th, known as the Devil's Cauldron, was not part of Thompson's original plan. He had no intention of using this area of the extensive property. However, during the winter of 1927, when heavy snows and bitter temperatures had halted construction work, an avalanche created a new glacial lake. When Thompson returned to Banff he spotted the lake and immediately grasped its potential as the basis for a world-class short hole.

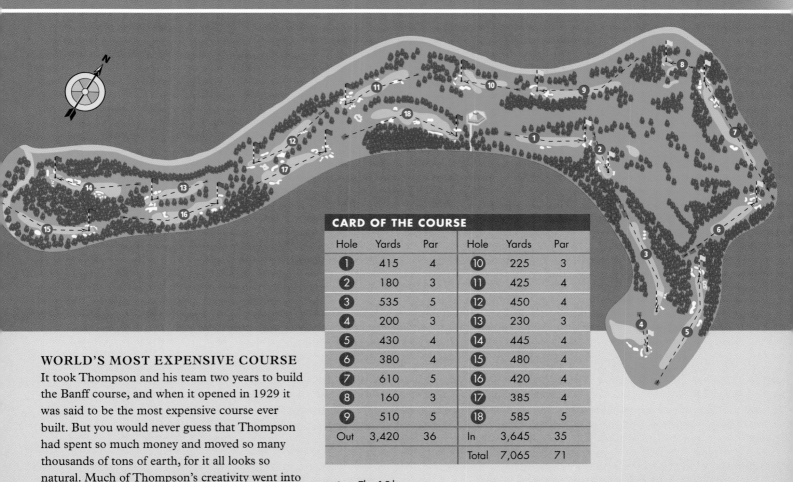

CARD OF THE COURSE

Hole	Yards	Par	Hole	Yards	Par
1	415	4	10	225	3
2	180	3	11	425	4
3	535	5	12	450	4
4	200	3	13	230	3
5	430	4	14	445	4
6	380	4	15	480	4
7	610	5	16	420	4
8	160	3	17	385	4
9	510	5	18	585	5
Out	3,420	36	In	3,645	35
			Total	7,065	71

WORLD'S MOST EXPENSIVE COURSE

It took Thompson and his team two years to build the Banff course, and when it opened in 1929 it was said to be the most expensive course ever built. But you would never guess that Thompson had spent so much money and moved so many thousands of tons of earth, for it all looks so natural. Much of Thompson's creativity went into ensuring that manufactured features, such as bunkers, raised greens and mounds, were perfectly scaled to the grandeur of the surrounding forests and mountains. As a result of such empathy, the course is not overwhelmed by the scenery.

In recent years a new clubhouse has been erected and the original order of playing the holes abandoned. So the course now starts with a hole that throws the golfer straight into the forests, while the next two holes turn to face Mount Rundle. Thompson needed dynamite to blast away enough room to build the 3rd fairway and to clear the site for the 4th green, but it was well worth it, for the 4th is a world-class short hole (ranked in the world's top four by *Golf Magazine*), calling for a drop-shot down over a glacial lake to find a well-bunkered green on the far side. After three more holes in the forests the course emerges for a sequence of beautiful holes beside the Bow River.

Thompson's original opening hole is now the 15th and many an experienced golfer has stood on that tee and been knocked off their game by the sight ahead, with the sparkling Spray River far below and the tree-lined and bunker-strewn fairway uncomfortably distant on its far side.

Below The 15th, once considered to be the grandest opening hole in the world.

Barnbougle Dunes

Barnbougle Dunes, Bridport, Tasmania, Australia

One of the most exciting golf courses to have been built in Australia in recent years is unexpectedly far from the usual tourist resorts, being located on Tasmania's north coast on what was an otherwise unusable stretch of land on an extensive potato farm. Its owner had no interest in golf, but a young man called Greg Ramsay spotted the potential of the thin strip of duneland and, after much persuasion, convinced the owner that a great course might be built there. It fell upon vogue designer Tom Doak to realize the land's potential, which he has done brilliantly.

The ground on which Barnbougle Dunes is built is a very narrow coastal plot, reminiscent of the traditional 18-hole out-and-back courses such as Royal Aberdeen or the Old Course at St Andrews. Here, however, instead of the clubhouse being located at one end of the course it has been built in the middle, thereby providing two loops of out-and-back nines. Every hole, with the exception of the 2nd, is thus provided with a border of sea and/or dunes on both sides of the fairway.

Fortunately, Doak's style is to create wide fairways that have enough space to allow the high-handicapper to cope with the demands of the omnipresent wind, while also offering multiple

Below A great short par 4, the 4th is a fine example of Tom Doak's skill in creating wonderfully appealing holes that, nevertheless, have a sting in the tail.

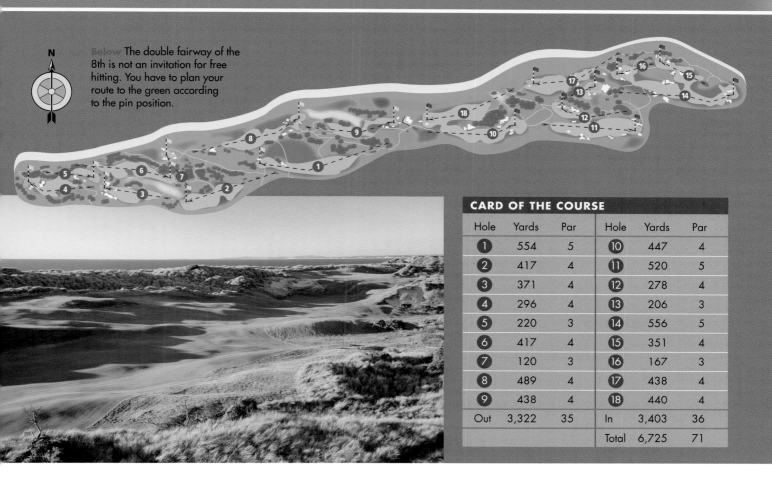

N

Below The double fairway of the 8th is not an invitation for free hitting. You have to plan your route to the green according to the pin position.

CARD OF THE COURSE

Hole	Yards	Par	Hole	Yards	Par
1	554	5	10	447	4
2	417	4	11	520	5
3	371	4	12	278	4
4	296	4	13	206	3
5	220	3	14	556	5
6	417	4	15	351	4
7	120	3	16	167	3
8	489	4	17	438	4
9	438	4	18	440	4
Out	3,322	35	In	3,403	36
			Total	6,725	71

'I hated those dunes, it was just land where I couldn't grow potatoes.'

RICHARD SATTLER, OWNER OF BARNBOUGLE DUNES

● Barnbougle Dunes is unusual for a contemporary, world-ranked course in having two par 4s (4th and 12th) measuring under 300 yards/274 m from the very back tees.

● Accommodation for visiting golfers is provided, not in a hugely expensive hotel, but in a row of charming cottages in the style of traditional beach huts.

playing options to the golfer proficient enough to be able to utilize them. Such options are particularly appealing when the architect has been confident enough to employ them on a short par 4, such as the 296-yard/271-m 4th.

You cannot preplan how to play the 4th hole. You simply have to wait until you get there, find out what the wind is up to and where the pin has been cut and start plotting back from there, taking into account your own strengths and weaknesses. Holes of this length and of such distinction are rare. It is to be hoped that it is never lengthened, whatever developments of club and ball may lie in the future.

The par-3 5th is another timeless hole, calling for a tee shot that rolls on landing, letting the contours feed the ball to the pin.

ARCHITECTURAL BRILLIANCE

What makes Tom Doak one of the outstanding architects of our time is his willingness to be unconventional if it results in the right hole for the right place. There is a prime example at the 13th, a substantial par 3 of 206 yards/188 m. With modern equipment this is well within reach of a long iron for most, but what sets the hole apart is the green. It is so imaginatively contoured that the normal high, stopping shot is simply not right. Control of length and shape of shot is required, to feed the ball into the correct part of the green to allow the extraordinary contours to carry it onto the section of putting surface on which the pin is located for the day. Thanks to Doak's vivid imagination golfers are required to respond with equal imagination in the way they tackle each hole.

At Barnbougle Dunes Doak was joined by Michael Clayton, a tour golfer turned course designer with an equally original architectural mind. We should expect more mould-breaking courses to emerge in Australia in the future.

Blue Canyon

Canyon Course, Blue Canyon Country Club, Phuket, Thailand

Thailand is awash with golf courses, some good, some very good. The most celebrated of them all is Blue Canyon, a country club with two brilliant courses, situated in a heavenly spot looking out on to the blue waters of the Andaman Sea, with the Phang Nga mountains creating an inviting terrestrial backdrop. It is fabulously beautiful, but it was not always so. In former times this was a tin mine and rubber plantation.

When it was decided to develop a golf course here, Yoshikazu Kato was engaged as course architect, with a brief to keep the shifting of earth to a minimum and to utilize the natural features of the property. He had been given a helping hand with honouring his brief because huge quantities of earth had already been moved in the tin-mining days, and the abandoned workings had filled with the rainwater that falls so abundantly in Thailand to form a network of lakes and ponds. In this climate the rapidly growing vegetation has also assisted in softening the once stark features. Kato began with the Canyon Course, which was built in 1991. The Lakes Course followed in 1999 and more than lives up to its name – there are water hazards on 17 of the 18 holes.

Below The 14th is a deceptive hole, playing shorter than you think because of the big drop from tee to green, and it can be complicated by crosswinds.

CARD OF THE COURSE

Hole	Yards	Par	Hole	Yards	Par
1	390	4	10	392	4
2	218	3	11	600	5
3	449	4	12	440	4
4	407	4	13	390	4
5	398	4	14	194	3
6	556	5	15	586	5
7	205	3	16	357	4
8	412	4	17	221	3
9	561	5	18	403	4
Out	3,596	36	In	3,583	36
			Total	7,179	72

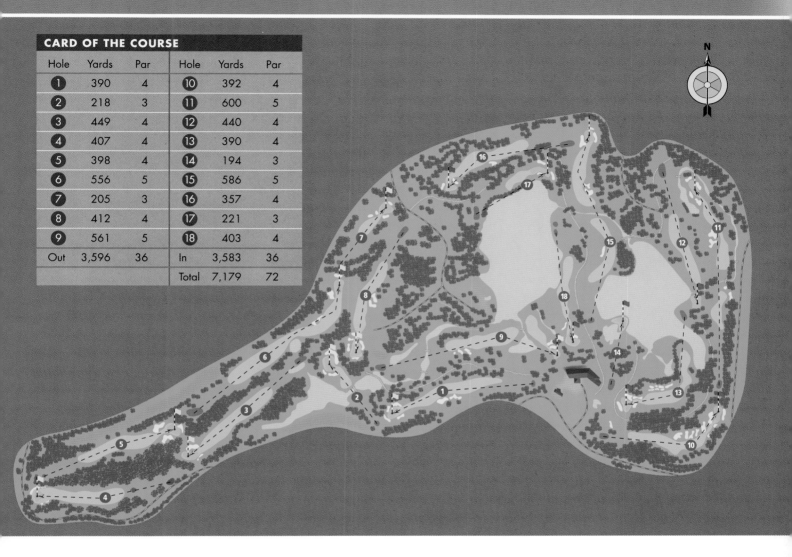

THE CANYON COURSE

After a reasonably straightforward opening hole, water is encountered for the first time on the 2nd hole, a par 3 of some length. On the 3rd a huge calabash tree, standing in the middle of the fairway, confronts the golfer. Which way round it do you go? Accuracy off the tee and precise approach shots to tiered greens are called for on the otherwise fairly short par 4s going to the turn, while the stiff par 5s are a foretaste of the challenges ahead.

The sea views from the 10th tee are superb, while the hole itself is a manageable dogleg to the left. Then comes a 600-yard/549-m monster of a par 5, with water adding complications for the long hitter. Water is present on the next hole as well, and there are strategic decisions concerning water to be made on the par-3 14th, with its kidney-shaped island green, and on the 15th, too. The 17th, squeezed between trees to the left and water to the right, is an outstanding short hole, while the water-troubled 18th ensures that the pressure is kept up right to the very end of this delightful course.

TIGER TRIUMPHANT

The 1994 Johnnie Walker Classic was played on the Canyon Course. Greg Norman stormed round the course on the final day in 64 for victory. Finishing in a tie for 34th place was a young amateur, Tiger Woods. In 1998, Woods, now a professional, returned to Blue Canyon for the Johnnie Walker Classic. Beginning the last round nine shots behind the leader, Ernie Els, he dug deep and caught up with Els on the final green. Woods won the play-off. It was an immensely popular victory, not least because Tiger's mother is herself from Thailand.

Cape Kidnappers

Cape Kidnappers Golf Course, Hawke's Bay, North Island, New Zealand

For many years New Zealand has been something of a golfing sleeper. Despite the natural advantages of climate and setting, few courses realized their true potential, Paraparaumu Beach being one of the exceptions. Now there are two spectacular modern courses – Kauri Cliffs and Cape Kidnappers – that have raised the bar enormously, just as their American developer, Julian Robertson, has raised the bar in golf tourism in New Zealand.

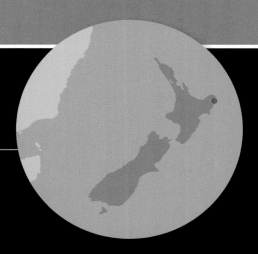

The name, Cape Kidnappers, is sufficient to suggest that here are to be found stunning seascapes and any number of fabulous holes exploiting them. But the key to maximizing the potential of a site of this kind is what you do with the rest of the course. It would be disappointing to have to play dull holes on dull ground simply as a means of getting to the exceptional holes. In choosing Tom Doak as the designer, Robertson was on to a winner, for Doak is a master at routing a golf course, ensuring that every hole is of golfing interest, that there is a good balance between sorts and styles of holes and that the entire course is memorable. He and his team walked the site many times before setting to work, taking in the enormity of the task, getting to know every detail of the ground and simply coming to terms with the magnificent canvas he had been given to work on. Here, Doak was able to exploit his talent for locating stunning green sites.

Below The spectacular setting of the stretch of holes from the 14th to the 17th is wonderfully captured in this aerial photograph. The 14th and 17th greens are in the foreground.

CARD OF THE COURSE

Hole	Yards	Par	Hole	Yards	Par
1	440	4	10	430	4
2	540	5	11	224	3
3	215	3	12	460	4
4	544	5	13	130	3
5	420	4	14	348	4
6	225	3	15	650	5
7	453	4	16	500	5
8	182	3	17	463	4
9	403	4	18	480	4
Out	3,422	35	In	3,685	36
			Total	7,107	71

'The 15th is quite possibly the most difficult, intimidating, and dangerous long hole in golf.'

MICHAEL CLAYTON, *WORLD ATLAS OF GOLF*

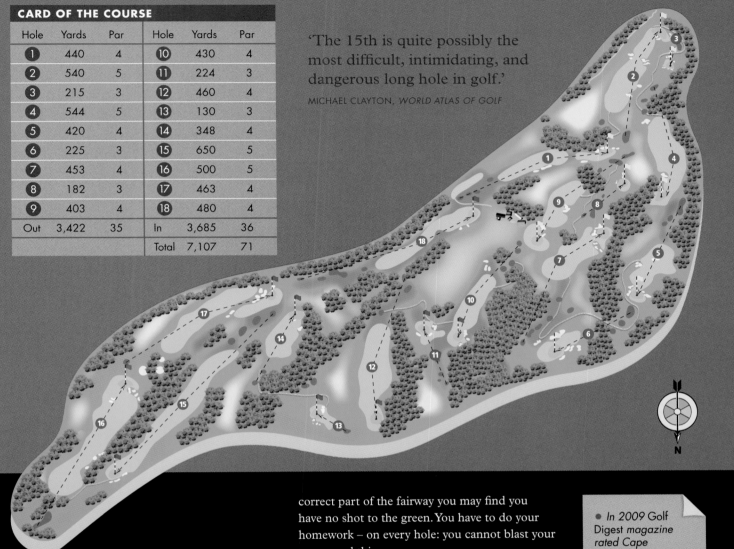

WIDTH AND OPTIONS

Doak has rebelled against the 'total' architecture of many of his contemporaries: not for him narrow fairways that call for target golf on every shot. Instead, where possible, Doak provides width, just as Alister MacKenzie did in the early twentieth century. And, just as MacKenzie's greens were defended cleverly, so that you had to conjure up a different kind of approach shot depending on where you were on the fairway, Doak requires you to use your imagination by giving you choice.

You are, for instance, given a lovely wide fairway on the 1st, tempting you into a big drive. But the green is angled across the line of the fairway, and it is cleverly bunkered. Unless you are in the correct part of the fairway you may find you have no shot to the green. You have to do your homework – on every hole: you cannot blast your way round this course.

Cape Kidnappers would be a fine course even if it consisted solely of holes comparable with the early ones, but it is at the 12th that it becomes exceptional, with a string of breathtaking clifftop holes. And that 12th green – sitting on the skyline between heaven and hell! It is followed by a short hole on the very edge of the cliffs and then a clever drive-and-pitch hole made particularly devilish by a demon of a pot bunker. This gives way to a 650-yard/594-m par 5 of incredible beauty and great treachery: to the left there is a vertiginous drop to the ocean; to the right a ball-swallowing ravine. Although a stroke might be rescued at the 16th, the two closing holes are decidedly tough, with Doak making you think until the very last putt has dropped.

● In 2009 *Golf Digest* magazine rated Cape Kidnappers the 13th best course in the world outside the United States – a significant accolade for a course opened only in 2004.

● Captain Cook named this spot Cape Kidnappers in 1769, following a Maori's attempt to abduct his cabin boy from his ship, HMS Endeavour.

Carnoustie

Championship Course, Carnoustie Golf Links, Angus, Scotland

Is Carnoustie the toughest course on the Open Championship roster? The way it was prepared for the 1999 Open, played in the wind and rain, it certainly was, Paul Lawrie's winning score being six over par. It was more sympathetically prepared for the 2007 Open, when Padraig Harrington and Sergio Garcia tied on 277, seven under par, Harrington winning in a four-hole play-off. What most observers were agreed on was that this set-up displayed all the greatness of this historic links, and in particular that there were often two or three different strategies for playing a particular hole, depending on a golfer's strengths and weaknesses, the wind and the weather.

Below The Barry Burn, snaking across the 17th and 18th. Jean Van de Velde's skirmishes with it cost him a seven in the 1999 Open Championship, when a six would have won it.

It is not certain when golf began in Carnoustie (probably over 500 years ago) but it was some time around 1842 that Allan Robertson – the pre-eminent golfer at that time – was brought from St Andrews to lay out a ten-hole course on the Barry Links. Another St Andrews stalwart, Old Tom Morris, made considerable alterations in 1867, expanding the course to 18 holes, and James Braid made the final significant changes in 1926.

THE LONGEST BRITISH OPEN COURSE

Carnoustie hosted its first Open Championship in 1931, with Scottish-born American Tommy Armour coming from five behind to win. As a championship course it has always been among the longest. For the 2007 Open it measured a daunting 7,421 yards/6,778 m, the longest ever, with two par 4s reaching almost 500 yards/457 m, yet such is the prowess of today's professionals with modern equipment that many forsook their drivers, taking long irons from the tee. They did it simply because you cannot blast your way round this course. You have to plot your way around it. The bunkers are deep, gathering and perfectly positioned; the rough can be savage; out of bounds threatens on several holes; and the Jockie's and Barry burns were brilliantly incorporated into the design, especially on the last two holes.

Jockie's Burn, for instance, limits the length of the tee shot on the challenging 5th, putting

pressure on the approach to a snaking, multi-level green, cunningly bunkered and over 50 yards/46 m deep. Out of bounds waits to wreck scores on the long 6th, causing many an errant tee shot to be pushed into the deep rough on the other side. Of all the hazards it is the Barry Burn that is most feared, very largely because it comes

into play viciously on the last two holes, hard on the heels of the 16th, a seriously long par 3 on which only the straightest of tee shots can pierce the bunkered mounds guarding the front of the green. Birdies here are rare, dropped shots frequent. The 17th then strikes out over the burn, which meanders hugely, creating almost an island fairway, with length restricted where the burn crosses it.

Still to come is the scariest drive of them all, back over the Barry Burn to another narrow fairway, once again bounded by the burn. Even after a successful drive, there remains the long second to the green, which lies perilously close to the out-of-bounds fence and is, naturally, only just beyond yet another meander of the dreaded burn. What a tough hole!

● Almost 300 young men from Carnoustie have emigrated to the United States to work as golf professionals. The Smith brothers from Carnoustie had an enviable professional record: Alex was twice US Open champion, Willie once, and Macdonald came second to Bobby Jones in both the British Open and the US Open in 1930.

CARD OF THE COURSE

Hole	Yards	Par	Hole	Yards	Par
1	406	4	10	466	4
2	463	4	11	383	4
3	358	4	12	499	4
4	412	4	13	176	3
5	415	4	14	514	5
6	578	5	15	472	4
7	410	4	16	248	3
8	183	3	17	461	4
9	478	4	18	499	4
Out	3,703	36	In	3,718	35
			Total	7,421	71

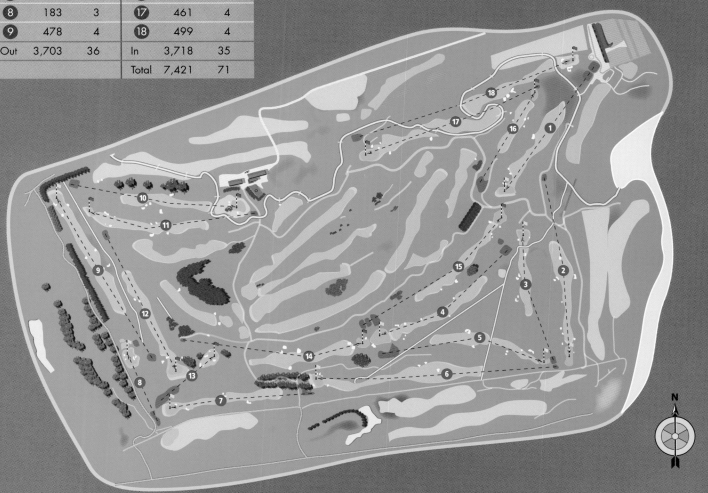

Fancourt

The Links, Fancourt Hotel and Country Club, George, South Africa

Late on 23 November 2003, the Links played host to one of golf's greatest duels. The US and International teams of the President's Cup, tied at the end of four days of golf, sent one player each to settle the match with a head-to-head, sudden-death play-off. As darkness fell on the picturesque course, an estimated 800 million people worldwide watched Ernie Els and Tiger Woods battle for the cup.

With the first two holes halved, both players faced long par-saving putts on the third play-off hole. Tiger holed out from 15 feet/4.5 m to leave Els with a putt of 8 feet/2.5 m to keep the match alive. Opposing captain Jack Nicklaus later said, 'There wasn't anybody in the world who wanted to see you miss that putt.' Els holed out, and captains Nicklaus and Player epitomized the spirit of the game by agreeing to a tie and sharing the cup.

Designed by Gary Player, this strikingly beautiful course sweeps through mounds at the feet of the Outeniqua Mountains, the dunes creating a links-like experience. These mounds are often assumed to be natural because they seem so in keeping with the surrounding mountains, but they are actually the result of a huge amount of earth moving. In fact, from the mounds down the right of the 13th, there is a good view of the flat farmland that is the land's natural state. But natural or not, the course plays like a links, those carefully created mounds enveloping the fairways, and fierce pot bunkers protecting tough greens.

Below The key to producing a links-like playing experience is scaling the artificial undulations so that they are not overwhelmed by the mountain background, as demonstrated here on the 15th hole.

CARD OF THE COURSE

Hole	Yards	Par	Hole	Yards	Par
1	396	4	10	408	4
2	236	3	11	161	3
3	469	4	12	481	4
4	494	4	13	533	5
5	549	5	14	361	4
6	341	4	15	477	4
7	476	4	16	584	5
8	202	3	17	186	3
9	609	5	18	616	5
Out	3,772	36	In	3,807	37
			Total	7,579	73

RISK AND REWARD

Gary Player's trademark design features – risk and reward, playability to all skill levels – exist throughout the course. Powerful hitters have opportunities to make long carries on most holes, and there is temptation to drive both short par 4s: the 6th and 14th. However, the drives must be perfect, because the holes are cleverly designed, with large pot bunkers and thick rough on the dunes ready to gobble up wild shots.

Multiple tees successfully keep the course interesting to all golfers, so an exciting contest will arise between a long hitter and a short accurate player. On all too many other courses the holes are consistently too tight for the long hitter, or too long for the player relying on accuracy. It is this element of the design that made the course perfect for the match play of the President's Cup, as one player could lay up safely in the fairway, allowing his partner to take on the aggressive lines.

The long par-4 15th is reminiscent of the 18th at Sawgrass, doglegging left around marshland. However, the unsung hero is the par-3 17th. With a stone-walled burn short and left, most golfers play out to the right, leaving themselves a tough chip across a slick green. Trees behind the green add confusion about wind direction. This is when you should turn for advice to one of the caddies at Fancourt, said to be among the best in the world.

FANCOURT'S FOUR COURSES

The Links is the highest-profile course of four at Fancourt. The Montagu has been upgraded by David McLay Kidd, designer of Bandon Dunes in Oregon, USA, while the Outeniqua is a 7,000-yard/6,400-m Gary Player design. To play these courses you must be a guest at the resort. The public-access course is Bramble Hill, designed by Player to give 'golfers of every level a Fancourt experience'.

Kiawah Island

Ocean Course, Kiawah Island Golf Resort, South Carolina, USA

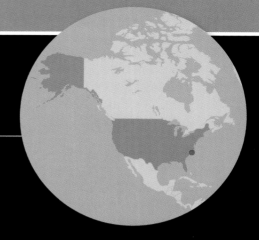

Never has a name rung so true as 'The Ocean Course', for the Atlantic Ocean is in view on every single hole. Ten holes are directly on the coast – the greatest number of seaside holes on any course in the northern hemisphere – and the other eight play parallel to them. This remarkable feature not only provides some of the most scenic golf imaginable, but also means the course is massively affected by the wind. As with the 17th at Sawgrass, this trademark was not intended by the designer Pete Dye, who had planned to sit the course behind the dunes until his wife and co-designer Alice suggested raising it in order to provide the stunning sea views.

Below The sand areas are not considered hazards, so you may ground your club. This is the par-4 9th hole.

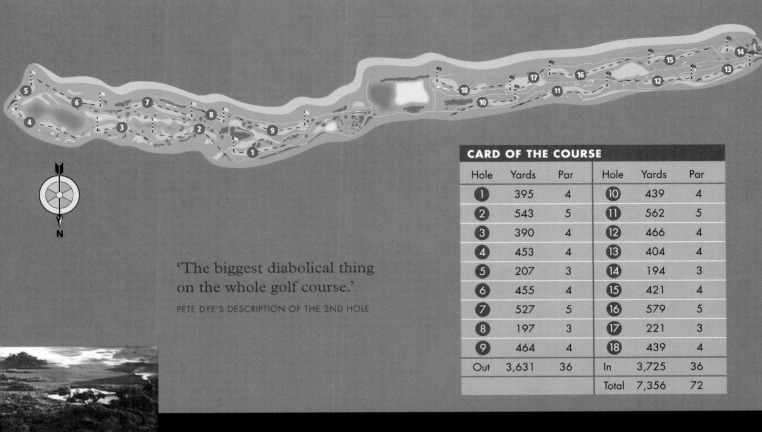

'The biggest diabolical thing
on the whole golf course.'

PETE DYE'S DESCRIPTION OF THE 2ND HOLE

CARD OF THE COURSE

Hole	Yards	Par	Hole	Yards	Par
1	395	4	10	439	4
2	543	5	11	562	5
3	390	4	12	466	4
4	453	4	13	404	4
5	207	3	14	194	3
6	455	4	15	421	4
7	527	5	16	579	5
8	197	3	17	221	3
9	464	4	18	439	4
Out	3,631	36	In	3,725	36
			Total	7,356	72

The unbelievable beauty of the course disguises its brutal difficulty. Dye made use of the natural environment, with dunes and tall grasses devouring poor shots. The most distinctive design feature is that different shot options are always available. Many holes reward daring carries, but players are never forced to take these lines. From the tee and fairway, players must pick a shot to suit their ability and the conditions.

The wide range of options makes for innovative golf, and it is also mandatory on a course so affected by the wind. It has been estimated that wind changes can alter club selection by up to eight clubs, so there needs to be a route for every strength and direction of wind.

CREATIVE CHALLENGES

Extensive lakes and vast tracts of sandy waste await the inaccurate shot, making this a fine match-play course but the very devil on which to keep a medal card going. The par-5 2nd hole is a good reflection of the course. From the tee, players will be struck by the epic view towards the ocean. But they will also be faced with golfing dilemmas in choosing the correct angle from the tee to cross the marshland, which spells golfing disaster if you come up short. A safe shot plays out right for the less bold. If the drive was overly cautious, the second shot must be laid up short of another marsh, 110 yards/101 m in front of the green. Good players should be able to get around the green in two, but that is not the end of the story, as the green is a difficult raised shelf, rolling away into a deep bunker. After a gentle opening hole, the 2nd can be a real nemesis, and even the professionals rack up big scores here. In the 1991 Ryder Cup, Seve Ballesteros won the 2nd with a double bogey to Wayne Levi's 8!

Like a true links, the options for shot making are endless, and the longer holes tend to offer a route in on the ground, as well as an airborne approach. You are continually challenged to think hard and pick the right shot. With the design so demanding of creative golf it is no surprise that the Ryder Cup was such a success, and that the course was selected to host the 2012 US PGA Championship.

Les Bordes

Les Bordes, Saint Laurent-Nouan, France

When the sun rises above the Sologne forests and illuminates the rolling fairways and shimmering lakes, there are few places better to wake up than in the traditional Loire Valley cottages that provide accommodation at Les Bordes. The location is hard to beat, and the quality of golf is such that Les Bordes is consistently ranked as one of the finest and toughest courses in continental Europe.

For centuries, monarchs, politicians and wealthy industrialists have chosen to live in the Loire region, for it combines idyllic tranquillity with easy access to Paris. Les Bordes, opened in 1986, was the brainchild of industrialist Baron Marcel Bich, who made his fortune from his ballpoint pen company, Bic, and his trading partner Yoshiaki Sakurai. They decided to build a course in the grounds of the Baron's hunting lodge. Although the project might have seemed risky, as the area had no golfing history, these captains of industry knew that their 'dream course' could be carved out of this beautiful area.

Robert von Hagge was the Texan architect chosen to transform dream into reality, drawing on his experience of over 200 courses to create a stunning design that makes full use of the natural features of the land. He went on to build up a distinguished portfolio of golf courses in France, and many cite his course at Seignosse in southwest France as one of his best.

Above The 7th is a wicked hole, almost turning back on itself. It is the sort of hole, making great use of water, that is now almost obligatory in resort golf.

SOLOGNE BACKWATERS

Establishing a golf resort in the backwaters of the Sologne was a bold move. This was not typical golf course country – the Sologne is famous in France for its winged game, prized by gastronomes as the best in the country. Baron Bich chose his architect well, for Robert von Hagge was not afraid of felling forests or creating minor lakes to carve his course out of unpromising material. The course is noted for its bold gestures, yet von Hagge succeeded in maintaining the Sologne country atmosphere.

A SUPREME LAKESIDE CHALLENGE

Sologne's lakes protect 12 of the holes at Les Bordes, while the forest and undulating mounds eat into the narrow fairways. Inventive bunkers are also common. Indeed all these troubles await the golfer on the 1st hole. An intimidating carry over a lake makes for a daunting first tee shot, and from there the fairway narrows and veers right, skirting the edge of the forest. Though the green is fairly large, it is almost surrounded by an enormous bunker. It's a tough opening hole, but a fair reflection of the challenges to come.

Baron Bich's favourite hole was reputedly the 7th. It epitomizes the marriage between design and landscape that makes Les Bordes so special. A solid tee shot is a must on this par 5, as the landing zone is well protected by water. The fairway turns at right angles, and, given a perfect

● Although the course is extremely demanding, it is impossible not to enjoy the round. The whole experience is uplifting, from waking up in that charming cottage, playing the teasing course, being at one with nature, to enjoying the region's traditional food and wine. The dream course is reality!

drive, the green is reachable in two. However, it calls for strong nerves as the second shot is played almost entirely over water. Even a lay-up requires a decent shot played to a severely angled fairway.

One of the few waterless holes, the 15th requires accuracy to avoid a long bunker on the right. Following the picturesque holes that sweep through lakes and forests, the 15th may appear to be somewhere to catch your breath. Far from it – the bunker provides enough difficulty from the tee and the approach shot is played through seemingly endless undulations before the bunkerless green.

CARD OF THE COURSE

Hole	Yards	Par	Hole	Yards	Par
1	439	4	10	512	5
2	522	5	11	399	4
3	388	4	12	413	4
4	165	3	13	185	3
5	435	4	14	558	5
6	385	4	15	437	4
7	507	5	16	215	3
8	156	3	17	454	4
9	390	4	18	447	4
Out	3,387	36	In	3,620	36
			Total	7,007	72

Merion

East Course, Ardmore, Pennsylvania, USA

'I love Merion. It is one of those old-time golf courses that doesn't have the length of some of the modern-day courses, but still stands the test. That's the mark of a great golf course to me.' That was Jack Nicklaus's opinion of Merion East, one of two distinctive courses at this great club on the outskirts of Philadelphia. It held the record for being the shortest course in modern times to host the US Open, which it last did in 1981. Happily, Merion has been reinstated on the US Open roster and will see the return of this great championship in 2013.

Merion's golfing beginnings lay, strangely enough, with the members of the Merion Cricket Club. Having formed a golf section, they laid out a nine-hole course in Haverford, but it soon proved too short and too restrictive for their ambitions. One of the club's young members, Hugh Wilson, had captained the golf team at Princeton, and in 1910 he was despatched to Britain for seven months to study the architecture of the best courses there. Perhaps it is no surprise, then, that there is a feeling of both English heathland and Scottish links about Merion, and the bunkering is every bit as formidable as that on any of the British Open links.

AN AURA OF PERFECTION
The distinguished golf course designer Tom Doak maintains that Merion's East Course is probably the only course that any major golf architect would find it difficult, if not impossible, to improve. That is quite a tribute to Wilson, who had never designed anything before.

Key to survival at Merion is to avoid the bunkers. There are 128 of them and a third of those are encountered in the first three holes. Key to winning at Merion is to overcome the subtleties of the greens, once described by Herbert Warren Wind, the doyen of golf writers, as wonderfully varied, 'plateau greens, bench greens, crown greens, sunken greens, large greens, small greens, two-level greens, three-level greens and greens that slope in a hundred different directions'.

One of the most intimidating opening tee shots is encountered at Merion, not because the hole is any more fearsome than the other 17, but because the tee is located right next to a terrace, under the awning of which members and their guests take their coffee, lunches and teas: the consequences of a snap hook are unthinkable. It is, in fact, a fine hole, calling for precise placement of the tee shot to give access to the cleverly angled green.

Below A ridge crosses the 9th green, making the putting surface uphill at the front and back but downhill in the middle, which Ben Crenshaw described as 'very tough to read'.

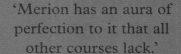

'Merion has an aura of perfection to it that all other courses lack.'

TOM DOAK

HOGAN'S COURAGE

Following a car crash, Ben Hogan played the 1950 US Open at Merion in great pain. On the 13th hole in the final round he told his caddie that he could not go on. 'I don't work for quitters. I'll see you on the 14th tee, Sir,' was the reply. Hogan laboured on and forced his way into a three-way play-off for the title, which he duly won.

CARD OF THE COURSE

Hole	Yards	Par	Hole	Yards	Par
1	350	4	10	325	4
2	556	5	11	367	4
3	219	3	12	403	4
4	597	5	13	120	3
5	504	4	14	438	4
6	487	4	15	411	4
7	345	4	16	430	4
8	359	4	17	246	3
9	206	3	18	505	4
Out	3,623	36	In	3,245	34
			Total	6,868	70

There are only two par 5s at Merion, but length is largely irrelevant here, guile being of the essence. Take the par-4 11th, for instance. Most of us would have no difficulty steering our tee shot downhill to the nominated landing zone, but the pitch to the green is entirely over deep rough; a stream bounds the green to the right and behind, and the putting surface is small and firm. It was on this famous green that Bobby Jones completed his Grand Slam in 1930 by winning the US Amateur Championship.

The finish from the 14th is memorable, with the 16th and 17th being played over the remains of an old quarry, and a formidable drive at the 18th up and over a rock face.

Muirfield

The Honourable Company of Edinburgh Golfers, Muirfield, Gullane, East Lothian, Scotland

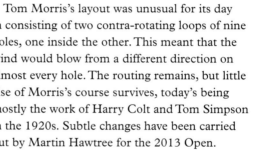

Muirfield is the third home of the Honourable Company of Edinburgh Golfers, who from 1874 began to host the Open Championship in rotation with Prestwick and St Andrews. In 1891 they moved from Musselburgh to Muirfield, nearly 20 miles/32 km to the east of Edinburgh, calling on Old Tom Morris to lay out their new course.

Only a year after it opened, Muirfield hosted its first (and the club's seventh) Open Championship. Fourteen further Opens have followed, as well as the Amateur Championship, Senior Open, Ryder Cup, Walker Cup and Curtis Cup. Some of the greatest names in golf have triumphed at Muirfield, including Vardon, Braid, Hagen, Cotton, Player, Nicklaus, Trevino, Watson, Faldo and Els – an impressive list.

Tom Morris's layout was unusual for its day in consisting of two contra-rotating loops of nine holes, one inside the other. This meant that the wind would blow from a different direction on almost every hole. The routing remains, but little else of Morris's course survives, today's being mostly the work of Harry Colt and Tom Simpson in the 1920s. Subtle changes have been carried out by Martin Hawtree for the 2013 Open.

● Jack Nicklaus, after winning the 1966 Open, said, 'It is essentially a fair course. It has more definition than any links that the Open is played on.' He went on to name the first course he created – in Dublin, Ohio, USA – Muirfield Village.

● It was at Muirfield, in 1892, that the Open Championship was first played over 72 holes. Previously it had been over 36 holes. It was also at Muirfield in 1892 that an entrance fee to play in the Open Championship was first imposed.

● Ben Crenshaw (former US Masters champion and a distinguished golf course architect) praised Muirfield for 'its beautiful honesty as a test of golf'.

Left Muirfield's 12th green is slightly raised, with downslopes and bunkers all around, and, as so often on this course, everything is visible as you play your shot.

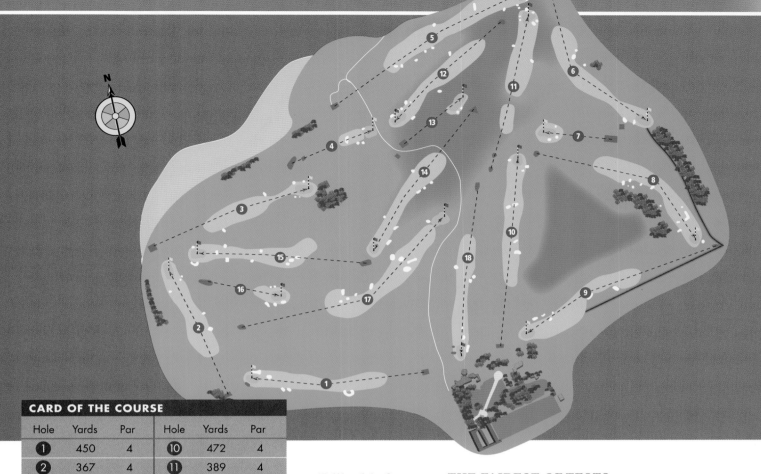

CARD OF THE COURSE

Hole	Yards	Par	Hole	Yards	Par
1	450	4	10	472	4
2	367	4	11	389	4
3	379	4	12	382	4
4	229	3	13	193	3
5	561	5	14	478	4
6	469	4	15	447	4
7	187	3	16	188	3
8	445	4	17	578	5
9	558	5	18	473	4
Out	3,645	36	In	3,600	35
			Total	7,245	71

'I liked it from
the first day
I played it.'

JACK NICKLAUS 1966

THE HONOURABLE COMPANY ON THE MOVE

It was in the Edinburgh suburb of Leith that the Honourable Company of Edinburgh Golfers first held a competition over its five-hole course in 1744. By the 1830s the game had become so popular that the course was overcrowded and members took to playing on the racecourse at Musselburgh. The Company moved there in 1836, initially storing its clubs under the grandstand. In the late nineteenth century overcrowding again became a problem and in 1891 the Company purchased another racecourse, at Dirleton, which was to become the Muirfield course.

THE FAIREST OF TESTS

The course is well respected by the top players, particularly for its fairness: there is little blindness and there are few capricious bounces. It is a good test of driving, the rough being particularly grasping, and some of its bunkering is ferocious. Jack Nicklaus has described the bunkers as 'the most fastidiously built bunkers I have ever seen, the high front walls faced with bricks of turf'.

Perhaps of all the Open courses, Muirfield has no 'stand-out' hole, for it is a very evenly distributed examination of the game, but most players would agree that the 6th, 8th and 18th are among the best long, two-shot holes in links golf. The 13th, too, is a white-knuckle short hole with a long, narrow green perched above five terrifying bunkers. A brilliant escape from one of these set up Ernie Els's Open win in 2002.

From the visitor's point of view, it is worth noting that the club does not introduce temporary tees or winter greens in the off season. You get to play the real course, and for a reduced green fee, to boot.

Oakmont

Oakmont Country Club, Pennsylvania, USA

Oakmont is a family course, owing its whole concept and being to Henry Fownes and his son William. Henry was an exceedingly wealthy steel magnate who purchased a large plot of land near Pittsburgh in 1903 with the idea of creating a world-class golf course. William subsequently became one of America's best amateur golfers, winning the 1910 US Amateur Championship and twice playing in the Walker Cup; he was also very influential in the political sphere of the game. Between them, they created something approaching a golfing behemoth, and had the clout to ensure that it was used for the most prestigious tournaments.

As first built, the course at Oakmont was long but not particularly difficult. It was William Fownes who beefed it up in the 1920s, making it so unforgiving that it has since been called the toughest course in America. For starters he set about rebunkering the course. At one time there were 220; today about 175 remain. For these Fownes devised a venomous rake; it created golf-ball-sized furrows in the sand, which were drawn across the line of play to make escape almost impossible.

And then there were the greens, which were quite unlike any others – a remarkable assortment of sizes and shapes and, in particular, slopes. To make them the most terrifying greens in the world Fownes had them rolled with huge barrels of sand, and insisted that absolutely no watering was done to them. The greens were also cut phenomenally low – shaved – and with the deep, clinging rough grown in to narrow the fairways for a major tournament the course fully justified its macabre reputation. Today's professionals are used to tricked-up courses with lightning-fast greens, but, with the exception perhaps of Augusta, they rarely play courses with such contours to the greens.

Even so, when the US Open was held at Oakmont in 1973, Johnny Miller scored an unbelievable 63 in the last round to win the championship. It is considered by many to be the greatest round of golf ever played.

Above The famous Church Pew bunkers separating the 3rd and 4th fairways. As can be seen from this photograph, the bunkers to the right of the fairway are hardly less intimidating!

'A shot poorly played should
be a shot irrevocably lost.'

WILLIAM FOWNES

CARD OF THE COURSE					
Hole	Yards	Par	Hole	Yards	Par
1	482	4	10	462	4
2	340	4	11	379	4
3	428	4	12	667	5
4	609	5	13	183	3
5	382	4	14	358	4
6	194	3	15	499	4
7	479	4	16	231	3
8	288	3	17	313	4
9	477	5*	18	484	4
Out	3,679	36	In	3,576	35
*4 in men's majors			Total	7,255	71

● Describing
Oakmont's one-time
bunker rakes, which
left furrows 2 inches/
5 cm deep, the
American golfer
Jimmy Demaret once
remarked, 'You could
have combed North
Africa with those and
Rommel wouldn't
have got past
Casablanca.'

GREAT DESIGN

Surprisingly, Oakmont is not grotesque. It is
handsome (more so since the removal of a great
many trees that had threatened to choke the
course) and strategic, and responds to thoughtful
play. The 3rd hole, for instance, is famed for its
Church Pew bunkers – deep sandy trenches
separated by rows of treacherous grass ridges – but
the greater interest is provided by the green, which
is difficult to access, being raised up to repel
anything but the truest of approach shots. Miss
this green and that's when the scrambling starts.

A glance at the card might suggest that the
17th would be a pushover for today's powerful
champions, but it is not. It can be driven, but that
involves successfully carrying a minefield of
bunkers on the left (the direct line from the tee)
and somehow managing to squeeze the ball onto
the putting surface between another bunker and
deceptive low ground to the left. The hole can be
played conservatively, but it is dangerously
tempting to attack – as well as being remarkably
resistant to it. And that seems to sum up so much
about Oakmont.

Pebble Beach

Pebble Beach Golf Links, Pebble Beach, California, USA

Pebble Beach is universally regarded as one of the world's best public courses. It was chosen as the venue for the 110th US Open in 2010, the fifth time it had hosted the championship, yet anybody can simply book a tee time and play on this historic stage. There are, of course, two snags: it is very expensive and you must book long in advance.

Pebble Beach opened in 1919 and ten years later became the first course west of the Mississippi to host the US Amateur Championship. A young Jack Nicklaus capped an impressive amateur career here when he won the 1961 US Amateur; his affection for Pebble Beach never waned, and eventually he bade an emotional farewell to the US Open here in 2000, poignantly sitting on the fence behind the 18th tee, surveying one of the best finishing holes in golf.

The par-5 18th (par 4 for the pros) requires nerves of steel, as the entire hole teeters on the edge of the Pacific. It really should be played as a three-shot hole, often with a 3-wood from the tee. In the 2000 US Open, even Tiger Woods, who would coast to victory by a margin of 15 shots, managed to pull his tee shot into the sea.

Tom Watson showed the perfect way to play the closing holes in the 1982 US Open. With one of golf's most famous chip-ins, he made birdie from the rough on the par-3 17th to claim a one-shot lead over Nicklaus. Sensibly Watson hit a 3-wood for position from the 18th tee and laid up with his second shot in the fairway with a 7-iron to leave himself a short iron approach. Again he played safely, approaching the heart of the green as the pin was tucked behind the front bunker. From there he finished in style, rolling the 20-foot/6-m putt into the cup for a birdie-birdie finish.

GLORIOUS COASTAL HOLES

Stunning holes are abundant here, and from the 4th there is a fabulous sequence of seven consecutive oceanside holes, including the amazing 7th – with wind blowing into your face and the ocean awaiting if you overhit your shot, the prospect from the tee is nerve-racking. The sequence from the 8th to the 10th is one of the greatest trios of consecutive par 4s in world golf. At the 8th, after an exciting drive, you play an awesome approach shot across a corner of the ocean to the typically small and unreceptive green.

Throughout the round you are presented with daunting drives at undulating fairways, but it is the approach shots that call for ingenuity. On one hole with wind behind, only a high fade will stop on the tiny green, but on the next you may be playing straight into the wind and having to hit a low punch shot. The course is designed for inventive golf and backed by breathtaking views. As Billy Andrade once said, 'It's the Holy Grail for us.'

Below Bucking the trend that holes need to be outrageously long to be testing, the diminutive 7th is a mere 109 yards/ 100 m long. Its difficulties are plain to see.

'If I had only one more round to play, I would choose to play it at Pebble Beach.'

JACK NICKLAUS

CARD OF THE COURSE

Hole	Yards	Par	Hole	Yards	Par
1	380	4	10	495	4
2	502	4	11	390	4
3	404	4	12	202	3
4	331	4	13	445	4
5	195	3	14	580	5
6	523	5*	15	397	4
7	109	3	16	403	4
8	428	4	17	208	3
9	505	4	18	543	5
Out	3,377	35	In	3,663	36
*4 in men's majors			Total	7,040	71

Pinehurst

Pinehurst No. 2, Pinehurst Resort, North Carolina, USA

Pinehurst No. 2 stands as a pinnacle of classic golf course design in the United States. Because any major changes to the course happened in its infancy and were overseen by its legendary architect, Donald Ross, the holes share a remarkable harmony.

Ross learned his trade from the best, serving an apprenticeship under Old Tom Morris at St Andrews following a youth spent at Dornoch on Scotland's Sutherland coast. His career then took him to the United States, where he was soon employed at Pinehurst. In 1907 Ross's signature course was completed. His affection for it was such that he built himself a house next to the 3rd green, and the course evolved under his watchful eye. In 1934 the greens were converted from compressed sand (which was common in the southern states at that time) to grass, and in 1935 the layout was altered for the last time until a year-long facelift was carried out under the

Below The daunting approach to the 5th green on Pinehurst No. 2. The putting surface is raised up in typical Ross fashion, repelling all but the most truly struck golf shots.

supervision of Ben Crenshaw for the 2014 US Open and Women's US Open. Championship tees were extended, fairways widened and rough replaced with areas of hardpan, sand, pine straw and wiregrass, in order to reflect the course's original design and strategic values.

'FUN GOLF'

No. 2 has no 'signature holes' as such. It is the collection of all 18 holes that makes this a great course. Wide fairways and large greens reflect Ross's links influence, although here the fairways amble through tall pines. 'Turtle back' greens have always been a feature of the course, rolling away poor shots uncompromisingly. In the 1999 US Open, the professionals demonstrated the difficulties, finding just 52 per cent of the greens in regulation on the first day.

Pinehurst has hosted many great tournaments, but it is the 1999 US Open for which it is best remembered. All the big names were in the hunt at the end, with Woods, Vijay Singh and Phil Mickelson challenging. After playing precision golf all week, Payne Stewart needed a putt of 15 feet/ 5 m on the last to win. 'When I looked up, it was about two feet from the hole and breaking right into the centre of the cup,' he recalled. Stewart was the first person in US Open history to hole a sizeable putt on the last to win.

Woods sums up the attributes of the course: 'I play courses on tour and we all see it – miss the green, atomic lob wedge, hack it out of the rough. That for me is not fun golf. Fun golf is Pinehurst.'

Below The par 3s on Pinehurst's No. 2 course are perhaps less celebrated than the par 4s, but they are each handsome, requiring intelligent and subtle play to tame them. This is the 15th.

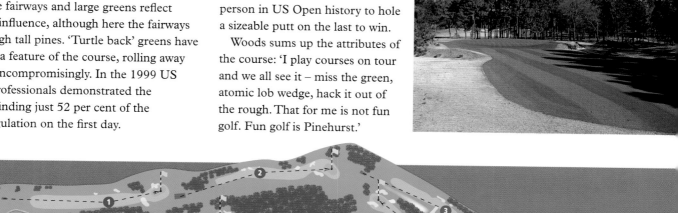

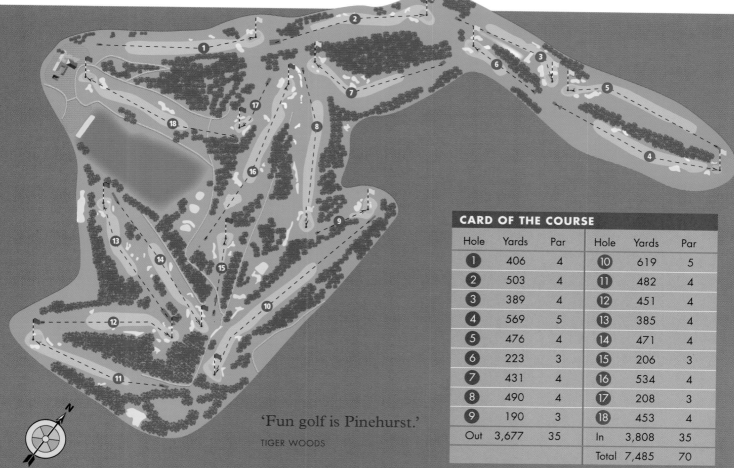

'Fun golf is Pinehurst.'
TIGER WOODS

CARD OF THE COURSE

Hole	Yards	Par	Hole	Yards	Par
1	406	4	10	619	5
2	503	4	11	482	4
3	389	4	12	451	4
4	569	5	13	385	4
5	476	4	14	471	4
6	223	3	15	206	3
7	431	4	16	534	4
8	490	4	17	208	3
9	190	3	18	453	4
Out	3,677	35	In	3,808	35
			Total	7,485	70

Royal Birkdale

Royal Birkdale Golf Club, Southport, Merseyside, England

There is refreshingly little pomp for a club and course with such an august history. The respect of being chosen for the 100th Open Championship and a consistent ranking in the UK Top 10 are quite sufficient for Royal Birkdale.

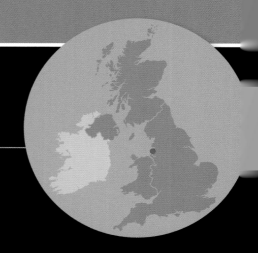

A striking sight greets visitors to Royal Birkdale: a white Art Deco clubhouse resembling a ship sailing on a tossing sea of sand dunes. It was designed in 1935 to replicate the superstructure of the ocean liners that in those days steamed out from Liverpool in considerable numbers, heading for all corners of the British Empire. Within the clubhouse, however, its creature comforts most definitely belong to the twenty-first century.

True links golf is played in partnership with nature, and Birkdale's course uses little trickery or human intervention to create its challenges, the difficulties arising instead from subtle design and substantial distances. Thick rough and willow scrub devour errant shots, and act as a wonderful haven for a wide variety of wildlife. However, the design (evolved over the years by the Hawtree family of golf course architects) is actually very simple: holes weave through valleys between sand hills, creating flat fairways (for a links!) that offer the reward of a lengthy roll on a well-struck shot, and a good stance for the next shot. The crests and troughs of that tossing sea of sand dunes are omnipresent, but you are troubled by them only if you stray off line. There are some fine tee and green sites high on the dunes, such as the 11th tee and the 12th green.

Above Overlooking the final green, Royal Birkdale's unique clubhouse resembles an ocean liner, so many of which used to steam past the course on their way out from Liverpool.

A PROUD MOMENT FOR GOLF

One of golf's great gentlemen, Jack Nicklaus generously conceded a short but missable putt to Tony Jacklin on the 18th green at the climax of the 1969 Ryder Cup at Birkdale – a gracious gesture that allowed them to halve their match and for the home team to tie with the Americans. 'I am sure you would have holed, but I was not prepared to see you miss,' was Nicklaus's brotherly remark to his opponent.

A LONG AND DISTINGUISHED CHAMPIONSHIP HISTORY

Host to the Open Championship on nine occasions between 1954 and 2008, Royal Birkdale always proves to be an outstanding venue, with its fair nature rewarding good play, while the sand hills lining the fairways create a set of perfect natural grandstands for spectators – the best of any course on the Open roster. The overriding feedback from every Open is that the course is hard but fair, and it is a consistent favourite with the professionals.

The difficult 1st, a long, left-hand dogleg, sets the precedent that accurate hitting is key, with out of bounds right, the infamous 'Jutland' bunker on the left, and characteristic mounds that block approaches to the green from poor positions. Although the trees are never a factor in regulation play, they often provide a handsome backdrop,

such as when they top the dunes behind the 2nd green – a green cunningly contoured and guarded by pot bunkers.

As with all good designs, planning from the tee is essential to allow the correct approach shot to the green, such as on the tough 6th, on which one must flirt with a huge bunker on the right to leave a decent angle to the elevated green. The holes twist and turn through the dunes, allowing the prevailing wind to strike from every angle.

There is good variation to the holes, with short par 4s such as the dogleg 5th and downhill 11th both requiring good management. The greens, which were completely rebuilt by Martin Hawtree in the 1990s, are a fine test, with mounds, hollows and clever bunkering around them calling for an imaginative short game, summed up by Seve Ballesteros's famous chip-and-run between the bunkers on the 18th in 1976.

● The rough can be brutal for Open week. In 1971 Lee Trevino joked: '...at 15 we put down my bag to hunt for a ball, found the ball, lost the bag!'

CARD OF THE COURSE

Hole	Yards	Par	Hole	Yards	Par
1	450	4	10	408	4
2	421	4	11	436	4
3	451	4	12	184	3
4	201	3	13	499	4
5	346	4	14	201	3
6	499	4	15	544	5
7	178	3	16	439	4
8	457	4	17	572	5
9	414	4	18	473	4
Out	3,417	34	In	3,756	36
			Total	7,173	70

Royal County Down

Royal County Down Golf Club, Newcastle, County Down, Northern Ireland

On the coast of Dundrum Bay, backed by the Mourne Mountains, 18 holes weave purposefully through dunes and gorse to create, in the words of Tom Watson, 'a pure links'. For over 100 years, Old Tom Morris's routing has changed little, and there is a sense that the course has always been here, quietly tucked away in this beautifully unassuming place.

Don't make the mistake of assuming that the age and tradition of the course have left it obsolete in today's game. Though quite capable of hosting major tournaments, Royal County Down has opted to avoid these events, fearing that the course and indigenous wildlife would suffer from trampling spectators and media villages – the Senior British Open and Walker Cup have been the biggest events held here in recent times. It is especially impressive, therefore, that many of the game's great players have made the pilgrimage to this wonderful course simply to experience it. Famously, Tiger Woods has chosen the holes of Royal County Down to sharpen his links skills before an Open Championship.

A PERFECT NINE?

The front nine is commonly regarded as the best front nine in golf (not to say that the back nine is shabby). A great starting hole, the par-5 1st is reachable in two, but one must carry the ball long down the left-hand side to take advantage of the sloping fairway, which bounds the ball forwards towards the green. As poor drives are punished with dunes on both sides and the beach on the right, this hole sets the precedent that control is a necessity. Another somewhat daunting feature during the round is that of playing tee shots over dunes, blind or semi-blind.

After the first couple of drives, which play in the same direction over intimidating hills, when guests reach the 4th tee members often allow them to set up with driver aiming over the dune before pointing out that this is a par 3 played in the opposite direction! Looking in the correct

direction from this elevated tee, one is blessed by a gorgeous view of the mountains and sea, but the player can also see the countless challenges ahead. After a carry over gorse bushes, nine brutish bunkers surround a green with large drop-offs to both sides and the back.

Possibly the best hole on the back nine is the 13th. Bunkers plague the dogleg on the right-hand side, and a decent hit down the left is rewarded with lengthy run on the mounds of the firm fairway. If the drive is too short, sight of the green is blocked by the gorse-banked dune on the dogleg. The broad, sloping green is nestled among dunes to create its own amphitheatre, backed by swathes of lilac heather. The strength of holes like this, coupled with picturesque scenery and legendary hospitality, have led Royal County Down to a consistent ranking as one of the world's Top 10 courses.

Below Slieve Donard, the highest of the Mourne Mountains, overlooks Dundrum Bay and the historic Royal County Down links. This is the excellent 3rd hole, viewed from behind the green.

- In 1933, in the Irish Open Amateur Championship, Eric Fiddian recorded two holes-in-one in the final, yet he still lost.

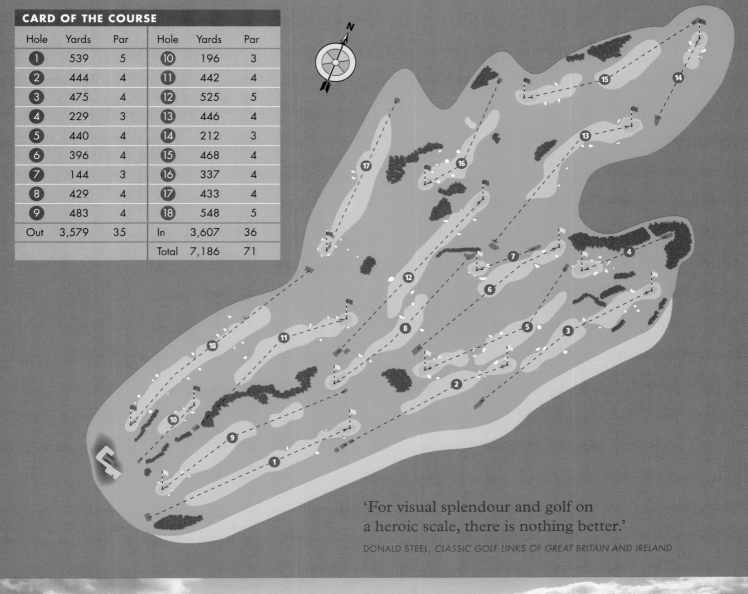

CARD OF THE COURSE

Hole	Yards	Par	Hole	Yards	Par
1	539	5	10	196	3
2	444	4	11	442	4
3	475	4	12	525	5
4	229	3	13	446	4
5	440	4	14	212	3
6	396	4	15	468	4
7	144	3	16	337	4
8	429	4	17	433	4
9	483	4	18	548	5
Out	3,579	35	In	3,607	36
			Total	7,186	71

'For visual splendour and golf on
a heroic scale, there is nothing better.'

DONALD STEEL, *CLASSIC GOLF LINKS OF GREAT BRITAIN AND IRELAND*

Royal Liverpool

Royal Liverpool Golf Club, Hoylake, Wirral, England

Founded in 1869, Royal Liverpool (popularly known as Hoylake) is one of England's oldest golf clubs. Golf was first played here alongside amateur horse and pony races, for this was the site of the Liverpool Hunt Club. Naturally, the horses were not expected to charge up and down the sand dunes, so, for the most part, Hoylake is an unusually flat course. But appearances can be deceptive, especially here.

In no time at all (in 1872), Hoylake had attracted its first professional tournament – in fact the first of any significance outside Scotland. The first prize was almost double the prize for the Open Championship. It attracted a small but distinguished field, with Young Tom Morris emerging victorious. Next up was the inaugural Amateur Championship (1885), followed by its first Open Championship (1897). The winner on this occasion was Royal Liverpool's own Harold Hilton; he and his club companion John Ball were the only amateurs to win the Open Championship until the emergence of Bobby Jones, who won at Hoylake in 1930. This was to become the second leg of his extraordinary 'Grand Slam', when he won the Open and Amateur Championships of the United States and Britain in the same year. The Open returned to Hoylake several times, but after Roberto de Vicenzo's victory in 1967 there was a lengthy gap.

Below The 12th green presents a difficult target, raised up on top of the dunes, but it gives wonderful views over the Dee Estuary to the Flintshire hills.

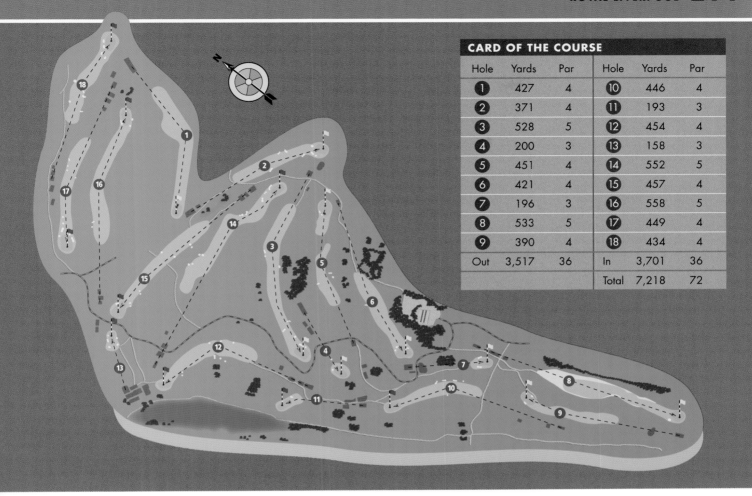

CARD OF THE COURSE

Hole	Yards	Par	Hole	Yards	Par
1	427	4	10	446	4
2	371	4	11	193	3
3	528	5	12	454	4
4	200	3	13	158	3
5	451	4	14	552	5
6	421	4	15	457	4
7	196	3	16	558	5
8	533	5	17	449	4
9	390	4	18	434	4
Out	3,517	36	In	3,701	36
			Total	7,218	72

WOODS – THE GREAT STRATEGIST

When Hoylake next hosted the Open, in 2006, Tiger Woods showed everybody else how to play the course. As he had done the previous year at St Andrews, Woods analysed the course from the point of view of his own strengths, deciding that it was too dangerous to use the driver prospectively from the tee. He reckoned correctly that if he played for position rather than length, making sure that his tee shot landed in the best spot from which to approach the green, his long-iron play to the green would get him close to the hole.

The order of the holes was altered for the Open, but more usually Hoylake begins with a unique hole, a bunkerless par 4 on which it is possible to drive out of bounds on either side. The green adjoins a 'cop' (a grassy bank, typical of Hoylake) which is also out of bounds. Like the first hole, most of the early holes are level, but there is a relentlessness about the probing that never lets up. The wind rarely lets up either.

As the round progresses the character of the course changes gradually until the 8th, when the pitch is made steeply uphill to a rolling green standing on top of the dunes, giving way to a glorious sequence of seaside holes with expansive views. The pick of these must be the 12th, a majestic par 4 beginning with a drive to a low, curving fairway, followed by a long second shot uphill to a brilliantly sited green, repelling all but the finest approaches. Woods solved its problems on the second day of the Open by pitching in for an eagle. His approach, stone dead, on the final afternoon was breathtaking. Great golf on a great course! The Open will return to Hoylake in 2014.

'I know no better golf course anywhere in the world.'

BERNARD DARWIN

● For the 2006 Open Championship a number of alterations were made to the course, including a brand new 17th hole (which was played as the 1st for the championship). The old green had been so close to a road that it was not unknown for players to putt out of bounds.

● The 6th hole is unusual among championship courses in that the drive is made over the corner of an orchard.

Royal Lytham

Royal Lytham & St Annes Golf Club, Lancashire, England

English golf is full of surprises, and one of those surprises has to be Royal Lytham. It lies on a somewhat unprepossessing chunk of land, the Fylde, whose principal conurbation is the holiday resort of Blackpool. Hopes are not raised by the immediate surroundings of the club, with neither a sand dune nor a breaking wave to be seen. In fact the club is enclosed by housing and a railway line. Yet there is no denying that this is one of England's great clubs with one of its finest courses, well worthy of its frequent hosting of the Open Championship, including the 2012 Open.

Lytham made an auspicious start to its Open career. The year was 1926 and the winner was none other than Bobby Jones, the greatest amateur player the game of golf has known. No further Opens were held there until after World War II, when an illustrious list of champions was produced: Bobby Locke, Peter Thomson, Bob Charles, Tony Jacklin, Gary Player and Seve Ballesteros (twice). Yet there were no Americans in that group. Amends were made in 1996, 70 years after that first American triumph, when Tom Lehman emerged as champion, and reinforced in 2001, when David Duval realized the full potential of his talent.

Each one of those great champions needed abundant grit and determination, for Lytham never lets up. It is a very well-defended course and utterly unforgiving.

Below The 7th hole follows a gentle right-hand dogleg towards a slightly sunken green. Those looking for a birdie here should beware the heavy bunkering on both sides of the fairway and around the green.

NOTHING IS ORTHODOX AT LYTHAM

It is not that Lytham is eccentric – far from it! But it is unusual in opening with a par 3, and to have three par 4s well under 400 yards/366 m on the back nine is far from today's norm. Yet that back nine is fearsome. Scores made on the way out are more often than not lost on the way home.

Lytham is relentless. For the average player it is probably the most testing of all the Open courses, largely because of its prolific bunkering. As Open has succeeded Open, and equipment has developed and player prowess grown, new bunkers have had to be added each time. The old ones have been left intact. They threaten shots of every length on each hole.

It is an educative experience following great players over the closing holes. Of the 15th hole Jack Nicklaus once exclaimed, 'God! It's a hard hole!' The fairway is angled across the line of the drive, narrow and well bunkered. A conservative drive leaves a blind shot, against the wind, to find the green. In 1979 Seve Ballesteros played an amazing recovery shot from a car park to the right of the 16th green for an unlikely birdie on his way to winning the championship. For the rest of us the best approach is from the left.

Bobby Jones made an astonishing recovery on the 17th on his final round in 1926 – so remarkable a shot that a plaque is set in the ground to the left of the fairway bunkers to commemorate it. With two diagonal lines of bunkers crossing the fairway, the final drive is one of the more nerve-racking in golf, and many a championship has been thrown away on this hole.

EUROPE'S RESURGENCE

When Tony Jacklin won the Open at Lytham in 1969 it proved to be an influential moment in British and European golf, because it signalled a resurgence in self-belief. No longer did the Europeans fear the Americans, Australians and South Africans who had dominated world golf. It paved the way for wins in majors by Sandy Lyle, Ian Woosnam, Seve Ballesteros, Bernhard Langer, José María Olazábal, Nick Faldo, Paul Lawrie, Padraig Harrington, Graeme McDowell and Martin Kaymer.

CARD OF THE COURSE

Hole	Yards	Par	Hole	Yards	Par
1	206	3	10	334	4
2	436	4	11	540	5
3	457	4	12	196	3
4	391	4	13	340	4
5	210	3	14	443	4
6	494	5	15	464	4
7	555	5	16	358	4
8	417	4	17	467	4
9	164	3	18	410	4
Out	3,330	35	In	3,552	36
			Total	6,882	71

'It's a beast but a just beast.'
BERNARD DARWIN

Royal Melbourne

West Course, Royal Melbourne Golf Club, Black Rock, Victoria, Australia

The Royal Melbourne Golf Club has been – and still is – the most influential golf club in the Australian game. The man who made it so was a visitor, none other than Dr Alister MacKenzie. He had been sent by the R&A following a request from Royal Melbourne for advice on the laying out of a new course. MacKenzie arrived in October 1926 and stayed for two months, during which time he also visited a number of other courses, making suggestions for improvements to these, too.

MacKenzie's lasting influence was his recruitment of 1924 Australian Amateur champion and Royal Melbourne member, Alex Russell, and the club's greenkeeper, 'Mick' Morcom. MacKenzie was not going to be in Australia long enough to oversee the changes he suggested for so many clubs, nor to supervise at Royal Melbourne. Russell and Morcom quickly assimilated MacKenzie's architectural principles and were able to carry out a revolution in strategic design – and bunker design in particular – that has lasted to this day, especially in the Melbourne sand belt.

MODEL BUNKERS

Some years ago, when Nick Faldo, then just starting out in the golf design business, was in Australia to play in a number of tournaments, he was not to be found on the practice range in his down time. He was seen, instead, standing in, walking around, photographing and measuring many of the bunkers at Royal Melbourne, so impressed was he by their enormous variety and the huge influence they still exert on playing strategy, even though modern professionals are so expert at bunker play.

● Tournaments are played on a Composite Course drawn from the West and East Courses, allowing play to be kept within the main club grounds and avoiding roads.

Below The two courses intertwine engagingly. Viewed from the back of the 2nd green on the East Course, the West's famous 6th is seen stretching into the distance on the right.

THE EAST COURSE

In addition to the five Australian Opens played on the Composite Course and two on the West, two Opens have been contested on the East Course. A very fine course in its own right, it was laid out by Alex Russell and Mick Morcom in 1930–31. They were clearly influenced by Alister MacKenzie's visit in 1926, for stylistically it has much in common with the West Course, most particularly in its bunkering. Russell and Morcom obviously had something of MacKenzie's gift for identifying great green sites, and both courses are superb tests of approach play. The short holes are particularly appealing, the 201-yard/184-m 4th being as tough as any short hole on the West Course. It plays long as it runs uphill through serious bunkers and it's hard to judge the distance.

'This is one of the great courses in the world, but there is a fear factor to it.'
NICK FALDO

CARD OF THE COURSE

Hole	Yards	Par	Hole	Yards	Par
1	429	4	10	312	4
2	480	5	11	455	4
3	354	4	12	476	5
4	507	5	13	147	3
5	176	3	14	366	4
6	428	4	15	477	5
7	148	3	16	221	3
8	379	4	17	439	4
9	416	4	18	433	4
Out	3,317	36	In	3,326	36
			Total	6,643	72

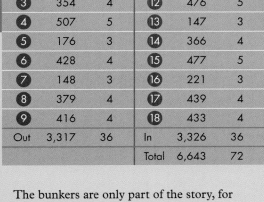

The bunkers are only part of the story, for the real genius of the West Course is the way MacKenzie routed it to take maximum advantage of the topography. For example, the sequence of holes from the 3rd to the 10th makes brilliant use of two big sandhills and two smaller ones. The 4th is a magnificent hole, whether played as a short par 5 or ultra-long par 4, with a drive over cavernous bunkers to a distant hilltop followed by a long second shot, very likely played from a hanging lie, along a curving fairway to a heavily bunkered, distant green. Then comes the 5th, as gorgeous a short hole as you could wish for. The 6th is one of the world's great two-shot holes, with a drive over serious bunkers to set up an approach shot to a deliciously bunkered, ledge green cradled in the dunes of one of the bigger hills.

Little attention is usually given to the short 7th, which is a better hole for being routed up a hill rather than over an adjacent pond, while the 8th green is unreceptive, being sloped down towards the back and attendant bunkers. A mid-length par 4 follows, with a tricky pitch uphill to the green, and then comes the fabulous 10th, a wonderful short par 4, tempting the long hitter to drive the green and mercilessly punishing even the slightest failure. Despite today's superior clubs and balls it remains a great hole.

Royal St George's

Royal St George's Golf Club, Sandwich, Kent, England

The Open Championship was a Scottish monopoly for the first 33 years of its existence, but in 1894 the championship was allowed to be played south of Hadrian's Wall for the very first time. It could hardly have ventured much farther south, for it came to the Kent coast at Sandwich, where the Royal St George's Golf Club had been established (by two Scotsmen, of course) in 1887.

Our two Scotsmen (Dr Laidlaw Purves and Henry Lamb) had travelled along much of England's Channel coast in an attempt to find a piece of ground that resembled the great links of their native land but was reasonably accessible to London golfers. They were beginning to despair of discovering what they were searching for, when in Sandwich Bay they found a wild, tumbling wilderness in which an exciting and exceedingly challenging course could be built.

A NATURAL COURSE
On such land, Purves and Lamb had no need to engage in lengthy and costly earth moving. It was merely a matter of finding as varied a routing out and back as they could, through, across and along the dunes. They did such a good job that the course follows much the same route today. There have been changes, however, not least the elimination of blind shots and one particularly blind par 3 – known as the Maiden.

Below The 6th green, right in the heart of some of the finest duneland on earth. Farther along the shore lies Prince's Golf Club, host to the 1932 Open Championship.

● *A little bit of golfing history was made on the 16th hole during the 1967 Dunlop Masters tournament, when Tony Jacklin holed his tee shot in one: it was the first time an ace had been broadcast live on British television.*

'It is just about the ultimate in leave-it-as-the-lord-made-it courses.'

JACK NICKLAUS

Of all the Open Championship courses, it is Sandwich – venue for the 2011 Open – that feels the most removed from everyday life, with its clubhouse apparently sitting in fields at the end of a track. That sense of remoteness continues on the opening hole, striking far out into the wide expanses. On the 4th the first-time visitor might be somewhat perplexed at the prospect from the tee, for a giant sand dune bars the way to the distant fairway, and in its face are set two of the most fearsome bunkers imaginable. It is the beginning of a wonderful sequence of holes taking play to the sea shore.

There is respite of a kind around the turn, but it is a white-knuckle run home from the 14th. Indeed, that 14th has ruined many an Open aspirant's chances, with an out-of-bounds wall worryingly close to the fairway all the way to the green. (Prince's

Golf Club, where Gene Sarazen won the 1932 Open Championship, lies on the other side of the wall.) Sturdy hitting is required to surmount the difficulties of the three remaining long two-shot holes, very exposed to the wind as they are, yet the delicate 16th is no pushover, despite its being the shortest hole on the course.

CARD OF THE COURSE

Hole	Yards	Par	Hole	Yards	Par
1	444	4	10	415	4
2	417	4	11	243	3
3	240	3	12	381	4
4	495	4	13	459	4
5	419	4	14	547	5
6	178	3	15	496	4
7	564	5	16	163	3
8	453	4	17	426	4
9	412	4	18	459	4
Out	3,622	35	In	3,589	35
			Total	7,211	70

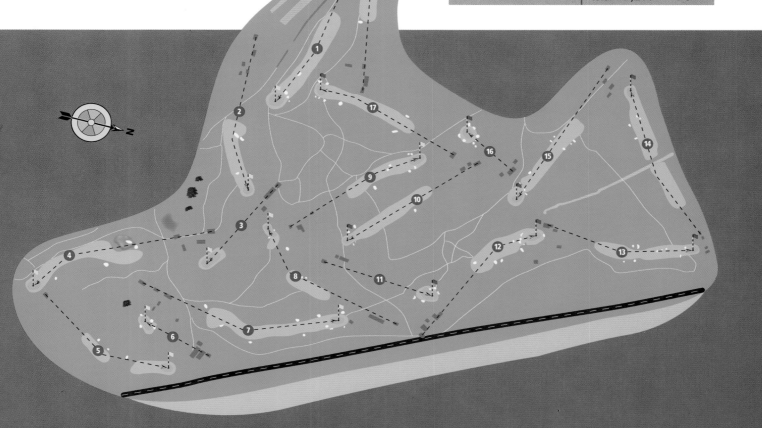

Shinnecock Hills

Shinnecock Hills Golf Club, Southampton, Long Island, New York, USA

One of the United States' oldest championship courses, Shinnecock Hills was founded in the affluent Hamptons on Long Island back in 1891. By 1896 it was ready to host its first important championships, the US Amateur and US Open, both being held for only the second time. After taking its place at the top of the pecking order, Shinnecock faded into the background for nearly 100 years, its golf being entirely social.

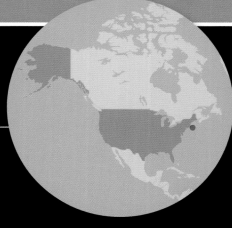

Below The routing of Shinnecock Hills brings the 9th and 18th holes back in parallel to deliciously sited greens on the slopes beneath the club's splendid clubhouse.

A revised layout was completed in 1916, but the club did not seek further public attention at that time, or when the building of a new highway on Long Island forced further changes in 1930–31. The new layout was ignored for national championship play until 1986, when the golfing world at large was awakened to the magnificent course that had been hidden from public gaze for so long. The US Open returned, and it was clear that this would not be a one-off affair – there were repeat visits in 1995 and 2004.

To create this long-concealed gem, the club had called on William Flynn, an architect who had previously worked mostly in the Philadelphia area. He and his business partner Howard Toomey are now recognized as one of the most imaginative partnerships in what was a particularly creative era of American golf design, between the two World Wars. Flynn retained two holes from the previous course (designed by another great partnership, Charles Blair Macdonald and Seth Raynor) but the rest was brand new.

A GENUINE LINKS?
Shinnecock Hills has been described as the nearest America gets to a true links, as exemplified by Britain's ancient links. Is this so? The answer has to be 'No' on two counts. First, there are 'inland links' far from the sea, such as Sand Hills in Nebraska, which play more like the Old Course than Shinnecock ever can. Second, the sea is not really a factor in how play is made, how the shots must be shaped, as it is (if often indirectly) on a true links. And yet, in so many ways, Shinnecock is

reminiscent of a links. Its wide spaces are windswept, and the direction of the wind is often hugely important in how the play of an individual hole may change from day to day, or hour to hour. And Shinnecock is far hillier than Dornoch, Royal Aberdeen and St Andrews put together.

It would be invidious to single out any particular hole at Shinnecock, because it is the collective strength of all 18 holes that makes this such an outstanding course. It might be by far the shortest of recent US Open courses, but part of its strength is the way the course is maintained, with firm-and-fast conditioning demanding great skill in approach work allied to formidable rough –

the sort of thing the R&A conjured up for the infamous 1999 Open at Carnoustie. At Shinnecock that is normal.

This is, in golfing terms, a favoured corner of Long Island, with the famous National Golf Links literally next door and the Jack Nicklaus/Tom Doak Sebonack adjoining that.

● *Shinnecock's clubhouse, designed in 1892 by the fashionable architect Stanford White (whose womanizing led to his murder in 1906), was the first purpose-built clubhouse in the United States and is still in use today.*

'Each hole is different and requires a great amount of skill to play properly. Each hole has complete definition.'

BEN HOGAN

CARD OF THE COURSE

Hole	Yards	Par	Hole	Yards	Par
1	393	4	10	412	4
2	226	3	11	158	3
3	478	4	12	468	4
4	435	4	13	370	4
5	537	5	14	443	4
6	474	4	15	403	4
7	189	3	16	540	5
8	398	4	17	179	3
9	443	4	18	450	4
Out	3,573	35	In	3,423	35
			Total	6,996	70

St Andrews

The Old Course, St Andrews, Fife, Scotland

There is no more famous golfing town than St Andrews. It is, after all, the Home of Golf, and the game has been played there since the fifteenth century. Overlooking the Old Course is the handsome clubhouse of the Royal and Ancient Golf Club (R&A) – a comparative newcomer to St Andrews, having been founded in 1754. Nowadays the R&A governs the game throughout the world, with the exception of North America, and every five years it brings its Open Championship (or British Open, as it is commonly known to the wider golfing world) to the Old Course, producing winners of the calibre of Tiger Woods, Jack Nicklaus, Severiano Ballesteros and Nick Faldo in recent years and James Braid and Bobby Jones in the distant past.

Jones was one of many golfers who found that it takes time to appreciate the many subtleties of the Old Course. It has humps and hollows here, there and everywhere; hundreds of bunkers, many in the unlikeliest of places and some, such as Hell, Strath, Hill or Road, terrifying to even the world's greatest players; huge, rolling greens – all but four of them double greens shared by holes playing in opposite directions; and a wealth of history in every blade of grass. All the greats of golf have played at St Andrews, and the locals will happily recount fantastical tales of derring-do and catastrophe everywhere on the course. The first-time visitor would be well advised to employ the services of a good local caddie, not only to unravel the mysteries of playing the Old Course but also to share in some of those numerous St Andrews legends.

Below One of the most famous views in golf, looking across the 17th green and the Swilcan Bridge towards the clubhouse of the R&A (left) and the wide expanse of the 18th green (right).

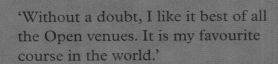

'Without a doubt, I like it best of all the Open venues. It is my favourite course in the world.'

TIGER WOODS, BRITISH OPEN CHAMPION
AT ST ANDREWS IN 2000 AND 2005

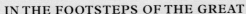

CARD OF THE COURSE

Hole	Yards	Par	Hole	Yards	Par
1	346	4	10	386	4
2	453	4	11	174	3
3	397	4	12	348	4
4	480	4	13	465	4
5	568	5	14	618	5
6	412	4	15	455	4
7	371	4	16	423	4
8	175	3	17	495	4
9	352	4	18	357	4
Out	3,554	36	In	3,721	36
			Total	7,275	72

IN THE FOOTSTEPS OF THE GREAT

There is no simpler drive in golf than that on the 1st hole of the Old Course – at least, that would be the case if the tee were anywhere other than right in front of the R&A clubhouse. It is a hugely broad fairway shared with the 18th, and there are no bunkers. However, there is the sinuous Swilcan Burn to be cleared to reach the green. Thereafter the course makes its way out, in the shape of a shepherd's crook, to the Eden Estuary, turning in a loop before retracing its path alongside the outward holes on wide shared fairways and greens. The space, which appears to invite uninhibited driving and cavalier approach play, is deceptive. Such are the ingenuities of the course's defences that how the hole is played from tee to green depends on exactly where the pin is located.

However much you may be enjoying your round you cannot relax until you have passed the 17th, the Road Hole, dominated by the treacherous Road bunker. Get in there and there may be no escape! But all is surely alleviated by the walk up the 18th: the most famous walk in golf.

BOBBY JONES AND ST ANDREWS

Strangely, Bobby Jones hated the Old Course on his first visit, tearing up his card during the 1921 Open Championship, but he came to love it as he got to know it better, eventually saying, 'I could take out of my life everything except my experiences at St Andrews and I'd still have a rich, full life.' It was on the Old Course in 1930 that Jones won the Amateur Championship, defeating Roger Wethered 7 and 6. In this remarkable year he also won the US Amateur at Merion, the US Open at Interlachen and the Open Championship at Royal Liverpool, a feat described at the time as storming 'the impregnable quadrilateral of golf'. At the end of that season Jones, at the age of 28, retired from competitive golf.

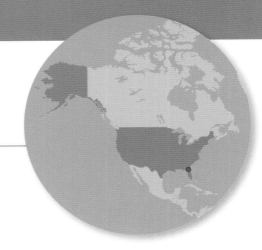

TPC Sawgrass

Stadium Course, TPC Sawgrass, Ponte Vedra Beach, Florida, USA

When the two-year-old course hosted its first tournament – the Players Championship of 1982 – the professionals were almost unanimous in their verdict: they hated it. While the design had always aimed to be tough, it was clearly too much, and Pete Dye, the renowned US golf course designer, modified the course slightly to soften the greens and change particularly brutal bunkers. The changes worked and the Players Championship has now become the unofficial fifth major.

The professionals' opinions were especially important at Sawgrass as TPC (Tournament Players Club) courses are owned by the PGA (Professional Golfers' Association) for the purpose of hosting tournaments. The course is respected by the professionals because its clever design does not favour a specific type of player. Long hitters such as Davis Love and Tiger Woods have won the Players Championship, but so have those who rely on accuracy, such as Hal Sutton, Justin Leonard and Tom Kite. Adam Scott won at the age of 23; the following year Fred Funk won, aged 48.

THE ISLAND GREEN
The PGA ownership is reflected in the design, in that the course was created specifically for tournament golf. Huge amounts of earth were dug out of the site and used to create spectator mounds surrounding the fairways and greens, the deep holes left from excavation being filled with water to create plentiful lakes. Such is the fame of the island-green 17th, one of golf's most feared short holes, that an American sports channel devotes itself to showing uninterrupted coverage of the hole during the Players Championship.

Below The 17th hole has acquired a notoriety all of its own. On the opening day of the Players Championship in 1984, in blustery conditions, no fewer than 64 balls were hit into the water. The stroke average was 3.79, making it the hardest par 3 in Tour history to that date.

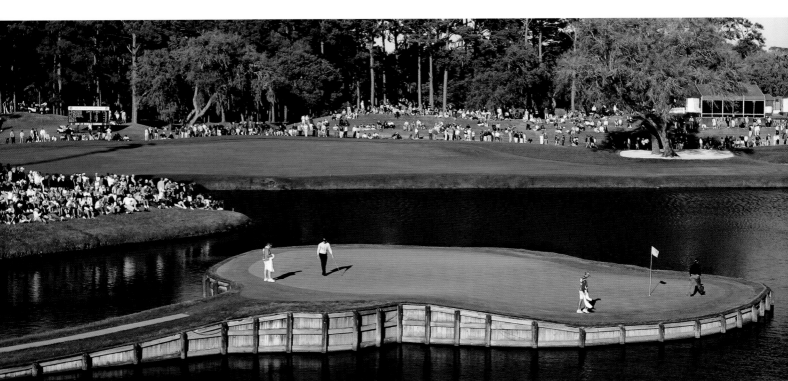

Interestingly, Dye did not originally intend the 17th green to be surrounded by water. He was planning to make it a giant bunker until his wife Alice suggested the island.

Water comes into play on most holes, notably on the brutal 18th. With a lake on the left of this tough dogleg, players are faced with a 'bite off as much as you can chew' concept from the tee. If the drive is not perfectly placed you must lay up the approach, as an aggressive second shot, especially from the clingy rough, tends to be water bound.

You don't have to hold your breath until the 17th for the course to kick in. One of the best holes is the reachable par-5 2nd. With palm trees lining the fairway, an accurate draw is required from the tee. The hole is deliberately kept at a realistic length so that it is hittable in two, but the second shot is played to one of Dye's trademark small greens, with penalizing rough and pot bunkers offering ample protection.

Recent alterations to the course have emphasized the 'hard and fast' style of the design. The result of this is that a wayward shot now has even more chance of running away into trouble, which has been increased through the addition of 200 newly planted trees. The course's length has changed little since it was first built, only about 200 yards/183 m having been added in nearly 30 years. The emphasis, then, is on creating exciting golf through reachable distances – refreshing in an era when too many other courses are put on steroids for Tour events. The biggest change is a new clubhouse in the 'stately home' style.

'We have seventeen pretty good holes at TPC and one bad one – the 17th.'

TOM KITE

- The weight of the Spanish tiles on the roof of the Mediterranean-style clubhouse is equivalent to that of two jumbo jets.

- It is esimated that over 100,000 balls are scooped out of the water on the 17th every year.

CARD OF THE COURSE

Hole	Yards	Par	Hole	Yards	Par
1	392	4	10	424	4
2	532	5	11	535	5
3	177	3	12	358	4
4	384	4	13	181	3
5	466	4	14	467	4
6	393	4	15	449	4
7	442	4	16	507	5
8	219	3	17	137	3
9	583	5	18	447	4
Out	3,588	36	In	3,505	36
			Total	7,093	72

Turnberry

Ailsa Course, Turnberry Hotel, Turnberry, Ayrshire, Scotland

Turnberry's Ailsa Course enjoys the most spectacular setting of the half-dozen courses on the Open Championship roster. Often compared to California's Pebble Beach, it made its Open debut in 1977 and immediately produced a classic. Yet twice in its history this most majestic of courses has been on the brink of extinction.

The railways played an important part in the spread of golf throughout Britain (America, too, for that matter). They were also responsible for the establishment of some of the country's finest hotels, not least Gleneagles, Cruden Bay and Turnberry. It was in the early 1900s that the Glasgow and South Western Railway negotiated a lease with the Marquis of Ailsa to enable them to construct a hotel at Turnberry. Already in existence on site was the Marquis's private 13-hole course, and a further 13 holes were added so that

by 1906 Turnberry could, with justification, call itself a golf resort. It was good enough to host the British Ladies Championship of 1912, and a promising future seemed certain.

Unfortunately, progress was halted by World War I, when the course became an airfield. After that war, restoration was undertaken and the thread of development resumed. Worse destruction came in 1939 in the form of a major air base, a vital part of the defence of transatlantic shipping lanes. It must have seemed the end for Turnberry.

Below The short 11th, with the lighthouse and Ailsa Craig – the very essence of golf at Turnberry, a scene far removed from the runways of a wartime aerodrome.

A REMARKABLE RESURRECTION

It was not the end, however, in the mind of Turnberry's manager, Frank Hole. He managed to garner sufficient compensation from public funds, and support from the newly formed British Railways, the hotel's owners, to turn the air base into a fine golf course. Scottish designer Philip Mackenzie Ross produced one of Britain's most visually attractive courses.

Turnberry then worked its way up the tournament ladder and in 1977 it got its just reward – its first Open. It turned out to be one of the greatest Opens of all, the famous 'duel in the sun', with Tom Watson and Jack Nicklaus going head-to-head to produce some of the most spectacular golf ever seen.

It could be argued that the first three holes of the Ailsa Course sail under the radar a little, because the player is already anticipating the stretch of shoreline holes from the 4th to the 11th, which are worthy of comparison with those famed seaside holes at Pebble Beach. The seascapes are stunning, especially at sunset, but the golf requires full concentration, with some holes threaded down valleys between the dunes and others (such as the short 4th and 6th holes) fully exposed to the wind on top of the dunes. Arguably, the curving 8th is the best of these demanding par 4s, but the visitor cannot wait to be photographed on the peninsular 9th tee, the drive being made over enough of the ocean towards a distant clifftop fairway to cause trepidation in many an otherwise proficient player.

Perhaps the austerities of postwar Britain suggested to Ross a minimalist approach to bunkering, but this aspect was tightened in preparation for the 2009 Open, Turnberry's fourth. This proved to be another classic, with Tom Watson, at the age of 59, coming agonizingly close to becoming the oldest major champion.

NAMING OF HOLES

Following a custom common to many Scottish golf courses, Turnberry's holes are named as well as numbered. The 2nd, for instance, is Mak Siccar ('make sure'), the 3rd Blaw Wearie ('out of breath'), 6th Tappie Toorie ('hit to the top'), 10th Dinna Fouter ('don't mess about'), 13th Tickly Tap ('a tricky little hit'), 15th Ca Canny ('take care') and 17th Lang Whang ('good whack').

CARD OF THE COURSE

Hole	Yards	Par	Hole	Yards	Par
1	354	4	10	456	4
2	428	4	11	175	3
3	489	4	12	451	4
4	166	3	13	410	4
5	474	4	14	448	4
6	231	3	15	206	3
7	538	5	16	455	4
8	454	4	17	559	5
9	449	4	18	461	4
Out	3,583	35	In	3,621	35
			Total	7,204	70

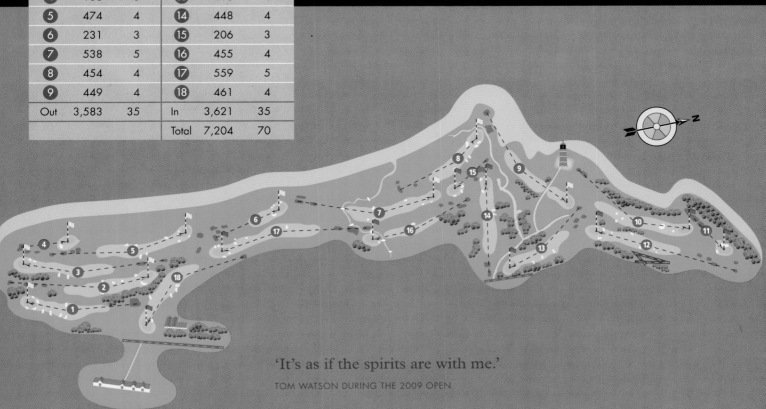

'It's as if the spirits are with me.'
TOM WATSON DURING THE 2009 OPEN

Valderrama

Club de Golfe Valderrama, San Roque, Cadiz, Spain

Regarded by many as the top golf course in continental Europe, Valderrama is inextricably linked with the Volvo Masters, until 2009 the European Tour's end-of-season flagship event. In 1997 the course also hosted one of the most closely fought Ryder Cups, with Seve Ballesteros's European team managing to withstand the comeback of the Americans on the final day to retain the Cup by a margin of one point. Despite its high profile, and the menacing reputation of the 17th, Valderrama prides itself on being playable by all skill levels. A large range of tees ensures not only widely differing distances, but also different routings, to cater for various abilities. Credit must go to the inventive design of the course, which, interestingly, was designed twice by the same man.

Valderrama began its life as the New Course at Sotogrande, in turn becoming Las Aves, before being bought by rich Bolivian industrialist, Jaime Ortiz-Patiño. Keen to host high-quality tournament golf, Ortiz-Patiño called back the designer of the course – the prolific architect Robert Trent Jones – to make the necessary alterations. The most significant of Trent Jones's changes was to reverse the two nines, so that the hardest run of holes would become the finishing stretch. A massive drainage programme was also initiated and, later, a lake was introduced in front of the 17th green. The conditioning of the course is always impeccable.

Below This view of the short par-4 10th shows why distances are irrelevant, even at professional level, if the topography of the site and the intuition of the architect are in harmony.

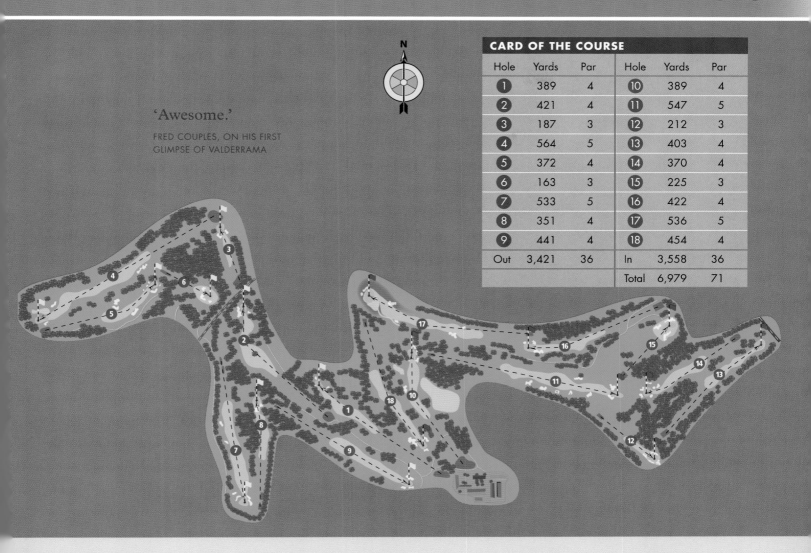

'Awesome.'

FRED COUPLES, ON HIS FIRST
GLIMPSE OF VALDERRAMA

N

CARD OF THE COURSE

Hole	Yards	Par	Hole	Yards	Par
1	389	4	10	389	4
2	421	4	11	547	5
3	187	3	12	212	3
4	564	5	13	403	4
5	372	4	14	370	4
6	163	3	15	225	3
7	533	5	16	422	4
8	351	4	17	536	5
9	441	4	18	454	4
Out	3,421	36	In	3,558	36
			Total	6,979	71

SHADES OF AUGUSTA

Overall length has never been a priority at Valderrama, but the challenges are considerable. The course is hilly, wind is a constant factor – and a variable one, with two prevailing winds changing the characteristics of the course from day to day – and a proliferation of trees makes particularly high demands on straight hitting. The trees remove options from play: usually there is only one specific route to the green, meaning that this is target golf.

One of Ortiz-Patiño's aims was to replicate the feel of Augusta, both in condition and design, and this is achieved well on the 10th. Despite its short length there is little room for error, as the tee shot must be faded past a lake on the right and short of a bunker that devours a tee shot hit too straight. From here there is a magnificent view of the green, surrounded by white sand bunkers and a ring of cork trees. But, like the 9th at Augusta, the approach must be hit positively, as a weak shot will roll backwards off the green and often back down the fairway.

The environment plays an important role in the Valderrama experience, and the natural beauty of the course is a shining example to others. An active involvement in ecology means that there are twice as many species of plant and a third as many more types of bird to be encountered on the course than in the surrounding countryside. While many courses resort to fertilizer, pesticide and even dyeing the lakes blue, Valderrama has maintained quality without neglecting the environment. In fact, 1997 US Ryder Cup captain Tom Kite claimed the greens to be among the best he had ever putted on.

● Huge sums are spent each year on maintaining the course in peak condition. It has 4,600 sprinklers, compared with around 600 on the average course in the United States.

Glossary

ACE A hole played in one stroke; a hole-in-one.

ADDRESS The position a golfer assumes over the ball before making his or her strike.

AIR SHOT A swing and a miss.

ALBATROSS A score of three strokes under par on a hole; also known as a 'double eagle'.

ALIGNMENT The position of a golfer's body in relation to an imagined ball-to-target line.

APPROACH A shot played to the green from the fairway or rough.

BACK NINE The second set of nine holes on an 18-hole course.

BACKSPIN The backward spin imparted to the ball, usually with a lofted club to make it check up on the green.

BACKSWING The initial part of the swing, starting from address, away from the ball to the point where the 'downswing' will begin.

BIRDIE A score of one under par on a hole.

BITE The action of a ball hit with backspin as it lands on the green.

BLADE A traditional iron with the weight distributed evenly across the back of the club. Also, when the ball is struck midway up by the bottom part of the club: a 'thin'.

BLIND SHOT OR HOLE A situation where the golfer cannot see his or her target.

BOGEY A score of one over par on a hole.

BUMP AND RUN A low approach shot often used on links courses when there are no hazards between the golfer and the green, designed to land short of the green and then roll up to the flagstick.

BUNKER A natural or man-made depression on a fairway or around the green, usually filled with sand, but sometimes with earth or grass.

CADDIE A non-player who carries the golfer's bag and is allowed to give advice on club selection and strategy.

CARRY The distance from where the ball is struck to the spot where it first lands on the ground – especially when a ball is hit over water or a bunker.

CASUAL WATER Temporary standing water on a course caused by heavy rain or melting snow, from which a player can take relief.

CAVITY-BACKED IRONS Modern irons with the weight removed from the back of the clubhead and distributed around the perimeter of the clubface; also known as perimeter-weighted irons.

CLOSED STANCE An alignment generally used to hit a draw, with the front foot closer to the target line than the back, and arms, shoulders and hips parallel to that angle.

CLUBFACE The area of the clubhead used to strike the ball.

CLUBHEAD The lower part of the club, which is attached to the end of the shaft and used to hit the ball.

CUT A score designated at a set point in a competition to reduce the field of players. Those who score the same or better 'make the cut.' Also, a shot played with a left-to-right ball flight.

DIVOT A slice or piece of turf cut away by the clubhead when a shot is played, usually on the fairway.

DOGLEG A hole where the fairway bends sharply, generally from a point where a tee shot would land.

DOUBLE BOGEY A score of two strokes over par.

DOWNSWING From the top of the backswing, the movement back towards the ball, then through to impact. It is often initiated by a gradual turn of the hips towards the target, followed by the shoulders, arms and hands.

DRAW A shot in which the ball starts slightly to the right of the target then curves back to the centre, usually landing with some forward roll.

DRIVE A shot played from a tee.

DRIVER Generally the longest club in the bag and one with the least loft; used for hitting the ball the maximum distance off the tee.

DUCK HOOK An errant shot in which the ball moves violently from right to left and drops sharply or never gains much height; sometimes known as a 'snap hook'.

DUFFER A high-handicap or unskilled player; also known as a hacker.

EAGLE A score of two strokes under par on a hole.

FADE A shot where the ball starts slightly to the left of the target, then curves back towards the centre, usually landing softly with little roll.

FAIRWAY The closely mown area leading from the tee to the green.

FAT Hitting the turf behind the ball first, drastically reducing distance; also known as a 'duff'.

FLAGSTICK Also known as the pin, the flagstick sits in the hole and marks the golfer's target.

FOLLOW-THROUGH The final part of the swing after the ball has been struck. In a full swing, the arms and hands come up over the shoulders to a finished position.

FORE A warning shout given when a ball is headed towards other players on the course.

FOURBALL A competitive format in which pairs of players use only the better of their scores on each hole; also known as 'better ball'. Also, four golfers simply playing together.

FOURSOME A competitive format in which teams of two golfers play alternate shots.

FREE DROP A drop of the ball without penalty away from an obstruction, in accordance with either the local rules of a club or the general rules of golf.

FRINGE The short-cut grass that surrounds the green.

FRONT NINE The first nine holes on an 18-hole golf course.

GREEN The putting surface; an area of short, tightly mown grass around the hole.

GRIP The upper part of the club, covered in leather or rubber, that the golfer holds. Also, the manner of holding the club and arranging the hands and fingers.

GROUND UNDER REPAIR A part of the course marked by the committee from where a player will be entitled to a free drop.

HALF In match play, a score equal to an opponent's on an individual hole. Also, a tie in a match play contest, when, at the end of a round, the opponents have won an equal number of holes.

HANDICAP An official number issued by a club or society to a golfer, designating how many strokes he or she usually plays over par, with the opportunity to deduct those strokes from a gross score in competitive play. It is designed to measure and reflect a golfer's abilities and enable him or her to play against any other player.

HANGING LIE A lie in which the ball rests on a downward slope.

HOLE A general term for the entire area between tee and green; also, the hole into which the ball is finally putted, also known as the cup.

HONOUR The right to drive or play first, as determined by the lowest score on the previous hole.

HOOK A shot that starts right or straight at the target, then bends sharply to the left.

HOSEL The socket that connects the clubhead to the shaft.

HYBRID A utility club with the characteristics of both an iron and a wood, for use from the tee, the fairway or to escape the rough.

IMPACT The moment when the clubface meets the ball during the full swing.

INTERLOCKING GRIP A grip favoured by players with small hands or short fingers, in which the little finger of the right hand intertwines with the index finger of the left hand.

IRON The metal-headed clubs, including wedges, used for most shots between tee and green.

LATERAL HAZARD A hazard, usually a water hazard, that borders a fairway or green, defined by stakes or painted lines on the ground.

LAY-UP SHOT When a golfer chooses to play short of the green or an intermediate target to avoid trouble, such as a bunker or water.

LIE How the ball rests in relation to the ground, grass, sand or other surface. Also, the term for the angle between the clubhead and shaft.

LINE The direction along which a golfer aims to hit the ball.

LINKS A golf course found by the sea, traditionally situated in the fallow area between the beach and the more fertile land farther from the shore.

LIP The edge of the hole or the front rim of a bunker.

LOB SHOT A short, high-trajectory shot played into the green to avoid a hazard and stop the ball short with backspin.

LOCAL RULES Rules unique to a particular golf course, printed on the scorecard.

LOFT The angle of the clubface, which determines how high and far a ball travels. Also, a term for the height a golfer puts on a shot.

LOOSE IMPEDIMENT A natural object, such as a stone, leaf or branch, that can be removed without penalty so long as it and the ball do not lie in the same hazard.

MATCH PLAY Competition between two players or sides that is determined by the number of holes won or lost – as opposed to stroke play.

NEAREST POINT OF RELIEF In the event of a free drop away from an obstruction, it is the point closest to where the ball originally came to rest where the obstruction no longer interferes with the swing or stance.

NET A golfer's score after the deduction of any handicap strokes.

OBSTRUCTION Anything artificial on the course, including roads and paths, that the committee has not defined as an integral part of it.

OPEN STANCE An alignment used to hit a fade, with the front foot farther from the target line than the back foot, and the arms, shoulders and hips parallel to that angle.

OUT OF BOUNDS Beyond the boundaries of the course, as defined by the committee.

OVER-CLUBBING Selecting a club that sends the ball a greater distance than was intended.

PAR The standard score for any given hole that a scratch handicap player is expected to make, usually based on the length of the hole.

PENALTY STROKE An extra stroke that must be added to a score after hitting out of bounds, losing a ball or violating a rule.

PITCH A short approach shot usually from 100 yards/91m or less into the green, generally played with a wedge.

PITCHING WEDGE A short iron with a high degree of loft, used to hit approach shots into the green or for chipping.

PITCHMARK A small depression or divot-like slash left by a shot hit into the green.

PLAY THROUGH When a group slows down and holds up play, it is expected to allow faster groups behind 'through' to play before it.

PLUGGED BALL A ball embedded in the ground or sand.

POT BUNKER A small, round, deep bunker, most commonly found on links courses.

PREFERRED LIE Usually a local rule that allows golfers to move a ball a short distance to an improved position on the fairway in order to avoid wet/muddy lies.

PRE-SHOT ROUTINE A consistent procedure a golfer goes through prior to playing a shot.

PROVISIONAL BALL A second ball hit when the golfer believes his or her first shot may be out of bounds or lost.

PULL An errant shot that flies straight left.

PUNCH A low shot usually hit to approach a green and keep the ball under the wind.

PUSH An errant shot in which the ball travels straight right; also known as a 'block.'

PUTTER A club that has a blade with very little loft, primarily used to roll the ball along the putting surface to the hole.

READING THE GREEN When a golfer examines the slope and contours of the putting surface to judge the probable line and speed of a putt.

RECOVERY SHOT A sometimes risky shot executed from the rough, trees or other trouble, in an attempt to land in a more favourable position for the next shot.

ROUGH The grass or other vegetation outside the fairway that can vary considerably in height and is meant to penalize the golfer who shoots off-line by making the next shot more difficult.

RUB OF THE GREEN When the ball is deflected or stopped by an outside agency, such as a tree.

RUN How far the ball travels once it hits the ground.

SAND WEDGE A highly lofted iron used for playing out of bunkers and for some chipping and pitching when a high ball flight is required.

SCORECARD A card listing the local rules for a course and the par for each hole (with its handicap or degree of difficulty), with space to record scores.

SCRATCH PLAYER A player with a handicap of zero.

SHAFT The long extension of the club from grip to clubhead.

SHANK An errant shot hit off the neck or hosel of the club, causing the ball to fly violently right.

SHORT GAME All shots from around 100 yards/91m in to the green, including pitching, chipping, bunker play and putting.

SKY An errant shot that flies high into the air with little distance.

SLICE A shot that starts left or straight at the target and then curves violently to the right.

SOLE The bottom of the clubhead.

STANCE The position of the feet before striking the ball in relation to the imaginary ball-to-target line, whether square, closed or open.

STROKE The action of swinging a club through the ball. Also, the method of keeping score: each stroke executed must be recorded.

STROKE PLAY Competition in which the winner is the player who completes the round (or rounds) in the fewest strokes; also known as medal play.

SUDDEN DEATH An extra hole or holes played when a competition ends in a tie, with the overall win going to the golfer who records the first better score than his opponent on any subsequent hole.

SWEET SPOT The most effective hitting area on the clubface.

TAKEAWAY The start of the backswing; the initial movement away from the ball.

TARGET LINE An imaginary line from the ball to the target.

TEEING GROUND A closely mown area that designates the starting point of a hole.

TEE PEG A small plastic or wooden shaft used to hold the ball off the ground for a tee shot.

TENDING THE FLAG Holding the flagstick while it is in the hole to help someone else's aim while he or she is putting, then removing it after the ball has been struck while it is rolling towards the hole.

TEMPO The timing and rhythm of a golfer's swing.

THINNING THE BALL Hitting the top half of the ball with the leading edge of the clubhead, producing a shot that flies low and will roll a long way, but with little accuracy.

THROUGH THE GREEN The whole area of a course except teeing grounds, greens and hazards.

TOE The tip or end of the clubhead, opposite where the shaft and clubhead join.

TOPPING THE BALL Hitting the top part of the ball with the bottom edge of the clubhead, which causes it to drive into the ground momentarily, then pop out and fly forward.

UNPLAYABLE LIE A ball that a player cannot take a swing at, usually because of a nearby obstacle such as a tree or bush. The golfer should declare the ball 'unplayable' to his playing partners, then move it clear and drop it elsewhere at the expense of one penalty stroke.

VARDON GRIP The most common grip in golf, in which the little finger of the right hand overlaps the forefinger of the left; named after the golfer Harry Vardon.

WATER HAZARD Any lake, river, stream, ditch or other body of water such as a swamp defined by stakes or lines painted on the ground. Specific rules govern play in or around all hazards.

WOOD A club generally used for longer shots off the tee or fairway. Once made of wood, most such clubs now have shafts and clubheads of steel, titanium or graphite.

YIPS A vague anxiety condition in which the golfer becomes so tense while putting that he or she has trouble stroking the putter comfortably, usually resulting in a jerky stab at the ball.

Index

Main entries are shown in **bold**

abnormal ground conditions, 252, 253, **255**
address, **90–95**, 252
chipping, 196, 200
driving, 110–11, 117
fairway woods, 128–29
hybrids, 130
iron play, 153
putting, 222, 224
shot shaping, 156
splash shot, 173
alignment, 90–91, 116, 123
alignment sticks, 91, 124, 142, 163, 227
Amateur Championship, 15, 52, 286, 298
Anderson, Willie, 38, 39
animal droppings and scrapes, 255
Apollo moon landing, 23
Armour, Tommy, 24, 47, 276
Asian Amateur Championship, 53
Asian Tour, 51
Augusta National, 19, 20, **42–45**, 63, 76, 172, **264–65**, 288, 315

backspin, 105, 135
backswing, 96–97, 101
balance, 102–103, 109
Ball, John, 15, 35, 298
Ballesteros, Severiano, 6, 25, 29, **72**
Masters Tournament, 44, 45
Open Championship, 24, 36, 37, 295, 300, 301, 308
Ryder Cup, 49, 76, 281, 314
ball, golf, 12, 16, 18, 21
at rest moved, 251, 252
deflected, 252
design, 22, 24, 25, 27
featherie, 15
gutty, 15
Haskell, 16
identifying marks on, 105, 123, 150, 154
losing, 256, 258, 295
marking, 251, 252, 253
out of bounds, 258
plastic, 157
practice, 217
premium, 209, 217
provisional, 258, 259
unplayable, 259
Wilson 'Staff', 21
Ballybunion, 266–67
Banff Springs, 268–69
banks, hitting up, 199

Barnbougle Dunes, 270–71
Barnes, Jim, 46
baseball drill, 114
Berg, Patty, 20
Bich, Baron Marcel, 282–83
Blancas, Homero, 22
blind shots, 160, 187
Blue Canyon, 272–73
Boros, Julius, 46
bottoming out, 134, 177, 178, 183
bounce, 173, 175, 180, 196, 201
Bradshaw, Harry, 21
Braid, James, 16–17, 35, 57, 60, **61**, 276, 286, 308
breathing, 103, 215, 229
British Amateur Championship, see Amateur Championship
British Open, see Open Championship
Brookline, 16
bump and run, 162, 198–99, 205, 206, 207, 219
bunker play, 19, **171–93**
address, 173, 191
altering the bounce, 175
blind shots, 187
bottoming out, 177, 190
club selection, 180–181
difficult lies, 182–83
distance control, 176–77, 179, 181
errors, 178–79
fairway bunkers, 190–93
greenside bunkers, 174–189
lie, judging, 186, 190
long bunker shots, 180–81
options, 184–85
plugged lies, 182, 184, 259
practice and drills, 176–79, 188–89, 192–93
practice swings, 179, 191
principle, 172
running bunker shot, 184–85
slopes, 183
strategy, 186–87
swing, 174
wet sand, 183
wrist hinge, 174
bunkers, 121, 158, 171, 175, 263
as 'lighthouses', 121
ball unplayable in, 259
casual water in, 255
function in layout, 171
loose impediments in, 254
raking 247
shuffling feet in, 191

Cabrera, Angel, 40
Caddyshack, 25

Campbell, Michael, 27, 40
Cape Kidnappers, 274–75
Carnoustie, 37, **276–77**, 307
cart paths, 248, 254
Charles, Sir Bob, 23, 29, 300
Chen, T.C., 250
chipping, 162, 195, **196–211**
address, 196–97
away from the green, 219
backspin, 208–209
bump and run, 198–99, 205
distance control, 204
errors, 202–203
feel, 204–205
flight control, 206–207
into a basket, 217
lob shot, 200–201
pace control, 204–205
practice and drills,202–203, 206–207
running chips, 198–99, 205
splash shot, 211
swing, 197
toe chip, 210
two balls, 203
using leading edge, 196
using bounce, 196
visualization, 207
with woods, 211
Cink, Stewart, 230
Clayton, Michael, 271, 275
clubs
custom fitting, 111, 113, 129, 147
development, 14, 16, 18, 21, 23, 24, 25, 26, 29
grips, 88, 161
grooves, 167, 209
permitted number, 19, 26, 127
selection, 138, 155, 164, 191
Collett, Glenna, 63
Colt, Harry, 286
Cotton, Henry, 18, 35, **64**, 286
Couples, Fred, 102, 315
Crenshaw, Ben, 25, 284, 286, 293
Curtis Cup, 19, 53, 286

Daly, John, 26, 47, 74
Davies, Laura, 76, 106
de Vicenzo, Roberto, 298
definitions, 248
distances, estimating 138
disturbance, 214, 246, 251
divots, 147, 155, 211, 246
Doak, Tom, 270, 271, 274, 275, 284, 285
Donald, Luke, 29
doorway drill, 105
double hit, 210, 250

draw, 107, 115, 156
drivers, 110, 111, 113
driving, **109–125**
absolute control, 119
address position, 109, 110–11
finding extra length, 118
practice, 123, 124–25
problems, 116–17
release, 115
swing, 112–13
tactics, 120–123
driving range, practice on, 114, 119, 124–25, 138, 142–43, 156, 162, 192
dropping the ball, 253, 255, 256, 259
Dubai World Championship, 51
Duval, David, 300
Dye, Alice, 281, 311
Dye, Pete, 280, 281, 310, 311

Eisenhower Trophy, 53
Els, Ernie, 40, **77**, 273, 277, 286, 287
etiquette, 245, 246–47, 251
European Seniors Tour, 51

fade, 143, 156, 157
Fairlie, James Ogilvy, 15, 34
fairway woods, 105, **127–143**
drills, 132–33
loft, 129
practice, 142–43
problems, 132–33
set-up, 128–29
Faldo, Nick, **73**, 286, 301, 302, 303
Open Championship, 25, 36, 308
Ryder Cup, 48
US Open, 45
Fancourt, 277–78
Faulkner, Max, 23, **67**
featherie ball, 15
FedEx Cup, 29, 50
feel, 215, 221
Ferguson, Bob, 14
Ferrier, Jim, 20
Fleck, Jack, 39
flicking, 168, 199
flight control, 119, 136, 162, 164
flop shot, 200–201
Fowler, Rickie, 80

Garcia, Sergio, 29, 48, 79, 276
Garrido, Antonio, 22, 24
Geiberger, Al, 23

Gleneagles, 61, 312
Goosen, Retief, 40
GPS devices, 121, 138
Graham, David, 47
Grant, Dr George Franklin, 17
Great Triumvirate, 16–17, 35, 60
greens, 263
condition, 212, 218
reading, 186, 188, 213, 234–35
two-tiered, 236
greenside bunkers, 172–89
grip, 88–89, 97, 116, 154, 178
gutty, 15

Hagen, Walter, 19, 35, 46, 48, 57, **62**, 286
Hak, Jason, 29
Harrington, Padraig, 47, **79**, 251, 301
Open Championship, 29, 36, 37, 252, 276
putting, 228, 234
Haskell balls, 16
Hawtree, Martin, 286, 295
hazards, 252
dropping in, 253, 255, 259
heel strikes, 152
hickory shafts, 14, 18
Hilton, Harold, 17, 28, **60**, 298
Hogan, Ben, 20, 21, 62, **66**, 68, 307
Masters Tournament, 45
Open Championship, 36
US Open, 38, 39, 285
Honourable Company of Edinburgh Golfers, 12, 262, 286, 287
hook, 90, 97, 116
Hoylake, see Royal Liverpool
Hutchison, Jock, 44, 46
hybrids, **127–143**
address, 130–131
drills, 134–35
loft, 131
problems, 134–35

illegal stances, 251
insects and heaps, 254
International Federation of PGA Tours, 51
iron play, **145–69**
errors, 152–53
making contact, 146–47
pitching, 164–69
practice, 162–63
punch, 154–55
release, 149
set-up, 148
shot making, 156–57

strategy, 158–59
swing, 148–49
weight shift, 150–51
irons, 105, 127, 145–69
blades, 151
blended sets, 153
cavity, 147
choice, 147
mid-cavity, 149
muscle-backs, 151
Irwin, Hale, 38
Ishikawa, Ryo, 28, 81

Jacklin, Tony, 23, 24, 28, 40, 48, 294, 300, 301, 305
James IV of Scotland, 13, 32
James VI of Scotland, 12
Janzen, Lee, 38
Japan Golf Tour, 51
Jiménez, Miguel Angel, 175
Jones, Bobby, 18, 19, 52, 57, **63**, 285, 301, 308, 309
Augusta National, 264, 265
Masters Tournament, 42, 44
Open Championship, 35, 298, 300
US Open, 38, 39
Jones, Dave, 121
Jones, Robert Trent, 262, 314, 315

Karlsson, Robert, 164
Kato, Yoshikazu, 272
Kauri Cliffs, 274
Kaymer, Martin, 29, 47, 50, **80**, 301
Kiawah Island, 280–81
Kingsbarns, 158, 159
Kite, Tom, 310, 311, 315
Kobe, 17
Kraft Nabisco Championship, 51

ladder drill, 206
Ladies Asian Golf Tour, 51
Ladies' British Amateur Championship, 52, 53, 312
Ladies European Tour, 51
Ladies Professional Golf Association (LPGA), 51
Lamb, Henry, 304
Langer, Bernhard, 25, 45, **72**, 231, 236, 301
lateral water hazards, 256
Lawrie, Paul, 29, 36, 99, 276, 301
Lee, Danny, 28
leg support drill, 179
Lehman, Tom, 300
Leitch, Cecil, 63
Leith Links, 12, 13, 287
Lema, Tony, 22, 36
Leonard, Justin, 26, 49, 310

Les Bordes, 282–83
Levi, Wayne, 281
lie, judging, 131, 133, 167, 186, 190, 201, 214, 257
lifting, dropping and placing, 253
lob shot, 200–201
local rules, 248, 254
Locke, Bobby, 21, 36, **66**, 300
loft, 129, 131, 153, 173, 174, 184–85, 197, 200–201
long par 4s, 140–141
loose impediments, 252, **254**, 255
Lopez, Nancy, 71
Love, Davis, III, 50, 310
Lowry, Shane, 28
LPGA Championship, 51
LPGA Tour, 65
Lyle, Sandy, 24, 25, 45, 301

McDermott, John, 38, 39
McDowell, Graeme, 28, 29, 40, 50, 123, 215, 301
McIlroy, Rory, **80**, 95
MacKenzie, Alister, 42, 264, 275, 302, 303
McLeod, Fred, 44
Manassero, Matteo, 81
marking your card, 247
Martin, Pablo, 28
Mary Queen of Scots, 13
Massy, Arnaud, 16
Masters Tournament, 19, 32, **42–45**, 63, 264
match play, 13, 33, 161, 193
Mayfair, Billy, 225
Merion, 284–85
Mickelson, Phil, 45, **78**, 79, 241, 259, 293
Miller, Johnny, 38, 288
Montgomerie, Colin, 27, **75**, 76
Morris, Old Tom, 57, 58, **59**, 263, 268, 276, 286, 292, 296
Open Championship, 15, 34, 35
Morris, Young Tom, 14, 34, 35, **59**, 298
Muirfield, 286–87
Musselburgh, 287

Nakajima, Tommy, 6
Nationwide Tour, 50
nearest point of relief, 253
Nelson, Byron, 20, 44, **64**
Newport Country Club, 39
Newport, 16
Nicklaus, Jack, 6, 62, **69**, 71, 78, 278, 284, 286, 287,

290, 291, 301, 305
Masters Tournament, 42, 44, 45
Open Championship, 36, 308, 313
Ryder Cup, 23, 24, 48, 49, 294
US Open, 22, 25, 38, 39
US PGA Championship, 46, 47
nine holes, 18 shots, 216
Norman, Greg, 25, 34, 42, 46, **73**, 273

Oakland Hills, 38
Oakmont, 39, 288–89
obstructions, 253, 254
Ochoa, Lorena, 28
Official World Golf Ranking, 25, 72
Ogilvy, Geoff, 40
Olazábal, José María, 26, 29, 45, 49, **76**, 301
Old Head Golf Links, 140
Olympic Games, 16, 29, 65
O'Meara, Mark, 26
Oosthuizen, Louis, 36, 50
Open Championship, 11, 14, 15, 16, 25, 32, 33, **34–37**, 38, 58, 59, 161, 276, 286, 294, 295, 298, 299, 300, 301, 304, 305, 307, 308, 309, 312
Ouimet, Francis, 17, 39
out of bounds, 254, 258

Palmer, Arnold, 20, 22, 36, 39, 44, 45, 46, 62, **68**
paper cut-out drill, 146
par 5s, 138–39
Park, Willie, Jr, 58
Park, Willie, Sr, 15, 33, 35, 57, **58**, 263
Pau Golf Club, 14
Pebble Beach, 40–41, 264, **290–91**, 312, 313
Penick, Harvey, 25
PGA, 17, 50, 60
PGA European Tour, 22, 50, 51
PGA Tour, 19, 50
PGA Tour of Australasia, 51
pin out, 213
pin placement, 159
Pinehurst, 292–93
Ping putter, 21
pitch marks, 251
pitching, **164–69**, 181
distances, 164, 166–67
problems, 168–69
placing a ball, 253
Player, Gary, 62, 66, **69**, 151, 278, 279, 286

Masters Tournament, 23, 42, 45
Open Championship, 21, 34, 300
US Open, 39
US PGA Championship, 47
Players Championship, 50, 310
plugging, 182, 184, 259
plumb bobbing, 235
positive recall, 122
posture, 94–95
pot bunkers, 184
Poulter, Ian, 102
pre-shot routine, 214–15, 241
President's Cup, 277, 278
pressure, 171, 217, 221, 231, 240–41
creating, 161
coping with, 103, 143, 185
Prestwick, 11, 15, 32, 34, 59, 286
Price, Nick, 42, **75**
Professional Golfers' Association, see PGA
Professional Golfers' Association of America, see US PGA
puddles, 212, 255
punch, 136, 154–55, 159, 162
Purves, Laidlaw, 304
putters
Anser, 224
belly, 230
face balance, 224
long, 230
putting, **221–241**
address, 222–23
alignment, 226, 227
along-the-line stroke, 224
angle of attack, 223
arcing stroke, 224, 225
body movement, 228
difficult putts, 236–37
distance control, 232–33
easy putts, 212
eye position, 222, 225
feel, 227
from off the green, 211, 219
grips, 199, 227, 230–31
how hard to hit, 228, 236
listening to the ball, 229
longer putts, 225
one-handed practice, 233
picking a line, 234–35
practice and drills, 238–41
problems, 228–29
rhythm, 226–27, 232
rules, 251
set-up, 227, 228
shoulder angle, 223
smooth strokes, 226–27

stability, 226
stance, 222
swing path, 224–25
using wrists, 223
visualization, 235
yips, 230–31

R&A, 12, 14, 15, 32, 34, 48, 52, 262, 308
rules, 16, 18, 20, 24, 248
Race to Dubai, 51
rain, 161
Rawlins, Horace, 16, 39
re-dropping, 253
release, 107, 115, 149
rhythm, 102, 109, 113, 215, 247
Roberts, Clifford, 42
Robertson, Allan, 15, 58, 59, 263, 276
Ross, Donald, 292, 293
Ross, Philip Mackenzie, 313
rotation drills, 106–107, 119, 135, 164, 175, 197
Royal and Ancient Golf Club of St Andrews, see R&A
Royal Birkdale, 294–95
Royal County Down, 296–97
Royal Liverpool Golf Club, 15, 52, 298–99
Royal Lytham and St Annes, 300–301
Royal Melbourne, 302–303
Royal St George's, Sandwich, 17, 121, 304–305
rules of golf, 12, 16, 17, 18, 20, 179, 245–259
local, 248
running chips, 198–99
Runyan, Paul, 46
Ryder, Samuel, 48
Ryder Cup, 18, 19, 20, 23, 24, 26, 27, 33, **48–49**, 50, 236, 255, 281, 286, 294, 314, 315

St Andrews, 6, 13, 32, 34, 35, 59, 171, 262, 286, **308–309**
Saint Andrews Golf Club, Yonkers, NY, 15, 16
sand wedge, 19, 173, 175, 181, 189
Sanders, Doug, 6
Sarazen, Gene, 18, 19, 39, 42, 44, 46, 47, 57, **62**, 172, 305
Sawgrass, see TPC Sawgrass
Schenectady putter, 16
Schlee, John, 23
Scott, Adam, 310
Se Ri Pak, 51
Senior British Open, 286, 296

shaft lean, 153
shank, 152
shaping shots, 125 137, 141, 143, 156–57, 162
Shinnecock Hills, 16, 306–307
shoes, 93
short game, 195–219
  practice and drills, 216–17
  pre-shot routine, 214–15
  shot selection, 212–15
  warming up, 218–19
sidespin, 88, 91, 97, 99, 114, 115
Simpson, Tom, 267, 286
Singh, Vijay, 26, 27, 38, 293
sixteen putts or better, 241
skying the ball, 117
slice, 90, 97, 99, 107, 114–15
slope drill, 115
slow play, 247
Smith, Horton, 44
snake drill, 240
snatching at shots, 117, 135
Snead, Sam, 19, 21, 35, 44, 45, 46, 57, **65**
soft-landing long shots, 137
Solheim, Karsten, 21
Solheim Cup, 24, 51
Sörenstam, Annika, 27, 51, 77
speed, 102–103
spike analogy, 191, 100
spike marks, 236
splash shot, 173, **174–75**, 180, 193, 211
  strategy, 182–83, 186–87, 193
sprinkler heads, 211, 254
Stableford scoring system, 18

stance, 92–93, 148, 165, 196, 250
  building, 250
  out of bounds, 258
  outside teeing ground, 249
  standing on another player's line, 246
Stewart, Payne, 26, 40, **74**, 293
Stimpmeter, 23
strategy, 120–21, 122–23, 139, 140–41, 158–59, 161, 186–87, 212–13, 247, 249
stroke play, 13, 33
stymie, 20
Sunningdale, 58
Sunshine Tour, South Africa, 51
Sutton, Hal, 310
swing, **87–107**, 148–49
  aim, 90–91
  balance, 103
  body rotation, 100–101, 106–107, 119, 201
  consistency, 97
  control, 119
  downswing, 98–99
  finish, 106–107
  holding the club, 88–89
  length, 119, 136, 162, 166
  making contact, 104–105
  posture, 94–95
  speed, 102, 129, 167
  spine angle, 94–95
  stance, 92–93
  starting swing, 96–97
  swing path, 97, 98–99, 157
  tempo, 99, 102–103
  train tracks visualization, 90
  weight shift, 101

swings, practice, 141, 203, 215, 250

Tait, Freddie, 17
targets, 121, 125, 215
Taylor, J.H., 16–17, 35, 57, 60
tee, 120, 246, 249
  rules, **249**, 252
tension, 201, 203, 217, 229, 233
thinning drill, 192
Thompson, Stanley, 268
Thomson, Peter, 21, 36, **67**, 300
toe chip, 210
toe strikes, 152
Toms, David, 46
torque, 100, 101
Torrance, Sam, 24
Tournament Players Club, 310
TPC Sawgrass, 120, 123, 278, 280, **310–11**
Trevino, Lee, 36, **70**, 286, 295
trigger move, 215
Troon, 36
Turnberry, 312–13
Tway, Bob, 46
twigs, 254
two turns and a hit, 101

United States Golf Association, see USGA
unplayable ball, 259
US Amateur Championship, 16, 39, 52, 53, 290, 306
US Open Championship, 16, 27, 32, **38–41**, 284, 285, 288, 290, 293, 306
US PGA, 46, 310

US PGA Championship, 32, **46–47**, 281
US Women's Amateur Championship, 16, 52, 53
US Women's Open, 20, 51
USGA, 16, 17, 20, 24, 38, 53, 248

Valderrama, 175, 314–15
Van de Velde, Jean, 27, 37, 276
Vardon, Harry, 16–17, 34, 35, 39, 57, 60, **61**, 286
Vicenze, Roberto de, 22
Villegas, Camilo, 234
visualization, 122–23, 143, 177, 207, 214, 217, 234, 235
von Hagge, Robert, 282

Walker, Mickey, 53
Walker Cup, 18, 53, 286, 296
Walton Heath, 61
Wanamaker, Rodman, 46
warm-up routine, 218–19, 238
water hazards, 120, 123, 138, 139, 249, 252, 255, **256–57**
  loose impediments in, 254, 257
water, casual, 212, 255
Watson, Tom, 25, 36, 40, 57, **71**, 266, 267, 286, 290, 296, 313
wedges, 164, 189
weight distribution, 92, 103, 130–31, 117, 183
weight shift, 101, 106, 150–151

Weiskopf, Tom, 38, 42
Westwood, Lee, 28, 29, 50, **79**
wet sand, 175, 183
Wethered, Joyce, 18, 53, **63**
Whitworth, Kathy, 68, **70**
Wie, Michelle, 28, **81**, 259
Wilson 'Staff' ball, 21
wind, 155, 161, 162, 164, 206
  crosswind, 141, 157
  in bunker play, 187
  moving ball, 252
Wind, Herbert Warren, 20, 42, 284
Women's British Open, 51
Wood, Craig, 44
Woods, Tiger, 25, 26–27, 28, 29, 47, 50, 62, **78**, 79, 123, 273, 278, 296, 310
  iron play, 145, 149, 299
  Masters Tournament, 26, 42, 43, 45
  Open Championship, 36, 37, 299, 308, 309
  putting, 228, 233, stinger, 136
  US Open, 26, 38, 40, 290, 293
Woosnam, Ian, 26, 45, 301
World Golf Championship, 50
worms and casts, 17, 254
Wright, Mickey, 68

Yang, Y.E., 47
yips, 72, 230–31

Zaharias, Babe Didrikson, 20, 53, **65**
Zoeller, Fuzzy, 265

Acknowledgments

The authors and producer would like to thank the Almanzora Group and all those at Desert Springs Golf Resort in Spain for allowing us to use their incredible course to illustrate the instruction section of this book. We would also like to thank PGA Professional Rob Leonard for advising on the coaching aspect of the book as well as for his tireless work in posing for the photographs. Thanks also go to photographer Paul Severn, who is responsible for the striking images that run through the instruction section. Thanks finally to *Golf Monthly* magazine's Top 25 UK Coaches, who together represent some of the finest golfing minds in the country.

Picture acknowlegments
The publishers are grateful to the following organizations and individuals for permission to reproduce the photographs in this book. We apologize for any unintentional omissions and would be happy to insert an appropriate acknowledgment in future editions. Key: l = left, r = right, c = centre, t = top, a = above, b = below.

Barnbougle Dunes Golf Club, pp 270, 271.

Corbis/Bettmann, pp 68b, 70a; /Mike King 151al.

Getty Images, pp 2, 4, 10, 18b, 19a, 21c, 23a, 23c, 24–8, 29a, 29bl, 30, 35a, 35b, 36b, 37b, 39b, 40, 41, 43, 45a, 46a, 48, 49, 50l, 51, 53, 54, 59, 60b, 62a, 63, 64a, 65a, 66b, 71, 72a, 74a, 75, 76a, 77, 78b, 79, 80, 81a, 92a, 95ar, 99b, 106a, 114ar, 121a, 123a, 136l, 140, 141ar, 159al, 175b, 187b, 214, 233r, 236l, 241a, 250b, 251b, 259a, 259bl, 260, 262, 264, 266, 268, 269, 274, 278, 282, 284, 286, 290, 292, 294, 296, 300, 302, 308, 310, 312; /AFP 37tr, 45b, 50r, 74b, 78a, 81c, 81b, 149ar, 164, 230a, 231b, 252, 255b, 259br; /Augusta National, pp 18c, 19b, 22c, 22b, 23b, 32, 44, 62b, 64b, 66a, 69a, 69b, 70b, 73a, 172; /Popperfoto, pp 17a, 34r, 61b; /Bob Thomas Sports Photography, pp 8, 20b, 29br, 36a, 37tl, 52l, 67a, 72b, 73b, 76b; /Time & Life Pictures, pp 20a, 22a, 39tr, 42, 68a; /Sports Illustrated, p 47; /US PGA Tour, pp 52r, 102a, 225b, 234.

Kiawah Island Golf Resort, p 280.

New York Daily News via Getty Images, p 56.

Nike, p 153.

Old Golf Images, pp 12–16, 18a, 19c, 21a, 21b, 34l, 46b, 58, 60a, 61a, 65b, 67b.

Phil Sheldon Golf Picture Library, pp 293, 304, 306; /Liz Anthony, pp 276, 288, 298.

Stefan von Stengel, pp 272, 314.

USGA, pp 17b, 38, 39tl.